D1211485

CLEMENTINA SUÁREZ

CLEMENTINA SUÁREZ

Her Life and Poetry

Janet N. Gold

University Press of Florida

Gainesville / Tallahassee / Tampa / Boca Raton

Pensacola / Orlando / Miami / Jacksonville

Clementina Suárez's poetry and material from the author's interviews with her are reprinted by permission of Clementina Suárez. Her photos and paintings are reproduced by permission of her heir, Alba Rosa Suárez.

Graphic by Anne Richmond Boston
Book design by Betty McDaniel

Printed in the United States of America on acid-free paper ∞

00 99 98 97 96 95 6 5 4 3 2 1

Library of Congress Cataloging-in-Publication Data
Gold, Janet N.
Clementina Suárez : her life and poetry / Janet N. Gold.
p. cm.
Includes bibliographical references and index.
ISBN 0-8130-1337-2
1. Suárez, Clementina—Biography. 2. Authors, Honduran—20th century—Biography. I. Title.
PQ7509.S78Z67 1995
861—dc20 94-34180
[B]

The University Press of Florida is the scholarly publishing agency for the State University System of Florida, comprised of Florida A & M University, Florida Atlantic University, Florida International University, Florida State University, University of Central Florida, University of Florida, University of North Florida, University of South Florida, and University of West Florida

University Press of Florida
15 Northwest 15th Street
Gainesville, FL 32611

For Stephen with love

and for Peter and Virginia Nowakowski

Contents

Illustrations

Following page 160

Acknowledgments

I cannot even begin to thank all the people in Central America who contributed in so many ways to make my work pleasant and productive—the numerous individuals who allowed me to interview them, who loaned me books, and who shared time and insights with me. My thanks to the members of Clementina's family who shared memories with me, especially her daughters, Alba Rosa Suárez and Silvia Rosa Suárez de Mercado, her sisters, Rosa Amelia Suárez de Maier, Dolores Suárez Zelaya, and Graciela Suárez Zelaya, as well as Victoria Buchard de Castellón, Ofelia Reyes Zelaya, María Suárez, Leda Suárez, Paula Heredia, Judith Burwell, and Elizabeth Mendizábal.

Zoë Anglesey, Ramón Luis Acevedo, Antonieta Máximo, Mario Argueta, and Julio Ponce provided invaluable bibliography and assistance in locating people I wanted to meet or write to. Many artists, writers, and scholars of Honduras were generous with their time and help, especially Rigoberto Paredes, Roberto Sosa, Eduardo Bähr, José Adán Castelar, Roberto Quesada, José Luis Quesada, David Díaz Acosta, Claudia Torres, Raquel Lobo Morales, Ada Luz Pineda, Aída Sabonge, Rina Villars, Roger Martínez, Francisco Salvador, Isidro España, Rafael Murillo Selva, Emma Moya Posas, Héctor Bermúdez Milla, Eliseo Pérez Cadalso, Raúl Arturo Pagoaga, Juana Pavón, William Lewis, María Eugenia Ramos, Filadelfo Suazo, Iris Piñeda, Anarela de Paredes, María Luisa Membreño, Josefina Coello, Helen Umaña, Napoleón Pineda, Roberto Castillo, Juan Domingo Torres, César Rendón, Dante Lazaroni, Mario Castillo, Gelasio Giménez, Dino Faconi, Luis H. Padilla, Julio Vizquerra, Aníbal Cruz, and Mario Zamora. Among the residents of Tegucigalpa who offered me their hospitality or charmed me with their recollections I would like to thank Alma Mateo, Consuelo de Torres, Carlota Reyes de Juhn, Aenna Dejá-Neuber, Lolita Garay, Julio Rodríguez Ayestes, Olivia Pastor de Borjas, and Anita Gómez Romero. I am especially indebted to Eva Thaïs for sharing with me the fruits of her research on Honduran women.

To doña Lety, a lady and a scholar, my heartfelt gratitude for opening the doors to her home, her library, and her heart, and to Felix and the rest of her wonderful family. The late afternoon *tertulias* in doña Lety's parlor provided me with the opportunity to meet many of the people whose conversation taught me so much about life in Tegucigalpa.

I am immeasurably grateful to María Elena Sánchez of Juticalpa for introducing me to her town, and to all the residents of Clementina's birthplace who shared their memories of times past and their comments on the present, especially Carlos Sarmiento, Marco Antonio Sarmiento, Salustio Hernández Urbina, Felix Cerna, Aura Noë Calix, Adela Mazzoni, Rafael Olivera Calix Herrera, Juana Colindres, Gallarda Colindres, Juan Enrique Cardona, Juan Darío Euceda, and Dora Vd. de Alemán.

From El Salvador I am indebted to César and Nelly Sermeño, Eugenio Martínez Orantes, Julio Hernández, Julia Díaz, Enrique Salaverría, José Mejía Vides, Matilde Elena López, and Ruth Moya.

In Costa Rica I was fortunate to be helped by Carolina Jiménez, Francisco Amighetti, Carmen Naranjo, Zayda Ureña Araya, Emilia Macaya, Marilín Echeverría, Julieta Pinto, Deida Castro Rawson, Alberto Ordóñez Argüello, and Luis Ferrero.

And Roberto Armijo and Otto Raúl González wrote me beautiful and descriptive letters from Paris and Mexico.

I would also like to acknowledge the University of Massachusetts and the Fulbright Commission for generous grants that allowed me to spend extended periods of time in Central America. Donna Roginski, cultural affairs officer at the U.S. embassy in Tegucigalpa, was a gracious hostess during my first weeks in town, and Martha McPhail, a sister Fulbrighter, was great company.

Finally, I would like to thank Javier Cevallos and Margo Culley for early readings of this manuscript, Nina Scott for her faith in my project and her affectionate encouragement, and the "wild women" of my Baton Rouge writing group for their friendship and enthusiasm for this book.

Introduction

If Clementina had died in January 1988, her small frame fragile on the queenly platform of her wide bed, the roots of her hair gray against her blue satin pillow, her friends and relatives hovering watchfully nearby, I would have had a different story to tell. I most likely would have sought out many of the same people to interview, read the same books, and visited the same places. But the Clementina I have created would have taken on her various masks and personalities without the entanglements that inevitably arise when two living people spend time together. I could have laid claim to biographical objectivity and presented ample evidence to substantiate my version of her life as being that based on the clearest perception, removed from the immediate and passionate response that her presence and personality inspired in most people who knew her.

For months I had been anticipating the moment of meeting her, constructing it in my imagination in a variety of ways. So when I arrived in Tegucigalpa in January 1988 and learned that she had been quite ill for almost two months, that her daughter had come from Mexico to be with her, that her friends feared she might not recover, that she was very weak and seemed to have lost the will to live, I wondered if perhaps my imagination would have to make do on its own, without the benefit of input from the poet herself.

I walked quietly into her darkened bedroom and sat in the chair beside her bed. She looked like a frightened little animal, much smaller and frailer than the woman I had pictured reciting her poetry on the stage of the National Theatre in Tegucigalpa in 1931. Her eyes were large, opaque pools. Her voice was cracked and complaining. She wasn't sure about me, but she agreed to let me visit again the following afternoon. I returned the next day, and the day after that. She began to look forward to my visits, and by the time I left Tegucigalpa two weeks later, I was determined to return and stay long enough to do the necessary research to write her biography, and she had agreed to help me in any way she could.

I first met Clementina as I walked between rows of books in the University of Massachusetts library, occasionally stopping, attracted by the rich color of a binding or the suggestiveness of a title: *La mujer en América escribe* (Women in America Write) stood out in red letters on a frayed and faded white paperback cover. It is a collection by Cuban critic Julieta Carrera of *semblanzas,* a word used in Central America to describe a short biographical sketch, typically in praise of the qualities of an outstanding national figure. The authors of semblanzas usually have a transparent desire to portray their subject as worthy of esteem. Statesmen and generals typically receive generous adulation for traits and accomplishments that have brought honor to the nation, while poets and artists are lauded for their emotional profundity and extraordinary sensibilities.[1] But while this genre can be seen as little more than empty praise, nonetheless, on the whitewashed wall of eulogy one can often detect cracks and rough edges, hints of a more complex relationship between the nation and its favored sons or between the author of the sketch and the supposedly superior soul of the poet. Blemishes can seep through onto the surface of these character sketches and allow the reader to savor the peculiar satisfaction that accompanies demystification.

Carrera's book is copiously indexed: a list of names in alphabetical order; a list of names grouped according to their predominant "tendency" (initiators, revolutionaries, essayists, novelists, surrealists, neoromantics); and an index grouping the women according to their country of origin. Under Honduras is a single name: Clementina Suárez. She also is included in the ranks of the "*neorománticas.*"

La mujer en América escribe is not unlike other volumes devoted to Latin American women in that it seems to have been motivated by a desire to right old wrongs or set the record straight. So little attention had been paid at that time (Carrera's book was published in 1956) to women writers in Latin America that there was an understandable tendency to include as many women as possible in encyclopedic volumes.[2] Her biographical sketches are not typical, however, of semblanzas, because she takes into account the social and political as well as personal ramifications of being a woman and trying to be a writer. She includes semblanzas of women who have been lionized (Juana de Ibarbourou, Claudia Lars) and women who have scandalized. When these semblanzas were first published, Clementina

Suárez probably scandalized more than she inspired praise or adoration, although she now swings comfortably in the balance between these two extremes.

In her semblanza of Clementina, Julieta Carrera understates: "Her biography is interesting." She elaborates: "Alone against society she took up writing . . . as if obeying an inner impulse, she took up traveling . . . she traveled alone . . . carrying with her rouge a handful of poems. . . . One day when she urgently needed money for one of her daughters, she announced that she was giving a poetry recital in which she would recite—among other works—her poem 'Dressed in Starlight,' attired only in nature's chaste raiment. . . . She struggled with clergymen and with men endowed with a harem psychology. . . . While preserving her lyricism, she adopts the cause of the proletariat. . . . At times morbid; at times diabolical, ever sensual, even while treading revolutionary paths, Clementina's poetry shocks and disconcerts."[3]

The poet on the page began to take shape in my imagination—she was young and attractive, her eyes were dark, her hair fell in a natural style to her shoulders. She was frail, but she strode willfully when she walked. I saw a knapsack with a lipstick and a notebook. I pictured her on a train, on a bus, walking down Bucarelli in Mexico City, sitting in a café in Havana plotting poetic revolutions. I wondered what she had written in that notebook.

Two volumes of Honduran semblanzas added tantalizing bits of information, each in its own exaggeratedly lyrical fashion. With the encouragement of such phrases as "crying changes nothing in life," "there are times when she lays down her lyre and picks up a hammer to forge ideals to redeem the workers and the hungry," and "of uncommon intelligence," I began to flesh out my first dramatic vision of Clementina.[4] Perhaps she was a revolutionary as well as an iconoclast. Did I dare imagine her as a declared feminist? What a find!

As I began to locate volumes of her poetry I was pleased to find a passionate and unapologetic voice. They were also replete with grandiose lyric gestures and tender turns of phrase. I began to picture her as my ideal revolutionary: tough yet tender, intelligent and committed. She now wore a beret, loose-fitting gabardine pants, and comfortable shoes. She sat in smoke-filled cafés with other members of the fledgling Central American communist parties and traveled in search of a lover as revolutionary and committed as she. I was still intrigued by that lipstick in her pack and particularly by that anecdote in Julieta Carrera's semblanza about reciting her poetry disrobed. And I was somewhat disconcerted when I learned that her first book of poetry bore the maudlin title *Bleeding Heart.* There were pieces of this human puzzle that didn't fit together neatly.

Another literary gem surfaced that modified some of my original notions about this woman who was gradually but insistently working her way into my imagination. In 1969 the National University of Honduras published a tribute to Clementina Suárez, a compilation of critical appreciations of her poetry and her person written over the years by writers and literary critics from various countries, accompanied by an amazing collection of eighty-nine portraits of the poet. A year after the publication of this volume, she was awarded the Ramón Rosa National Award for Literature, Honduras's highest literary tribute. I began to see that Clementina was neither a solitary, romantic wanderer nor a militant revolutionary, but a writer of stature, a woman well known and much commented on, not only in her own country, but throughout Central America and beyond. I was embarrassed to recall my initial pride in having "discovered" a new and interesting woman writer when I realized that it seemed such a find only because of my own ignorance.

It will come as no news that Central American literature is virtually unread and unstudied in universities in the United States. Beyond the obligatory recognition that Guatemalan Miguel Angel Asturias won the Nobel Prize in 1967 and that Rubén Darío was the founder and leading figure of *modernismo,* little is known of the literary life of these five countries (six if one includes Panama), although interest in the political turmoil in El Salvador and Nicaragua has helped writers such as Claribel Alegría and Ernesto Cardenal gain much deserved recognition. I realized that to tell the story of Clementina's life and poetry I also would have to reconstruct the social and cultural milieu that both nourished and stifled her. To gather the pieces of that picture it would be imperative to spend time in Tegucigalpa and, if possible, in the other places she called home at various times in her life. One reason for this is the difficulty of obtaining Central American materials through the U.S. library system. But this is not the most significant reason, as access to Central American bibliography, I learned, is almost as difficult in Honduras as it is in the United States. Some Honduran scholars in fact believe that the best collection of Honduran materials is in the Library of Congress in Washington. Honduran literary studies have not been systematized nationally, so to try to work systematically is an exercise in frustration. But once understood and accepted, this situation can then free one to be creative in exploring nontraditional sources of information as well as research methods tailored to the particular kind of information sought.

Many Honduran scholars have recently begun to adopt the practice of footnoting, quoting, and citing sources, but more common has been a self-assuredness with which writers have retold history, analyzed society, or evaluated literature, producing books and essays rich in ideas and information but devoid of documentation. José Francisco Martínez, for example, published in 1987 a literary history of Honduras titled *La literatura hondureña y su proceso generacional* (*Honduran Literature and its Generational Process*). In its 501 pages there is not a single footnote, and the bibliography consists of fifteen items: ten books, three journals, one newspaper, and the mysterious entry "others." The book fairly bursts with informative biographical and bibliographical information on more than a hundred writers, as well as excerpts from their writing. But a scholar who wished to verify or expand upon any of the information offered would be unable to retrace the researcher's route, so many scholarly efforts become primary investigations.

I, too, found myself starting from the beginning, trusting to luck sometimes, at other times to friends and newly established connections to get myself where I wanted to go. Access to private collections could only be obtained through proper introductions. Interviews, likewise, especially with people of Clementina's generation, often had to be arranged by someone trusted by the interviewee in order to be fruitful. And since no comprehensive studies of Clementina's life or work had been done, I worked with a perpetual sense of absence of closure. Every person with whom I spoke, every book I read, every visit with Clementina would suggest new avenues to explore, new people to meet, new questions to ask the people I had already interviewed.

As we compared notes on the frustrations and illuminations of researching a Honduran topic, a philosophy professor at the Honduran National

University observed that there is much that has been studied and written, but discovering that it was written, locating it, and finally gaining access to it constitute only a part of one's task. For there is also much that has not been written, and one must rely on the testimony of the living, of those who have witnessed or participated in events or known certain people personally. Their stories are the ephemeral raw material that must be collected while they are still able to recall them.

Most Hondurans love to gossip. Speculation as to the financial solvency and marital fidelity of friends, foes, and public figures provides as much of the popular entertainment of Tegucigalpa as of any other community. But Hondurans generally are also very respectful of one another's privacy, and the etiquette governing the public use of private information tends to be genteel and discreet. This may be why a tradition of biographical literature has never taken hold or developed in Honduras, or in any Spanish-speaking country, for that matter. Semblanzas, plus an occasional laudatory biography of a president or national hero, satisfy the collective curiosity or perhaps serve as the official façade behind which citizens are free to speculate in parlors and cafés about the real personalities and the true motivations of public figures. The kind and amount of information that can appear in print without offending friends or family is minimal and usually uninteresting: date and place of birth, elaboration of the family tree, public accomplishments, membership in honorary societies, and official marital history, mentioning only legitimate offspring. The unwritten rule not to offend friends or family in print constrains the efforts of the biographer who is also an outsider to gather truly useful and interesting information. But I was aided in my search for authentic stories by Clementina herself. She has led a colorful and controversial life, and not the least of her accomplishments has been her insistence on living as she pleased and hiding nothing from society's critical eye. Since she has always made it a point to flaunt her inconformity and has insulted everyone worth insulting at one time or another, many of the people who spoke to me felt uninhibited about recounting scandalous behavior that they might have chosen not to mention had the subject been anyone else.

So the methodology of my research has been a combination of following the expected academic avenues, such as endless hours in the reading room of the archives of the Honduran National Library poring over newspapers and magazines, coupled with adventuring into uncharted territory armed with little more than intuition, goodwill, luck, and curiosity. I was lucky, for example, to meet and interview the aging Salvadoran painter José Mejía Vides at "a good time," as he said, on a day when even in his blindness he was seeing things in all the glorious color of an oil painting. On that particularly lucid day, he was able to remember names and dates from the past, and he recounted his infatuation with Clementina when he was a young painter in Mexico City as if it had happened last month. And goodwill and curiosity, as well as a degree of ideological compatibility, sustained me through times when my feelings for Clementina ranged from love and tenderness to anger, resentment, and suspicion.

Clementina Suárez is a complex woman with seemingly contradictory facets to her willful and outspoken character. Not surprisingly, she inspires a broad range of emotional reactions in the people who know her. She is loved tenderly and angrily despised; she is admired by some and dismissed contemptuously by others. I do not think it would be an exaggeration to say that more than any other Honduran woman, she has created a place for herself in the collective consciousness of her country. In the Honduran psyche she has played the roles of liberated woman, fallen woman, femme fatale, prostitute, broken-hearted lover, muse, revolutionary poet, respected woman of letters, bohemian, and promoter of the arts. It is not surprising, then, that the stories about her sometimes seem like fictional narratives. As I listened to people's anecdotes I came to appreciate in a fresh way that veracity is a culture-bound creation, subject to variations in definition and social import. I began to realize that there would be no getting to the truth of Clementina unless I could privilege one story over all the others, and whose story could I judge as best? Clementina's version of herself? Mine? Her daughters'? But which of her two daughters? They are so different, and each sees her mother in her own way. Was the real Clementina in her poetry? Or perhaps in the portraits, which now number over one hundred? But which of the portraits is the most like her real self?

During that initial visit to Tegucigalpa I lost my biographical innocence. The naïveté with which I had anticipated getting to know Clementina was replaced with a fundamental questioning both of Clementina's ability or willingness to tell me the "truth" about her life, and of the possibility of being able to claim, ever, under any circumstances, that one truly "knows" another human being. I had imagined visiting her with my tape recorder, asking her questions about her life that she would answer. I expected that she would tell me what she had done, when she had done it, why and how she wrote, whom she had loved, where she had traveled and when. I expected that the people I interviewed would do likewise and that from this collective memory I would be able to discern the real Clementina. I would peel away the layers and arrive at the golden center, the truth about her life. I thought she would be able (and willing) to lead me there. I was alternately charmed and bemused, encouraged and thwarted in the presence of this woman who presented her life as an open book, yet who handed me pages and chapters in erratic and seemingly random chronology, reserving the right to censor. Selective memory has become Clementina's most cherished ally in her old age, helping her to reconstruct her past to suit the image she would like to leave for posterity.

So Clementina, who I hoped would be my last and best resource in times of doubt and confusion, was, after all, not always the best source of information about herself. The story she chose to tell me, knowing that I was writing her biography, is only one version of her life. I have attempted, drawing on the many sources available to me, to construct one more portrait. And just as I emphasize that no single version is innocent because no version is created or nourished in isolation but is inevitably contaminated by time and space and subjectivity, so too I insist on the relativity of my point of view. What makes my story unique, however, is that it is fashioned from the perspective of an outsider. Some things that shocked a particular sensibility or tickled a particular fancy of mine may have gone unnoticed by a Honduran observer. Conversely, something that seemed natural to me, such as Clementina's passionate will to be independent, has to be appreciated in the context of a society that situates independence and individuality on a lower level than mine in its hierarchy of values.

My knowledge of my subject is a canvas full of holes, gaps in time and information: the lapses in Clementina's own memory, the death of old friends, the selectivity exercised in remembering and retelling by those friends and family members still alive, the empty spaces on library shelves where books and journals should have been. Sometimes the testimony of individuals I thought would be key was a mere rehearsal of received information, or a retelling of an often-told tale about a figure who had become legendary. I do not feel that I have gathered all the information, but I have come to accept the impossibility of that goal and have used the empty spaces as an integral part of my narrative pattern. Of course the information gaps to which I refer are the missing pieces recognized as such. And there is also the spectre of all that I have not considered because I have not known enough to realize that it was missing or untrue. As Victoria Glendinning admits, "We do not have much choice about lies and silences. They accrue whether we will it or not."[5]

Whatever the technique and no matter how thorough the gathering of information, the prevailing biographical ethic has been to present another's life with any of a variety of focuses, but from a distance. The biographer's role has been that of observer, compiler, analyst, and sometimes judge and jury, but it has been assumed and expected that the life writer will maintain at least the appearance of objectivity.[6]

It has been suggested to me that writing this biography clearly had assumed larger than scholarly importance for me, but that at some point I might have to admit that the subject I had chosen, or discovered, as I liked to think originally, would prove to be not important or representative enough. Colleagues feared that I would devote much time and effort to describing a life not worth the trouble. Who, after all, cared about a woman poet from a poverty-stricken Central American country, and not even a politically correct country such as Nicaragua, but the nation that had harbored the infamous Contras? No one I knew had ever heard of her. In my own and Clementina's defense, and as a kind of apology for her life, as well as from a genuine enjoyment that talking about her afforded me, I would counter with what I considered fascinating tales about a headstrong woman whose notoriety crossed national boundaries. I would tell about her unwed motherhood, her outspoken presence at ceremonious occasions, her friendships with artists, her enormous collection of portraits of herself, and her unique role in Central American culture. My friends were always entertained by these stories, then would counter with another question: But is her poetry any good?

My inability to answer that question comes not from an ambivalence regarding my own response to her work, because her poetry has offered me insights and responses that range from self-validation and empathy to anger, pain, and delight. My ambivalence stems rather from the recognition that in my research of Clementina's life and work, I have committed the ultimate academic sin: I have lost my objectivity. I have eaten at her table and sat by her bedside. She holds my arm when we walk down the street. I have combed my hair at her mirror and heard her read her unpublished memoirs. When I read her poems, I converse in my inner self with the poet both as I have known her and as I have imagined her. I cannot forget her life when I read her poetry, and I admire and am bemused and intrigued by her life.

Why this connection has been forged between myself, a third-generation Polish-Italian New England woman from a working-class family, and an upper-class Honduran poet of my grandmother's generation, is a fact I cannot explain. My relationship with Clementina has moved from simple curiosity to identification with an imagined heroine to demystification to the complex involvements of friendship. As a friend, but also as a literary critic, as a daughter enchanted by the tales of a foremother, as a mother, even, nurturing and perpetuating another woman's memory, I hope to add a link in a chain that connects beyond me, into other spaces, writing so she will not die.[7]

But rather than apologizing for my personal involvement in my subject, I choose to embrace this relationship as a fundamental structuring dialectic of this biography. All biographies, like all novels, or any text for that matter, have a point of view. I agree with Phyllis Rose's assertion that "there is no neutrality. There is only greater or lesser awareness of one's bias."[8] There are times in this story when I presume to speak for Clementina and times when I have let her speak for herself. At these times I have relied on her poetry, on the self she has created and projected through inspiration and publication. I have also quoted from interviews, those published as well as my conversations with her, and from her "memoirs."

At this writing Clementina's memoirs have not been published. They sit on the night table beside her bed, handwritten whenever the spirit moves her in a series of small, paper-covered, school-exercise notebooks, ideas and memories sprawling out in her characteristically large script. Her plan is that they be a record of her consciousness—her motivations and influences, the growth and transformations of her spirit. She makes no attempt to be chronological, perhaps because, as a friend observed, her memory is affective: "When Clementina writes or speaks she avoids dates. She herself guides her remarkable memory, defining the periods of her life based on emotions."[9] And she has been reluctant to have them published, although there is great interest in Tegucigalpa to read them, because while she lives, there will always be more to write about; memoirs that do not include one's experiences of aging would be incomplete. To finish the writing would somehow end the life, especially for a woman who has built her identity around her writing. There is a good deal of speculation among her friends as to what might be in those memoirs. She insists they will not interest the gossips because they reveal her poetic sensibilities rather than her erotic adventures. But the artists and poets of Tegucigalpa won't believe it, they are sure she mentions them all, and probably not very favorably. They will be surprised (and perhaps relieved) to learn that indeed Clementina's memoirs are intimate, but they reveal her inner doubts and dreams, retold at random, with pages literally left blank and sentences occasionally unfinished.

Clementina never offered to let me read them, and I often wondered if indeed those phantom memoirs existed, or if they were simply another chapter in her living legend. Shortly before I left Tegucigalpa she took out those notebooks one hot afternoon and, leafing through them, read aloud to me passages from each of them, which she allowed me to record. I have thus used three sources—her poetry, interviews, and the recorded fragments of her memoirs—as autobiographical material.

This story is informed by a vision of biographical practice that chooses not to be trapped either in the old-fashioned romanticizing of the narrating self as essential and transcendent, or the more current romanticizing of the self as ethereal, displaced, inscribed only to be erased.[10] The realization that the notion of the essential self is potentially confining, and that the deconstructed self, taken to its logical conclusion, is ultimately not worth talking about but only experiencing, has prompted me to look beyond these extremes. The feminist imperative not to lose the female subject, but to reinscribe her in society and in literary history as well as in her own texts, to accept and try to understand her lies and silences, encourages me to liberate a space within critical practice where I have the freedom to be creative. For example, the accusation that all women's literature is autobiographical, which has in the past carried with it an implicit permission to disregard women's writing, can be read as a simple, nonjudgmental statement of possible fact that allows us to see and appreciate the fabrication of female subjectivity through language. Rather than conflating the life with the text, or reading the text as a reflection of the life, the possibility of seeing the text as a kind of workshop or studio, a space where a woman can be herself, be with herself, experience herself as subject, encourage herself to be or act, or develop strategies for survival, allows for a reading of Clementina's poetry as autobiography that is richly suggestive.[11] Or the notion that autobiography is never the "truth" but inevitably a fictional construct, a game of mirrors and masks, can allow us to appreciate why women would be drawn to self-construction through self-narrative, and to read their texts, be they poetry, fiction, letters, or art, as work sessions in the building of the self.

This portrait is painted with colors reflected from the mirror of a woman poet's workshop of words. It respects her right to name herself. It hopes to bring the woman to life, yet leave the legend intact.

That last sentence acquires an unintended poignance because, after this biography was written but before I had secured a publisher, Clementina died. Faced with the option of incorporating her passing into the text, I decided not to make the changes that would have turned Clementina into a dead woman, but to leave intact the illusion of presence and relationship that informed so much of the original writing.

In the six years that have elapsed since I began this project, the writing of women's lives by women has blossomed. Every month there are new biographies of women published. And what is even more encouraging to me are the number of feminist biographers who have come to question the traditional approach to life writing, who not only have taken on the countless challenges inherent in telling, validating, and revalidating women's stories, but who also are sharing their thoughts about their own relationship to their subjects.[12] I am proud to make a contribution to this renaissance in life writing.

CHAPTER ONE

A Childhood of Privilege

Wealth and Eccentricity

Shouting and commotion erupted in the quiet streets of Juticalpa as someone yelled, "Clementina has killed herself!" The children playing outside went running in the direction of the gunshot to the home of Eduardo Burchard and Blanca Mejía de Burchard, Clementina's uncle and aunt. Clementina's mother, doña Amelia, rushed from her house holding her bathrobe closed with one hand and brandishing a knife in the other. "My daughter!" she screamed. "My Clementina! Who has killed my Clementina?"

A more embellished version has it that doña Amelia was out of sorts that day, in one of her "difficult times," and when she came running from her house she lunged at the first person she saw, a curious neighbor who had come out to observe the excitement, and grabbed her neck, choking her and yelling, "They've killed my daughter!" Gasping for air, the poor woman barely managed to croak, "Clementina is alive!" Clementina, hearing her mother's impassioned cries, came out of her uncle's house wrapped in a coverlet she had whisked off a chair in the living room. "Look, Mother, I'm fine! Perfect! There is nothing wrong!"

Another account takes the story beyond its initial drama to find Clementina despairing at her failed attempt to end her life. She refused to let the doctor treat her, insisting that they should let her die. What good was she to anyone, after all? She had aimed for her heart but missed. Some say a bullet was lodged in her shoulder and that she was in bed recuperating for three months; others say it barely grazed the soft underskin of her upper arm and in three days she was as good as new.

Local speculation as to the motive for such scandalous behavior tended to be commonsensical and judgmental. Most people assumed that it was an act of passion: Clementina had been seeing a young medical student from the nearby town of Manto, he had jilted her, and in typical lover's anguish the wronged woman decided to end her torment with a sensational exit. There was general agreement that a man was behind it, but not everyone was convinced that Clementina was seriously trying to take her life. She had a reputation for being pampered, romantic, willful, histrionic. What a wonderful way to get attention: set the scene for suicide, but be sure the damage is minor and not disfiguring. She had always been spoiled by her father, the neighbors said; once he was gone, she missed being the center of someone's concern.

Clementina herself insists that it is all gossip, the invention of a backward, provincial town starved for entertainment. Yes, there had been a gun, but she had shot it out of simple curiosity at how the thing worked. The shot had frightened her and apparently everyone else, but the bullet never hit her. No, she had not attempted to end her life that day in Juticalpa during her twenty-first year, only months after the death of her father. But she has known despair, and there have been times in her life when she has lost the will to live. "*I have had enormous depressions. My father died and I felt not exactly suicidal but terribly afraid, a frightening loneliness. So I said, that's it, I die or I leave. My father's death was a terrible crisis. In the first place, I had never before confronted death. And it was the death of someone I loved so much, I was so attached to him. Leave or die, because I told myself I wouldn't go on living here. Cornelio Mejía offered to take me with him, but I didn't feel enough affection to leave with him, to live with him. It was when I was in that terrible state that he said, 'Come with me, if you like.' But I insisted that I had to solve this problem on my own.*"[1]

Clementina Suárez's father, Luis Suárez, died 29 September, 1923. Clementina had celebrated her twenty-first birthday on 12 May of that same year. She would have been an adult woman by contemporary North American standards, but in Juticalpa, capital of the Honduran province of Olancho, in 1923 twenty-one was not a significant age, and a woman of Clementina's position could still be considered a young girl. The prevailing upper-class social myth was that women were monogamous, maternal, and domestic. Before marriage, a girl was instructed in household management by her mother and provided for by her father. When she married, she became the mother who would instruct her own children, while being provided for by her husband. Always under the protection of a man, a female was considered a girl until marriage miraculously transformed her into a woman.

The phenomenon of protracted female childhood was of course limited to women of the privileged classes, for in Honduras women of the lower classes typically must work, often outside the home, from an early age and must accept the responsibilities of homemaking, child care, and support of their families. But Clementina was a child of privilege. In the words of her lifelong friend, Medardo Mejía, "Clementina Suárez came from a wealthy home. A feudal house of spacious parlors and patios, in a fertile valley. A house of landowners and cattle ranchers, people who throughout Latin America have directed society and been the proprietors of culture."[2]

Clementina's mother, Amelia Zelaya Bustillo, was the daughter of Nicolasa Bustillo and Adán Zelaya, members of two of the richest and most powerful families of Olancho. Long before Clementina began scandalizing Honduran society with her rebellious and independent ways, her family had achieved a certain notoriety not only because of its wealth but by virtue of its interesting and eccentric individuals. The Zelaya family name was among the first to make its mark on this Central American territory when it was still part of the Captaincy General of Guatemala, subject to Spanish colonial rule. The Zelayas distinguished themselves for their ability to accumulate land and wealth and for their determination to keep their wealth in the family. Clementina counts among her ancestors and current family members some of the most distinguished, benevolent, and ruthless citizens of Honduras. In 1540 the Spanish crown awarded title to vast stretches of land in Olancho to Jerónimo Zelaya, who accompanied the conquistador Pedro de Alvarado on his expedition in Guatemala and Honduras. Don Jerónimo was the first European to colonize the Guayape Valley, and his descendants exercised political, military, and ecclesiastical control over Olancho as well as in Tegucigalpa and surrounding areas.[3]

In Tegucigalpa, Father José Simeón de Zelaya distinguished himself as a powerful church leader, of liberal inclinations as concerned the behavior and customs of the Indians.[4] He is remembered as the motivating force behind the construction of the cathedral in Tegucigalpa, completed in 1765.

Don Pedro Mártir de Zelaya, Father José Simeón's half brother, was a well-known merchant and mine owner, thought to be the wealthiest man of his time in Tegucigalpa. Among his possessions he counted numerous haciendas, many of them located in Olancho, in the fertile Lepaguare Valley. Don Pedro never married but is thought to have fathered many children, to whom he referred as his grandchildren in his will. He remembered them all at his death with thoughtful if not overly generous gifts, yet the bulk of his lands and wealth went to family members who legitimately bore the family name. Don Pedro was a unique and self-made man, taking into account, of course, the fact that simply bearing the Zelaya name put him at an advantage in a society easily impressed by lineage. Unlike his brother the priest, who sponsored the construction of Tegucigalpa's cathedral and defended St. Michael the Archangel as the city's patron saint, don Pedro was a devout follower of the Virgin of Guadalupe, the dark-skinned Indian Virgin, and contributed handsomely to the construction of the Church of Los Dolores, built in the part of town known as Barrio Abajo, the same neighborhood where Clementina would live, many generations later, as she defied the proprieties expected from a woman who bore the Zelaya name. This neighborhood was populated mostly by Indians and mulattoes and was a hotbed of radicalism in the prerevolutionary decades of the late eighteenth and early nineteenth centuries. It was don Pedro's preferred part of town, its inhabitants his preferred company. Who knows how many of the mestizo and mulatto children who played in the streets of this neighborhood were his offspring?

Again, many of them were mentioned in his will but did not inherit sufficient wealth to rise above their marginalized status. They were, however, "protected" by their benefactor. In Honduras, as in other Latin American countries, protection is an important social relationship whereby the powerful or influential defend certain preferred individuals from the attacks of other powerful and influential individuals who happen to look less favorably upon the chosen one. The "protectees" in this case were favored because of a blood relationship, albeit an illegitimate one, but often those protected are favored because they are creative or talented persons whose financial situation or social position sets them at a disadvantage. Protection may take the form of financial largesse or of using one's prestige to fend off the enemy's verbal attacks or to counterattack with one's own verbal or written salvo. Protectionism is both powerful and subtle and is tightly woven into the fabric of social relationships in Honduras. It is as important today as it ever was, understood and revered by all. It helps one get a job; it produces favorable reviews of books; it opens doors to permissions and privileges. It has often played a significant role in Clementina's life, for, although she was born into privilege, her generation has witnessed the erosion of the old order, and the Zelaya family no longer commands the unquestioned respect that it did in the past.

Clementina's maternal great-grandparents, Felipe Bustillo and Apolinaria Ayala de Bustillo, have earned themselves a place in the folklore of Olancho, partly through the efforts of Honduran writer Medardo Mejía, who wrote down the story of the famous couple that had long circulated as part of the local oral tradition, with all the variations and embellishments that characterize often-told tales.[5] Family members and residents of Olancho may relate it in their own fashion, but don Medardo's version describes doña Apolinaria as a powerful matriarch who controlled poor don Felipe's every move—while he was at home. But he was a wealthy cattle rancher and frequently accompanied his men on long cattle drives to deliver his animals for sale in Guatemala. Once out of sight of his domineering wife, he rejoiced in his freedom. While his trusted employees looked after his cattle, he visited all of his favorite stops, leaving numerous little Felipes and Felipas along the way. But somehow doña Apolinaria always knew if her husband had behaved himself on his long trips. If he had been good, she would sit on a tall chair that resembled a throne and order her servants to decorate the hacienda for don Felipe's return. All manner of succulent food would be set out, musicians would be called in, and a celebration that lasted three days and three nights would be prepared. As his horse entered the stable, she would order a bath to be drawn for her husband and indicate that he was to bathe with scented soap. But if she learned that his behavior had been less than exemplary, from her thronelike chair she would order that his bath be prepared with lard soap and that he be served tortillas and beans for supper.

Don Felipe's fame was based on more than his curious relationship with his wife, however. Besides being a wealthy rancher and landowner, he served as congressman from Olancho during the government of Trinidad Cabañas, as vice-president of the Republic during the term of Juan Lindo, and as acting president of Honduras from October to December 1848.

Popular opinion in Honduras tends to revere certain figures unconditionally and to make sport of those lesser figures who have not attained heroic stature in the public estimation.[6] So Felipe Bustillo, for all his merits, is remembered as a man who was browbeaten by his wife and who, during his two months as acting president of the country, "spent half his time sleeping and the other half doing nothing."[7]

Doña Apolinaria and don Felipe were living their lives as provincial aristocrats when the North American businessman-explorer-writer William Wells left California to travel over one thousand miles by horse and mule from Nicaragua, across the border into Honduras, to Tegucigalpa, through Olancho, and back to Tegucigalpa. His stated purpose was "to report to a number of gentlemen in San Francisco, who had become interested in my proposed enterprise of procuring from the government of Honduras the right to work gold placers, and to establish commercial stations for the export of hides, timber, dyewoods, and other valuables, by the river Guayape or Patook, from the department of Olancho. But, upon considering how little was then known of Honduras, I determined, after my arrival, in addition to the duties I had specified for myself, to devote some part of every day to a diary or journal of passing events, embracing the peculiarities of character and customs, and the general occurrences of travel among a primitive and secluded people."[8]

Wells's journey lasted a year, and indeed he spent a great deal of time writing his observations of everything from the landscape and architecture to the physiognomy of President Cabañas to the flora, fauna, and climate. He describes the food, the festivals, the manners and morals of the people he met and who invited him into their homes. His view, of course, is that of the outsider, and his observations are at times colored by his racism and his belief in the innate superiority of the industrious North American, but the book that grew out of his diary is nevertheless an invaluable document of its time.

Wells wanted to explore Olancho because of its reputation as an area rich in gold. The California gold rush was still a warm memory, and there was also interest among certain sectors to turn all or part of Central America into the kind of slave states that were becoming increasingly less viable in the southern United States. Wells left Tegucigalpa for Olancho with letters of recommendation from President Cabañas and other high officials introducing him to General Francisco Zelaya, the current patriarch of the Zelaya family. He was warned by the Honduran president that the inhabitants of Olancho had a longstanding and well-deserved reputation for being ferociously independent. Separated from the rest of the Republic by a barrier of mountains, they considered themselves an autonomous entity and had refused to pay taxes or allow their young men to be conscripted into military service. The province had in fact gained a reputation of legendary proportions for being a land of gun-slinging cattlemen with a propensity for violence, fiercely loyal and regionalistic.

What Wells found, after a week-long trek by mule from Tegucigalpa, was an area of diverse natural beauty where jaguars, tapirs, wild pigs, and poisonous snakes were abundant. Toucans, quetzals, and the curious oropendula graced the treetops, and an impressive variety of plants and trees were cultivated or grew wild and untended in the wide, warm valleys as well as in the cooler higher altitudes. Fine horses, cattle, and mules were the pride of the province and expert horsemanship an important manifestation of virility. The social structure in Olancho in 1854 was of a semifeudal nature, with large haciendas owned by a small number of families. Of these powerful families, the Zelayas probably controlled the greatest wealth and exercised the widest authority. There were five Zelaya brothers: Francisco, known as General don Chico, the supreme patriarch, José Manuel, Lorenzo, Santiago, and José María. Clementina is descended from the first Zelaya to settle in Olancho, Jerónimo, through the branch of José María. Clementina's maternal grandmother, Nicolasa Bustillo Ayala, daughter of the legendary Felipe and Apolinaria, was married to Adán Zelaya, son of José María Zelaya.[9]

Contrary to the warning from President Cabañas, Wells was received by the Zelaya family with great dignity and hospitality. He was a guest at don Francisco's hacienda, which he depicts upon first seeing as "a scene of rare loveliness."[10] The enchanting vision he describes is one of pastoral simplicity, its seeming naturalness the product of a carefully nurtured class system. "Grouped trees stood far removed along the valley; the lowing of herds was borne faintly on the evening wind; voices, almost lost in the distance, came from the hacienda; a few horsemen appeared like specks on the plain. . . . A crowd of children, laughing and screaming, thronged about the gate, but ran hastily away as we approached. Wild mares and half-broken mules, fastened by hide tethers to logs, snorted as we jingled past; a noble black stud, with mane and tail flowing in the breeze, sprang away over the soft carpet of grass at the rattle of our spurs; wild-looking cows 'blew' at us as we neared them. . . . The placid-looking old Indian women engaged about the premises gazed curiously at us as we stopped, and a splendidly caparisoned horse, with silver-mounted *machillas, pistoleras,* and crimson *mantillas,* sidled proudly away from our shaggy mountain mules. . . . The master of the house, Don Francis Zelaya, then appeared . . . and placed his house and all in it at our disposition. Señor Don Chico is literally 'monarch of all he surveys.' He is tall and handsome, with a portly figure and commanding aspect, blue eyes, square forehead, and crisp, curling hair of iron-gray. In the affairs of his own country he does not lack sagacity or knowledge" (272–73).

Much of the land that Wells deemed richest in gold belonged to the Zelayas, and his ultimate goal was to return to the United States with a legal document signed by the owners of this land, granting him mining rights. On his visits to these sites he was surprised to find women wading ankle-deep in the rivers, laughing and smoking, sifting the sand and water through rustic sieves. Panning for gold was considered a woman's occupation, and don Francisco graciously allowed these women to work the rivers, insisting only that they request permission beforehand, permission that was apparently never denied, but the requesting of which had become a ritual formality scrupulously observed. Don Francisco insisted on this formality, Wells conjectured, "owing to the family jealousy of their ancient possessions, and their fear that any infringement upon them might eventually lead to the 'squatting' of unprincipled persons upon their territories. . . . Any women found washing gold without permission were invariably expelled, and never thereafter allowed to work on the estates" (280–81).

This is an example of the kind of benevolent feudalism on which the Honduran aristocracy has long prided itself. It is based on a clearly defined class system and a recognition and acceptance by all parties of their respective roles in the smooth functioning of this system. Members of the old landowning aristocracy of Olancho like to remember the days when people knew their place. There were those who were entitled by birth to the privileges of owning land and being served, and those whose birthright was to live on land owned by others and to serve them. Because people knew their place, they could without awkwardness be more familiar. The loyal servant could ask the *patrón* for a favor and expect that his request would be honored. Whole families lived on the patrón's land, and generation after generation would serve the patrón's family and his heirs after him. The patrón would often be the godfather to the newborn children of his workers. In fact, it is quite likely that many of the servant children playing on the grounds and in the stables of the haciendas were offspring of the patrón himself. Don Chico, like his predecessor don Pedro, was willing to share himself with the lower classes, if not his property. As Wells observed of his host: "Don Chico is a great rogue among the women, and the remarkable similarity to be traced in the features of several coffee-colored urchins running about the hacienda led me to suspect that they might claim a close relationship to our entertainer" (274).

But legitimacy was a very powerful myth and served to limit the number of descendants who could legally lay claim to the patrón's lands. Nonetheless, with each succeeding generation the Zelaya lands have been subdivided into smaller and smaller parcels.

There are still members of the Zelaya family who live and own land in Olancho. Clementina and Graciela sold their share of the family lands to their sisters Rosa and Lola, who moved to Tegucigalpa, although they and members of their families keep it productive and struggle not to allow it to be taken from them through the vagaries of agrarian reform. For all its long tradition of independence and isolation, Olancho has not been able to isolate itself from change resulting from the political forces of the present—popular revolutionary movements, labor unions, peasant organizations, agrarian reform. In 1975 a member of the Zelaya family, José Manuel, faced with the situation his ancestor don Francisco foresaw when he cemented his claim to his land by requiring that anyone wishing to pan for gold first request his permission, was unwilling or unable to deal with it as gracefully as don Francisco and was implicated in the infamous massacre of Los Horcones. According to the account of a peasant organizer, local cattle ranchers paid the military to prevent a union movement from pressuring the government to pass an agrarian reform law. Five demonstrators were killed at a union training center, and nine others, including two priests, were tortured and killed. Their bodies were found in a well on the ranch of José Manuel Zelaya.[11]

Nor has Olancho escaped ecological changes. A large part of this state that was once so lush with vegetation has suffered deforestation at the hands of farmers, cattle ranchers, international paper companies, and U.S. troops building roads through Olancho in the 1980s as part of their effort to aid the Nicaraguan Contras.[12]

Clementina's mother, Amelia Zelaya Bustillo, was the only daughter of Nicolasa Bustillo and Adán Zelaya. Although she had two brothers, Felipe and Próspero, being the only daughter made her the object of constant and loving attention, not only from her parents but from the numerous servants of all ages who lived in the patrón's house or on the hacienda. She had no responsibilites as a child and was pampered in even the smallest detail. Servants helped her bathe and dress; they brushed her hair and styled it using the elegant imported combs of which she was so fond. Because she was not required to participate in household chores, she never learned to cook or sew or perform even the simplest domestic tasks. Doña Amelia grew up on the family hacienda, San Roque, near Jutiquile, about eight miles north of Juticalpa. There she developed her even-tempered personality, her indolence, and her sense of superiority. Even after her marriage to Luis Suárez and the birth of her four girls, she continued to live the life of a spoiled only daughter.

There is the story of that first morning after her wedding to don Luis when he asked his new bride to fix him an egg for breakfast. She proceeded to put an egg, intact in its shell, into an empty pan and to put the pan on the fire, waiting for the egg to cook. Then there is the story of the time a chigger laid its eggs in the sole of her foot. She asked the girls who looked after her needs at San Roque to remove them because they were quite painful. They began the extraction with a pin, but doña Amelia complained that that method was painful and couldn't they get them out with cologne instead? It became a great joke, and whenever the children on the hacienda acted fussy or demanding their mothers would say, "Well, you must think you are Amelia, wanting to extract chigger eggs with cologne!"

She adapted to married life and motherhood with the same languorous amiability that characterized her childhood. She grew fat and lazy and declined to perform any tasks that felt like work, content to let her husband take charge of feeding and clothing the children while she swung in her hammock reading romantic novels or sat in a chair in her doorway dressed in her bathrobe, watching the provincial life of Juticalpa pass by. Whether from choice or from her inability to cook, doña Amelia's diet was unusual for Juticalpa. Olancho was known for its fine cattle, and the typical diet of those who could afford it was one of meat, milk, cheese, beans, and tortillas. But uninterested in either the consumption or the preparation of meat, doña Amelia ate mostly fruit and cheese, and her daughters did likewise.

The culinary style of doña Amelia's mother, doña Nicolasa, was more typical of the importance accorded to food and its preparation in Olancho. Froylán Turcios, one of the best-known Honduran writers of the early decades of the twentieth century, was born in Juticalpa and fondly remembered hearty breakfasts at the Bustillo home. Doña Nicolasa was his godmother, and he describes her in his memoirs as "a grand lady from the old days, open, intelligent, giving." He recalls her breakfasts: "Fresh fried eggs, excellent sausages, golden plantain tortillas, egg breads, pastries and numerous other dishes surrounded the hot, steaming cup of coffee and milk or the gourd of thick hot chocolate. 'Eat, my son,' she would urge. 'Eating with gusto is a pleasure.' In and out of the kitchen she went, bountiful and solicitous, bringing a bubbling pan of beans or a tasty avocado salad"[13]

Doña Nicolasa, the personification of the mythic nurturing mother, somehow failed in her responsibility to pass on the tools of adult womanhood to her daughter Amelia. The young girl who is magically transformed into the capable adult when she is passed from father to husband never quite materialized in Amelia. She in turn was incapable of passing on the traditional female skills to her daughters, although they have all managed to acquire a minimal domestic competence on their own, especially Clementina, who throughout her adult life has set up house and dismantled her living quarters countless times. She has been married twice and raised two daughters. Relatives marvel at her skill in cooking and sewing and are impressed by her neatness. These skills may seem commonplace, but for a woman of Clementina's background, they are symbolic of a life lived in opposition to tradition.

The marriage of Amelia Zelaya and Luis Suárez forms yet another chapter in the eccentric history of the Zelaya clan. The Suárez family was a large one, whose members, representing four main groups as of 1800, were spread throughout Honduras, El Salvador, Guatemala, Costa Rica, and the United States. Luis, the son of Angel Suárez and Julia Araya, was born in Cedros, a small town about 160 kilometers due west of Juticalpa, a distance that in the last decade of the nineteenth century in Honduras would have made it today's equivalent of being in another country. And, in fact, one of the objections of Amelia's family was that her suitor was a foreigner, because he was not from Olancho. At their father's death, the education of Luis and his two brothers, Pío and Angel, was assumed by an uncle from El Salvador, who saw to it that the three young men were educated at the University of San Carlos in Guatemala. Of the three brothers, Pío and Angel became doctors, while Luis studied law.

Young Luis Suárez arrived in Juticalpa with a government appointment as district judge. He owned no land and had no great personal wealth, but he quickly earned the respect and admiration of the community. He is remembered as an intelligent individual and a talented lawyer. It is said that he accepted only cases in which he acted as lawyer for the defense, refusing on principle to play the role of accuser. Amelia's father was not convinced initially that Luis was the best match for his pampered daughter, because Luis did not lay claim to an aristocratic lineage. There are family stories of Adán Zelaya whisking his daughter away to stay with her cousins in the north coast town of Trujillo in the hopes that Luis would not persist. But Luis and Amelia married, and the Zelaya family came to realize that what Luis lacked in land and wealth, he more than made up for in political astuteness and in the esteem in which he was held by all who knew him.

Luis Suárez, indulging in a practice familiar to many Honduran men, produced his first offspring, María Luisa, out of wedlock. He acknowledged his paternity and taught his legitimate children that María Luisa was their sister. Whether his egalitarianism extended into the realm of economic support is not clear, nor does it seem that the children of his marriage to Amelia Zelaya ever fully accepted this lesson, for they continue to refer to their family as comprised of four sisters, and María Luisa seldom surfaces in their family reminiscences.

Juticalpa, Provincial Capital

The legitimate family of Luis Suárez and Amelia Zelaya began with the birth of Clementina on 12 May, 1902, followed by three sisters: Rosa, born in 1904, Dolores in 1907, and Graciela in 1912. Clementina was born in a house on one of the streets that bordered the central plaza of Juticalpa. Her parents lived in this house, which was the property of her grandmother, for a few years after their marriage, but they later moved to another location one block off the plaza, this house becoming their permanent residence. It is important to emphasize the proximity of the Suárez home to the central plaza of Juticalpa, because in the hierarchy of provincial urban demographics in turn-of-the-century Honduras, the families of greatest prestige lived closest to the center. Their houses were large, often encompassing the area of an entire city block, with cool, spacious, high-ceilinged rooms with large shuttered windows looking onto the plaza. Their ample interior courtyards were lush with fruit trees and flowering plants and home to the usual barnyard animals. The residents of the area of town more distant from the center were, in the logic that follows the worldview that subscribes to knowing one's place and staying in it, not the aristocracy. They were merchants, tradespeople, and artisans. The Indians lived on the periphery, where town blended into countryside.

But while the homes in the center may have been "better located," larger, and more richly furnished, in fact there were certain conditions of life that everyone in Juticalpa, rich and poor alike, shared. When Clementina and her sisters were growing up, there were no paved roads in Olancho.[14] To travel from Juticalpa to the capital city, Tegucigalpa, was a journey of from five to eight days by mule. The length of time necessary for the trip varied because, as one resident of Juticalpa who remembers making the trip in his youth expressed it, "One traveled at the animal's pace." One took along a hammock and hung it in a friendly courtyard if one was available, otherwise under the stars. In Juticalpa there was no hospital, no interior plumbing, no electricity. Barefoot water carriers led their donkeys through town announcing that they had water for sale for those whose servants did not carry water from the river.

No one escaped the daily sights, sounds, and smells that were a constant reminder that Juticalpa was living a life lost in time, far from the changes that were bringing comforts and disquiet to the modern world. A native of Juticalpa remembers the sounds and discomforts: "Animals roaming the streets were part of the daily spectacle offered to residents and visitors alike. The sounds of a squeaking cart, the braying of donkeys, the barking of dogs, the croaking of frogs, the squawking and clucking of roosters and chickens, the crying of a young boy, the scolding of a grandmother, the knock at the door of the vendor selling supplies for the day's meals, carried in a basket or an old cooking pot. And the endless infestations of all kinds of insect pests: mosquitos, flies, horseflies, roaches, chiggers, without the aid of insecticides and using homemade smoke-bombs rather than fly-tox; bedbugs in the wooden beds lined with cowhide, scalding them periodically with hot water.[15]

Little was produced or manufactured in or near Juticalpa, except those wares absolutely necessary for basic survival in an agricultural and cattle-raising economy. Goods were brought in from Tegucigalpa to the south, or from Trujillo, the port on the Caribbean coast through which most merchandise imported into Honduras passed, a journey of fifteen days by mule to the north. Juticalpa at the turn of the century was a town of approximately six thousand inhabitants, although the population swelled considerably during major holidays such as 8 December, the Feast of the Immaculate Conception, or on market days, when people from neighboring towns and surrounding haciendas arrived to sell their wares.

Sunday was market day, when the town, saturated during the week with "a ghostly placidity," came alive with the calls of vendors announcing their wares, the smells of favorite regional foods being prepared in the streets, and the presence of numerous visitors buying, selling, eating, drinking, playing music, and generally being social.[16] Women in the market sold eggs, poultry, fruit, medicinal herbs, liquidambar, and flowers. They prepared *tapado olanchano,* a kind of stew made of fatty beef, *tostacas, empanadas* and *rosquillas en miel,* small, round, doughy rolls served with honey. They offered conserves of *palmito,* papaya, and pineapple. Men smoked, drank the local liquor known as *mistel,* gambled, and socialized. There were woven baskets from Tulín, tobacco from Guacoco, cloth from Río Tinto, and gold from Guayape. From Guarisama came articles made from the fiber of the maguey plant—ropes, bags, and harnesses for pack animals—while Catacamas and Gualaco were known for their coffee. The area produced fruits and vegetables, but not in the variety or abundance one would expect from a region of such temperate climate and fertile soil. As Froylán Turcios observed, "Besides watermelon and cantaloupe in the summer, and sapodillas, limes, bananas, guavas and some wild fruits, our region lacked, through negligence and lack of initiative on the part of its inhabitants, many of nature's delicious gifts. The pineapples, oranges and mangoes were very acidic" (59).

Sunday was also the day for rest and for excursions into the surrounding hills and countryside. People traveled to their Sunday destinations on foot, by bicycle, on horseback or muleback, or in ox-drawn carts called *carretas.* One of the most popular outings was the excursion in search of wine from the cohune palm, known as *vino de coyol.* Caravans of twenty or more young people would set out on foot or in ox carts at three or four in the morning to travel several miles to the place where the select palm trees grew that, when slit open in a particular fashion, provided a libation that inspired local pride. Clementina and her sisters often joined these outings and recall being allowed to drink the wine at social gatherings.

One could also attend the local military band concerts on Thursdays and Sundays in the Central Plaza. This public park served as a gathering place; residents came out and circled the plaza slowly, greeting and observing their neighbors as they performed the identical ritual. One of Clementina's fondest memories is going out every afternoon to stroll in the plaza with her father as the sun was setting.

A favorite pastime of the men in this quiet town was drinking. Women, of course, were not allowed to drink, at least not in public, although some probably did at home. But because drinking was (and is) considered such a characteristically masculine indulgence, it is not surprising that Clementina's imbibing has been so criticized.

Luis Suárez drank heavily, sometimes in the company of his friends, such as fellow lawyer Ramón Lobo Herrera. He was the kind of drinker who preferred companionship to solitary bouts with the bottle, so when his friends were unavailable, he often visited the local drinking establishments in the company of his little daughter Clementina. She remembers sitting by while he drank and talked. Sometimes she would stretch out on one of the rustic wooden benches and fall asleep, and when he was finally ready to leave she would take him by the hand and accompany him home over the dark, silent streets of Juticalpa.

Residents of Juticalpa whose requirements went beyond the local products sold at the public market or peddled door to door could satisfy their desires for the fine, the exotic, or the imported at one of the three major stores in the center of town. Two of them, Casa Siercke and Casa Rossner, were owned by citizens of German descent. Together with Casa Soto, they provided cloth, perfumes and lotions, china, hardware, and numerous other articles brought by mule train from Trujillo or Tegucigalpa. Luis Suárez at one time owned a small store near the center of town, but it was never his vocation to be a merchant, and the business was neither very lucrative nor of great duration.

Considering the difficulties of transportation, it is not surprising that even the homes of the well-to-do in the center of town were not sumptuously decorated, although some people still remember the piano that arrived by mule train, and some households managed to acquire ornate mirrors, carved bedposts, and reproductions of classical paintings. Froylán Turcios recalled his father's love of all things rare and beautiful and the superhuman efforts required to bring these rare and beautiful objects over the mountains to Juticalpa. He tells of three heavy mahogany dressers with large mirrors that arrived at the port of Trujillo from the United States. His father commissioned a laborer at the docks to deliver them to Juticalpa unharmed for two hundred pesos. He would have to carry them over eighty leagues of steep, rough terrain. Shortly after delivering the final dresser, he died of exhaustion.

Turcios described his family home, located two blocks from the plaza, as being the best house in town in the final decades of the nineteenth century. "It had two large courtyards. The main one, which was paved with stones, boasted three large trees. The most important rooms opened onto this courtyard: three bedrooms, the store and the parlor. It was surrounded, on the inside, by a spacious corridor that enclosed a bronze fence with graceful gates on either end. . . . The second courtyard, separated from the first by an adobe wall, was an orchard of oranges, custard apples, gourds and *izotes*. . . . There were the two large rooms used to warehouse the merchandise that came each month from Trujillo. Beside them, the room that housed the toilet, clean and hygienic, the only one of its kind at that time in the region" (17).

This mansion later housed the Colegio la Fraternidad, the local public secondary school, and is now a municipal building that has been allowed to fall into sad disrepair. Only a small plaque on its dark pink wall testifies to its former splendor. In fact, most of the sprawling homes in the center of town, which during Clementina's childhood covered entire city blocks, have been divided and subdivided to accommodate the exigencies of dwindling fortunes and the claims of the children and grandchildren to their inheritance. The house on the Central Plaza where Clementina was born is now a savings bank; the house a block away where she grew up is an auto parts store. It too was subdivided, split among Clementina and her three sisters when doña Amelia died in 1955.

Only a few people left in town remember a time when people knew their place and behaved accordingly, when life moved more slowly, and Tegucigalpa was very far away. Their reminiscences are unabashedly nostalgic and permeated with a sense of loss. One resident remembers the Festival of the Immaculate Conception in these terms: "Religion was at the heart of the fair; there wasn't the corruption then that there is now. Now the first thing one sees are gambling tables. They had them before, but it was more reserved; adults gambled, but not children. And very few women. Later when I went to Tegucigalpa, I was shocked to see gambling tables, and all manner of women, even from high society, were gambling. In those days people were respectful; it would have been unthinkable that anyone would dare to steal your wallet, to rob you. Inconceivable. Before, people used to leave their doors unlocked at night."

Being so isolated from other centers of population, Juticalpa developed its own culture, education, and entertainment. As one old gentleman remarked: "In those days one had to be knowledgeable. I know a bit of everything. I can play any instrument—piano, guitar, flute, mandolin. I learned it all myself." Acetylene lamps illuminated the Central Plaza at night, but the side streets and neighborhoods were dark, and even though oil lamps and candles provided light in homes, it was customary to retire early. Another resident recalls: "Juticalpa was a sad place; one would walk down the street and not see another living soul."

Another old gentleman remembers life in Juticalpa as being beautifully simple. "The outings to collect *coyol* with friends, and the dances, they were so much fun. The parties were high-class, society events, now everything's been ruined. It's no good any more. Now anyone who pays two dollars can get in and dance. Before, we danced to marimba music, but no more. Adult parties were serious: married couples only, a select crowd. The young people had their own parties. I remember Clementina used to go to those dances, but she wasn't a young lady who partied a lot. . . . We used to get a cart and go out into the country, about twenty of us. Some would ride in the cart, but most of us would walk, so we could talk with each other. It was nice. Everyone was happy, yelling and singing. Now, going out in a car, one doesn't experience the same pleasure."

This gentleman's brother also remembers slower, sweeter, more innocent times. "I used to take Clementina for rides on my bicycle, she liked going out with me and a friend of hers, María Rivera. So I would get a friend of mine and we would take the two girls out for a bicycle ride. It was so pleasant back then, we wouldn't try to make love to a girl or harm her in any way. We used to ride all around Juticalpa at night on our bicycles. And they were dark nights, because before there were no street lights here. Clementina wasn't a poetess back then, she was a young girl. Then she went to Tegucigalpa, she disappeared. At night we used to play cards at her house. Life was beautiful. There were exclusive dances, and the girls were very proper. You had to say to them, 'I beg your pardon, may I have this dance?' Now they just grab the girls and, 'Let's dance!' "

La Literata

Clementina and her sisters attended a public school that went through fifth grade. Girls and boys were segregated through grade three but received classes together the last two years. There were no private academies then in Juticalpa; occasionally a family would choose not to send their children to the public school and would employ a private tutor, but this was the exception and not the rule. Attendance was not obligatory, so it was not unusual for students not to complete the year, or to finish only through second or third grade. The local secondary school, La Fraternidad, founded in 1897, was an all-male institution until 1924. Trinidad Casco, Ramona Vanegas, and Teresa Lanza were the school's first female graduates, in 1927.

Girls who wished for a higher education before La Fraternidad permitted them to enroll had to seek instruction elsewhere. Many went to Tegucigalpa to attend the Escuela Normal para Señoritas, or women's teachers' college. Their parents or relatives accompanied them on the arduous trip to the capital in February and returned for them in November. During the academic year they lived at the school under the strict military-style supervision of the notorious headmistress "La Chilena," but they would normally return to spend vacation, which coincided with the Christmas celebrations, in Juticalpa or on the family hacienda. It seems logical that Clementina, with her wanderlust and love of books, would have wanted to join her friends at the Escuela Normal, but in fact this kind of regimen was unappealing to her. She has never stopped studying and learning, but her methods and materials have not fit into an institutional curriculum.

Notwithstanding the apparent informality of public schooling in Juticalpa, the town's older residents consider their education to have been superior to the instruction that children receive today. They remember their teachers as dedicated and hardworking; they recall a strict program of instruction in geography and history, and they are proud of the beautiful handwriting they were taught.

There was only one store in Juticalpa that sold books. The establishment of Carlos Gálvez displayed volumes that few people ever bought, so the genial Gálvez would loan his books to interested parties. Clementina remembers visiting his shop and being allowed to read the books without purchasing them. One could read magazines and newspapers brought in from Tegucigalpa, such as *Esfinge,* a literary magazine edited by Froylán Turcios. Turcios had moved from Juticalpa to Tegucigalpa in 1893 after his father's death and the family's subsequent change of fortune, and he was energetically involved in promoting "universal cultural values" in Honduras. Between 1912 and 1915 he helped found the writers' group El Ateneo de Honduras, serving as its president and directing its literary publication. He also founded and edited *Esfinge,* a biweekly anthology whose stated goal was "extracting the purest gold from the most beautiful volumes and selecting from the best journals that I received, beautiful paragraphs and refined sonnets." *Esfinge* was a slim, attractive publication in which one could read passages from Schopenhauer, Gabriel D'Annunzio, Baudelaire, Walt Whitman, and Kant in translation, as well as the work of noted writers in the Spanish language such as Rubén Darío, Julio Herrera y Reissig, Delmira Agustini, and Ramon del Valle-Inclán. To complete its offerings, *Esfinge* also included works by Honduran authors such as Juan Ramón Molina, Rafael Heliodoro Valle, Luis Andrés Zúñiga, and, of course, Froylán Turcios. Turcios continued his efforts to bring to Hondurans the gems of world literature with the publication of the journal *Ariel,* beginning in 1925.

There was of course no separate genre of juvenile literature, so Clementina read *Esfinge* and *Ariel* as well as everything else she could get her hands on. She remembers being especially entertained as a young reader by *Don Quixote,* and being captivated by the figure of Sancho Panza. It has also stuck in her mind that she read Juan Montalvo, the controversial Ecuadorian essayist, when she was scarcely nine years old. Reading permeated her life in Juticalpa: there were long, quiet days swinging in a hammock with a novel, weekends and vacations at San Roque when she would often wander into the countryside with a book. Books were her best friends, any and all books. In her collection of portraits a whimsical oil by Gines Parra depicts her as a young girl sitting at a desk reading, one hand propping up her chin, the other holding open a book. The background is blue, framing the concentration of the seated figure, which absorbs the space of the canvas. She is a little girl lost in a dream, living in her book. "*One always has inside oneself a personal secret, that is what it means to have a world complete unto itself, as in creation. One is born incorporeal, everyday, familiar. The world I invent, I live, and I make it live in my poetry. . . . How would it be possible to submerge myself in reality? I would like to be a woman like all the rest; it is painful to be unlike them. For me, what one lives, thinks, remembers, dreams, that is me. I belong to myself. Not invented, but drawn from myself. Since I was a child I have preferred the heights, and I read whatever book came my way. I arrived carrying Juan Montalvo, which earned me the mocking name of 'the literata' from my classmates. But I paid no attention to them, I kept myself occupied doing new and pleasurable things. The magic of Jules Verne held me captive. By this time I had begun to write, I don't remember what, but I used to write in little notebooks, which kept me isolated from the others. I had my favorite places, in the country as well as in town, where I was creating my separate world.*"[17]

Her father also sensed her precociousness, calling her "la literata," but his use of the term was affectionate and encouraging. As there was no public library at her disposal, Clementina turned to the private libraries of the residents of Juticalpa. Froylán Turcios describes his childhood of plundering the private libraries in town, probably in much the same way Clementina did. "By the time I was nine years old I had devoured my father's library, which contained six hundred works of various genres, as well all the novels in town I could get my hands on, by buying or borrowing. All the works by Verne, Sué, Mayne, Red, Walter Scott, Dickens, Balzac, Dumas, etc., that were to be found in Juticalpa, passed through my hands at that time, in rapid rotation, because my thirst for reading could never be satisfied. . . . My budding critical judgment was lost in those heterogeneous readings and I did not appreciate the quality of the authors." He claims with characteristic assuredness that at the time (c. 1885) there were fifteen hundred volumes in Juticalpa in various private collections. He was particularly impressed by the library of Pedro Rivera Bustillo, who introduced him to "Chateaubriand, . . . Victor Hugo, Lamartine, Racine, Corneille, Molière, Goethe, Schiller, Heine, Byron, Moore, Shakespeare, Milton, Dante, Petrarch, Tasso, Tolstoy, Dostoyevsky, Gogol, Ibsen, Björnson, etc., in total chronological disarray." He adds, "My greatest pleasure was to isolate myself in some agreeable spot with a few precious books. The insipid games of my schoolmates and neighborhood friends repelled me during that period of my youth" (36–39).

How similar this sounds to Clementina's recollections of her own childhood. The number of volumes in Juticalpa may have increased, and some of the books may have changed owners, but her method was the same: she read randomly and whatever she could find. During the long hours she spent with her father, they discussed the books she had read. He talked to her about ideas—philosophy, religion, ethics, law. She became his secretary, confidant, companion, and best friend. Luis Suárez had studied in Guatemala; he had traveled outside of Honduras; he was intelligent and well-read. He clearly did not find in doña Amelia the kind of intellectual companionship he must have craved, although their relationship seems to have been affectionate and considerate. So he turned to his daughter, his precocious Clementina, and began fashioning her into the kind of woman he would have liked for a soul mate. She remembers that he would say to her, using his affectionate nickname for her, "Nina, if you weren't my daughter, you would be my girlfriend."

The neighbors, of course, criticized Luis Suárez for the way he was bringing up his daughter. Perhaps because she was his and Amelia's first-born, perhaps because he perceived in her, even when she was quite young, the spark of something out of the ordinary, perhaps because he simply enjoyed her companionship—whatever the reason, over the years father and daughter developed a strong and complex bond.

Unlike most parents of the conservative Honduran upper class, Luis Suárez allowed his daughters ample freedom to explore life. His liberal attitude, combined with doña Amelia's carefree laziness, created an atmosphere that nurtured independence, self-assurance, and arrogance in the four girls. Each responded in her own way to these childrearing practices, but all four have grown up to be determined women who go after what they want. Clementina, however, is far and away the feistiest and most independent. While her three sisters clung more to their mother, Clementina always spent much more time with her father. She embraced her freedom energetically, ever pushing beyond the established limits. Her father taught her to ride at an early age, in the days when women in the Honduran countryside wore skirts when they rode and mounted sidesaddle in a way that allowed them to keep their legs covered in a ladylike fashion, called riding *galápago*. Clementina decided this modest method was cumbersome, so she abandoned the feminine saddle, donned pants, and rode to her heart's content. Sometimes she would even go riding with a young man, much to the consternation of relatives, but she chose to ignore their criticism. She earned the reputation of having been the first woman in Honduras to wear pants, which was but the first in a long series of dubious distinctions that have accumulated around her, the building blocks of a legend that has secured for Clementina a place in the national mythology. Clementina Suárez—she is the poet who writes about sex and revolution; she was the first woman to wear lipstick in Honduras, the first woman to wear nail polish, the first to wear shorts. She gave poetry readings naked in the National Theatre. She wrote a pornographic poem that circulated clandestinely in all the high schools of Honduras. She slept with Diego Rivera. She is a personal friend of Fidel Castro. A famous writer killed himself because she rejected his love. She has had love affairs with all the young artists of Central America. She is a Communist. She is an aristocrat.

She is penniless. She is wealthy. She is a great poet. The male poets write her poems for her.

It was customary in Juticalpa to celebrate Independence Day, 15 September, with speeches in the Central Plaza. Clementina on more than one occasion tried her hand at oratory, a difficult and respected art form in Honduras. The townspeople accused Luis Suárez of writing his daughter's speeches, but she insists they were her own. She also liked to participate in the local *veladas* or entertainments, not the formal productions under the auspices of La Fraternidad, but the more spontaneous, less pretentious ones that the young people put together among themselves to present to friends and relatives. What she really liked was organizing the neighborhood kids and being the star performer. "*I had a theatre group. I would put on my mother's dresses, I'd even wear her combs in my hair. We would perform in people's houses, in parks, anywhere. It was mostly the boys, because the girls were shy and didn't want to. We made everything up. I was always the star, the leader of the group. All the kids in the neighborhood. I was about ten years old.*"

The little girl lost in her books, the solitary dreamer, lived inside the stage performer. The inward retreat, the walks alone in the hills, the reading, writing, and pondering coexisted with the outward gesture of calling attention to herself as she acted out her personal drama on a public stage. Her need for solitude and independence was great, but so was her need to connect, to communicate, and to be involved. "*From the time I was a little girl I understood that I was different, because I wasn't able to communicate even with my sisters, or with the other children at school. I was always looking inward, interested in other things, that they didn't see. I could see the stars; the others did not have a sense of looking at nature, as I did through my eyes. Nor of seeing people. I was always interested in older people, because I was more interested in what they had to say than what children my own age talked about. So that's how I grew up, living apart, different, with no communication. This made me create my inner world, a world of dreams and fantasy. The others could not see this world, nor did they try to see it. Only I lived in this world.*"[18]

One of her favorite adult companions was also a great friend and colleague of her father. Ramón Lobo Herrera, born in Juticalpa in 1878, had studied law at the University of San Buenaventura in Tegucigalpa and participated in national politics as a representative to Congress from Olancho.

But his bent was philosophical rather than political, and he soon realized that the political intrigue and petty factionalism of the capital did not suit him. In 1907 he returned to Juticalpa and after that seldom left. He divided his time between his law practice, his house near the center of town, and his hacienda, La Oriental. Much like his friend don Luis, don Ramón became a big fish in a small pond. They both were respected lawyers, thoughtful, educated men whose opinions were solicited. Don Ramón was Clementina's godfather, and, like her father, he responded to her personality in a way that helped her develop her intellectual curiosity.

Ramón Lobo Herrera was tall and dark. He wore a Stetson hat and linen suit. "He was neither vain nor ostentatious nor severe, but rather a very natural man, anyone could tell they were in the company of a man who deserved their admiration and respect. He visited no one. But he did receive visitors in his grand, silent parlor. And there he would converse about things that were beyond the limits of the province, beyond the country, beyond boundaries even more remote. He didn't live in this place, but beyond it and quite far away. He knew about the scientific and social advances of the planet, often not from reading books and magazines, but because of his own piercing and audacious reasoning. . . . Lobo Herrera's conversation was that of an enlightened man. He always kept it on a high level, without extraneous comments or stumbling speech."[19]

Clementina was one of the visitors who frequented Lobo Herrera's grand, silent parlor. Don Ramón lived a solitary and dissipated life as a provincial bachelor. He had been married to a woman from one of the branches of the Zelaya family, but passions and infidelities led to a divorce, and he never remarried. He lived in the center of town with his two unmarried sisters, where he would spend hours in his hammock, reading, thinking, and drinking. When Clementina came to visit he would ask one of his sisters to make tea while he and Clementina discussed what they had been reading. He had style. As one resident of Juticalpa recalls, "Besides being a writer, he was a great orator. Once the local students elected Blanca Cubas de Rivera as their queen. He was in his hammock when he heard the students passing, parading their queen through the streets. The students called to him. One of his sisters was swinging the hammock. He got up and combed his hair. He was very handsome. He took the petals from a rose and held them in his hand, and when the crowd was outside his window, he said: 'Blanca, Blanca, youthful rose,' and tossed the flower petals down on her. He often gave speeches in verse, something you never hear anymore."

His library contained the works of Comte, Spencer, Darwin, and Bergson. If Clementina read and discussed these authors, she no longer remembers, but she does remember being influenced by the visits to Juticalpa of the young students who had gone away to study, in Tegucigalpa or elsewhere, and who would return for vacations, sometimes accompanied by school friends from other towns. One of these visitors was Arturo Martínez Galindo, writer and diplomat, who would later help Clementina realize her longed-for first visit to Mexico. She sought their company and their conversation, for they brought news from a larger world. From an early age Clementina dreamed of traveling to distant and wonderful places, so the young men who caught her fancy in Juticalpa were always individuals who had gone away to study or travel or who came from other places. Reynaldo Harder was German and managed Casa Siercke; the Montes brothers were merchants who traveled frequently to Trujillo. José María Martínez's uncle the archbishop had sent him to study in Philadelphia; Cornelio Mejía had studied in Tegucigalpa. Did she dream that they would take her away to see the world? Perhaps they were simply better company, because they had seen and done more than the local boys who never left town. Certainly they had an air of the exotic about them.

The call of distant lands, the promise of new experiences, the attraction of different landscapes and people have been determining factors in Clementina's dreams. What must those dreams have looked like colored by the hypersensitive imagination of a young girl from a provincial Central American town? To comprehend the world that nurtured her, it is important to establish a distinction between the geographic isolation of Juticalpa itself, and the collective life that took shape within this community. For all Clementina's feelings of solitude, it was actually impossible for her truly to be alone, for what happened to one, happened to all. People told and retold the comings and goings of their neighbors; everyone speculated on the fortunes and misfortunes of everyone else. The residents of Juticalpa were the actors in their own soap opera, with the most controversial characters providing the best entertainment. Events in Clementina's life passed from household to household, each teller adding narrative flourishes and coloring the details with interpretive innuendo. Clementina lent Ofelia her salmon-colored dress for the party, but you know she also stole Ofelia's beau at that same party. She said it was to color a skirt that she bought some red dye from one of the local stores, but the blood-colored water running from her house into the gutters looked like proof of a homemade abortion to her suspicious neighbors. Everyone knew that doña Amelia would sometimes not change out of her bathrobe all day long. The parrot in the grocery store repeated comments not meant to be overheard, to the delight and edification of shoppers. Everyone agrees that Clementina, deny it though she may, wrote a sexy poem about a girl losing her virginity that students pass down still from generation to generation. And everyone knew that she shot herself, although they may not agree on her motive.

It is a hot day in March. Clementina swings in a hammock reading one of her mother's novels. She kicks off her shoes and stretches her legs. Flies buzz, and the smell of latrines permeates the air. She calls to Servando to bring her some melon. Her uncle, Felix Cerna, stops by to greet doña Amelia. "Why do you let your daughter sit around reading, doing nothing? You ought to get her a broom and a grinding stone, teach her how to make tortillas." Clementina gets up from her hammock and slips out the door. She has heard this all before. She heads away from the center toward Barrio Abajo to visit her friends the Montes family. Her relatives consider this behavior inappropriate, but she doesn't care. She likes Justo, and she likes his friend José María Fernández. Her aunt tells her the Montes are low-class, rough people from the wrong side of town, but she visits then anyway. She goes out riding with them, and they go to the river on hot days. So what if she takes off her dress to go swimming with them? Besides, her father lets her do as she pleases. He wants her to make her own decisions and her own mistakes. He has told her she is special, and she knows it is true. So why should she listen to the conservative complaints of her small-minded relatives and neighbors? Someday her father will take her to Mexico, where there is light and energy, culture and revolution, freedom and ideas.

Her father never did take her to Mexico. Like his friend Ramón Lobo Herrera, he let the province swallow him. But he did take her to Tegucigalpa.

She accompanied him when he traveled to the capital to attend the annual sessions of Congress as deputy from Olancho, and he took her and her sister Rosa to attend the school La Instrucción, run by the Saravia family from Guatemala.[20]

The school was founded during the presidency of Manuel Bonilla (1903–6) and operated until its founder's death in 1915. It was a school of primary instruction where girls were taught the basics of mathematics, geography, and history. They wore white uniforms; they embroidered, memorized verses, and were taught the proper conduct of proper young ladies. Clementina was twelve when she studied there, and she remained for one year, until the academy was closed. She stayed in the home of her uncle Pío Suárez, Luis's brother, who lived in a large house near San Francisco Church, a short distance from Central Plaza with its small shops, its statue of national hero Francisco Morazán, and its cathedral. Her sister Rosa, two years younger, stayed at the presidential residence. The president of Honduras, Francisco Bertrand, was married to Victoria Alvarado Buchard, a cousin of Amelia Suárez, and she had arranged for Rosa to live with them and keep her daughter Victoria company.

Victoria Bertrand was born in Juticalpa in 1907 and moved with her parents to Tegucigalpa when her father assumed the presidency. She also studied at La Instrucción. Like Clementina, she had a romantic inclination and a desire to express herself in poetry. Her life followed a very different course from Clementina's, but she did write and she did publish at least one book of poetry, *Nómada,* in Costa Rica in 1937. Clementina and Victoria were contemporaries who had in common a childhood of privilege in a provincial environment and a gift for poetic expression. But Victoria was never able to project herself or her poetry; she never made herself known. She remained a marginal figure, unconnected and introspective, while Clementina burst out of the bubble of Juticalpa and connected herself through her poetry to a larger world.

End of Innocence

One of the facets of the Clementina legend is the image of the poet as a socially committed revolutionary. And indeed, Clementina's poetry records the ardent emotional involvement in social change and the attendant soul-searching fashionable among Latin American intellectuals in the 1930s and again in the 1960s. But the road to becoming a politically and socially integrated poet was a long and circuitous one, and politics was not central in Clementina's early development. In fact, it was not until she left Honduras that she was able to break through the mirror of self, to see out from the windows of her house of dreams, her "luminous solitude," her absorbing narcissism.[21] The magnitude of her self-involvement was great, so the social drama being played out around her did not significantly penetrate her consciousness. As an old woman looking back on her childhood, trying to recall the past to determine what was most important, she remembers herself as being different, separate from others her own age, able to see and appreciate with a special sensibility. Although at the time she had not yet channeled her difference into writing, a universe of poetry was growing inside her; it filled her with such wonder and pain that it eclipsed to a large degree the struggle that engaged the attention of so many of her compatriots. For Juticalpa may have been provincial, but it was not therefore immune to political rivalries and the violence that accompanies power struggles.

From the time of the wars of independence, when Honduras became a nation unto itself and no longer formed a part of the Captaincy General of Guatemala, local caudillos have vied for power in the provinces while national caudillos have done the same in a larger arena. The period 1883–1933 was one of protracted political instability, characterized by numerous conflicts that affected the entire country through forced military conscription, the economic repercussions of instability, or the emotional and psychological effects of chaos and violence. One resident of Juticalpa described the prevailing climate as a lawless free-for-all. "As far back as I can remember they were going at it. One minute it was General Llaves, the next it was Matías Funes, it was too much. In those days, that was how those people lived. Uncivilized. There were those who joined in because they couldn't get work, so they would get what they wanted at rifle point, or with machetes, going into towns, pushing around honorable people, looting the stores. Others got involved in these battles because they were criminals. There was no law and order. They would go into the town hall and burn all the records, to make sure their names didn't show up anywhere. Yes, I remember these things. Sometimes we lost a whole year of school. The children would have to stay at home, it was too dangerous to go out, with these bands running loose."

When Clementina recalls the political violence of her childhood years she remembers a horrific scene of a dead man being dragged through the streets of Juticalpa. But she offers these memories only if pressed. They are not the spontaneous memories that flow from her, because she does not associate herself with them: they were scenes in which she herself was not a protagonist. She would later come to identify very strongly with a larger social drama, but not until she had extended the boundaries of her self-image.

Nor does Clementina have particularly vivid memories of the brutal cholera epidemic that swept through Olancho in 1918. According to a lifelong resident of Juticalpa, "After the war with Germany there was a terrible disease here. At least ten or twelve people died every day. It was so bad that we couldn't bury them fast enough, everyone was getting sick. There was a man named Juan Sergio who had a cart. He would pass by the houses—no one closed their doors—looking inside to see if there were any dead bodies. He would pile the dead up on his cart and take them to the cemetery; they would bury five or six in each grave."

Another resident writes, "And how could the people of Juticalpa not be horrified when that cart passed by? It seemed as if Juan Sergio took pity on no one. He would search in every corner of every house and take out the bodies he found, whether on fine beds, on poor cots or on the floor. He would sling them over his shoulder and throw them in his squeaky cart. The only ones he left behind were those who could still talk; he would leave them for the next trip."[22]

Of Clementina's family, only the youngest daughter, Graciela, was stricken, but her case was not severe, and she recovered. A girlfriend of Clementina's was not so fortunate, and her death was the emotional inspiration for what Clementina recalls as her first poem.[23] There is no record of this poem; like the first scribblings in those early notebooks, it is only a memory. She showed those early notebooks to no one, not even to her father, for, although she publicly claims that she has nothing to hide, there are in fact secrets in her soul that she simply does not share.

Clementina's sisters, like many other one-time residents of Juticalpa, reminisce about their childhood with a twinge of nostalgia. But for them it is not time and its gradual changes that they lament, for the Suárez family's changes were quick and cruel. When Luis Suárez died, it soon became obvious that this slight man was the backbone that had kept the family together. Besides his law practice, his two terms as representative to the national Congress, and his store, he managed doña Amelia's land, cattle, and crops.

The youngest daughter, Graciela, who was eleven at the time, remembers her father's death as a dividing line between the carefree opulence of her childhood and an adult life in which her world was no longer cushioned, her needs fulfilled, or her whims satisfied. For when doña Amelia found herself without a husband, she was ill equipped to take charge. Eggs will not cook themselves if left sitting dry and unbroken in the frying pan, chiggers cannot be removed with cologne, and a hacienda cannot be run on good intentions alone. Rosa, the second daughter, married Juan Maier, and for a time her husband managed the family property. When doña Amelia died in 1955, the property was divided among the four daughters.

Clementina, being the oldest and probably the most capable, did her best to maintain a certain level of normalcy in the Suárez household. But the success of her efforts was minimal, because Luis Suárez's death proved to be an event of enormous significance in her personal life as well as in the collective life of the family. If his death was a dividing line between ease and struggle for her mother and sisters, for Clementina it came to represent the end of innocence. It brought her face to face with existential despair, closing the door on her childhood and opening the door to her poetry. The old-timers who are still around to remember those days mourn their passing because they are not pleased with what change has brought them. Most of them have lived their entire lives in Juticalpa, or, if they left, they keep Olancho in their hearts and identify strongly with their roots. Clementina, to the contrary, dismisses nostalgia with a characteristic curl of her lip and wave of her hand. Her memories of her parents are reverent, but when she talks of Juticalpa, of Olancho, and of the past, it is as if she has scraped all the romantic grime off the lens of time and is seeing her old environment with an incisive clarity. It nurtured her, but it also tried to strangle her. It respected her social position, but the same society that furnished her with respectability insisted that she conform to a life-style that was antithetical to her desires or forfeit her position and respectability.

Clementina has lived her life in a chronology the reverse of many of her contemporaries'. As a young girl she sought the companionship of adults. As a young woman she wallowed in the nostalgia and romantic angst of a person who has lived long and suffered enormously and for whom childhood innocence is a distant memory. Unlike the companions of her youth who in their old age have turned to nostalgia as consolation in life's weariness, Clementina in her eighties still agitates energetically for change. The decaying traditions of the past have no hold on her. If she regrets anything, it is that change has not come fast enough. In a world where all knew their places, there was no place for her. Why mourn its passing or long for its return?

In retrospect, Clementina tends to envision her decisions as made with swift determination. She looks back and recalls a time in Juticalpa when her life was balanced on a simple moment of fate: two roads, a choice—to take the road less traveled. She says she realized Juticalpa was not the place where she could spend the rest of her life. She was quite sure by then that she was different from the other girls her age with whom she had grown up. Different also from most of the boys, although she clearly identified more with masculine pastimes and pursuits and enjoyed the company of males, especially adult men, more than that of girls or women. She had outgrown Juticalpa; her father was no longer there to love her, protect her and encourage her; she had no refuge for her difference; so she left.

But where would she go? What would she do? How would she live? In the 1980s a young girl can run away from home in Honduras and make it on her own, albeit with great difficulty. She can take a bus to San Pedro, the industrial city on the north coast, or to Tegucigalpa, rent a room, and go out in search of a job as a clerk or secretary or housekeeper or babysitter. With perseverance and intelligence she can survive. But in 1923 in Honduras a young girl's prospects were significantly more restricted: anonymity was impossible, transportation problematic, and job opportunities limited in the extreme.

Job opportunities? In Juticalpa in 1923 the daughters of the ruling class did not think in terms of jobs, although a few earnest souls went to the Teachers' College for Women in Tegucigalpa to further their education and prepare themselves for the possibility of teaching primary school. It was a matter of masculine pride and family honor that females not work outside the home, because a wage-earning woman was tantamount to an admission that the patriarch was unable to support his family, and women too eager to work lost that patina of aristocratic languor. But Clementina's patriarch was dead, and the family finances in a state of confusion.

Local opinion holds that Clementina left town because of a romantic scandal. Some think she left because she was jilted by a lover and could not bear to remain in the same town as he. Others say she left because she had been dishonored in love and was too proud to stay around where everyone knew her shame. And there are those who insist that she left to have an adventure, an amorous affair with a handsome scoundrel who took advantage of her, and that after this taste of freedom she never wanted to return to her small hometown.

Any one of these may have been the surface reason for her leaving on a particular day, but the deeper reason was that Clementina was a poet. The decision to leave home may not have been a clear, conscious act of the will, carried out with the knowledge that it was the first step on the path of her destiny, as she chooses to reconstruct it in retrospect, because it may be that the decision had already been made or, more accurately, the decision was being made every day that she lived as her father's daughter. She perhaps after all had no choice but to leave, because previous choices, such as the stubborn determination to do as she pleased, were already being lived out.

She does not remember the day or the time or even the season when she left her childhood behind, but she claims that she left without her mother's permission and that subsequent to her departure she received no financial help from home. She managed somehow to get to Olanchito, a small town 684 kilometers northwest of Juticalpa, where she stayed in the home of a former schoolteacher of hers from Juticalpa. From there she made her way an additional 180 kilometers to Trujillo on the North Coast. She probably hitched a ride with Justo Montes, her old friend from Barrio Abajo. Justo made regular trips to Trujillo, where he delivered cattle and picked up merchandise from the port to bring back to Juticalpa. Clementina probably accompanied him part of the way on one of his trips, which took approximately fifteen days by mule. This was twice the distance from Juticalpa to Tegucigalpa, and as far from home as she had ever been. She had relatives in Trujillo with whom she stayed, but not for long. Once she got going, there was no turning back, and no stopping. The journey had begun, and she was never again to know the comfort of prosperity or the security of being pampered and protected. Which is not to say that she did not desire peace and comfort. Indeed, she has often made choices based squarely on this need. But her will to be free and her awakening sense of herself as a poet proved always to be stronger than her longing for security.

CHAPTER TWO

Forging a Poetic Identity

Early Poems

Clementina claims that from the age of ten she acquired the habit of filling small notebooks with her intimate outpourings. These notebooks unfortunately have been lost. The first evidence we have of her poetry is the book she published in 1930 in Tegucigalpa, *Corazón sangrante* (Bleeding Heart). Within a year she had published three more volumes: *Los templos de fuego* (Temples of Fire), *Iniciales* (Beginnings), and *De mis sábados el último* (The Last of My Saturdays), all in Mexico City. While these four books, as well as her next one, *Engranajes* (Gears), published in Costa Rica in 1935, vary in technique, they form an emotional unit. They are the expression of a young woman who has left home and is experimenting wildly and freely with her own power. Although *Bleeding Heart* was not published until 1930, it seems likely that she began writing it during these first years on her own, as a way of coming to terms with her life's changes. It is a tender, innocent, painfully anguished dramatization of her struggle with the harsh realities of her new life, a record of her soul in conversation with itself as it weeps and rejoices in its effort to communicate with the soul of the world. If this description of her early poetry sounds dramatic and excessively sentimental, it is because that is what it was—unabashedly romantic, ingenuous in its sincerity, devoid of irony, and apparently unaware of self-criticism. The emotions are tender, raw, wide-eyed, and histrionic. The gesture is sweeping and uncontained. The stance is that of an actress on stage.

A common criticism of women's poetry has been that so much of it is autobiographical. Exactly why this should be a cause for criticism is not self-evident, but it is a commonplace so often repeated that it has become accepted in some critical circles as a criterion for dismissing the poetry. Embedded in this rejection is the implication of a limited vision, of an absence of transcendence, and of the pitifulness of the delusion that one's own self could be interesting, important, or profound enough to serve as its own referent. But this kind of prescriptive criticism does not allow itself to see the beauty and complexity that baldly autobiographical poetry can attain. It is precisely the extreme self-referential nature of Clementina Suárez's poetry that makes it compelling, because poetry to Clementina is a vital occupation. With it she defines, articulates, and creates herself; it is the medium through which she hears her own voice and tells her own story.

Poetry is words arranged on a page, a configuration of language. It is a rhyming of words or an absence of rhyme. It is a feat of technical virtuosity or an innocence of structure. It is a subtlety, an irony, an exalted emotion, a romantic passion. It is so many things that it is finally nothing. It is a blank page and there are no rules, only the self and possibility. One covers the page or doesn't. One speaks or remains silent. She who chooses not to remain silent is a poet. Later comes outside criticism, when others decide if she deserves the name *poet,* but the primal decision to speak is the first and most important step.

In his prologue to *Temples of Fire,* Hernán Robleto notes that Clementina has published a great deal. This is a mistake, he believes. She does not discriminate but flings out her poems still wet with dew. She sings out at every opportunity and scarcely concerns herself with meter. She should hide some of her poems, be patient, and develop a more mature outlook, but alas, she doesn't listen to advice, either.

Fortunately, Clementina doesn't listen to advice. Luis Suárez taught his daughter that she had the right to be free, to set her own standards and behave accordingly. Amelia Zelaya's example taught her daughter that it was her birthright to be provided for and waited on. From these essential ingredients Clementina created her own poetic recipe, appropriating the territory with determined naturalness. With something akin to the self-assured willfullness of a spoiled child, she took it for granted that what she needed to express was poetic, that the workings of her heart, the permutations of her emotions, her awakenings, her angst, and her melancholy were the stuff of poetry. So she chose not to remain silent.

It was in Trujillo that Clementina first saw the sea. This initial meeting with its power and wonder was an event that touched something powerful and wonderful in her own self and released a veritable flood of sensuality, vitality, and hunger for experience. She included in *Beginnings* "Mi poema al mar" (My Sea Poem).

Kiss me!
Kiss me all over . . .
with dreams . . .
with poetry . . .
with tropical passion . . .
with a fierce soul . . .
with immortal delight . . .

Kiss me!
Kiss me all over!
my body is a pearl
in your sapphire depths,
for you it comes forth
wrapped in your waves
beneath their caresses
you will hear it moan.

I will be music,
soft whispers,
call me
and you will hear the harmony
of my soul
in a triumphant hymn . . .

———

Bésame! . . .
Bésame toda!
con ideal . . .

con poesía . . .
con ardor tropical . . .
con alma bravía . . .
con delicia inmortal . . .

Bésame!
Bésame toda!
que mi cuerpo es una perla
en tu fondo de zafir,
para tí ha de surgir
envuelto entre tus ondas
bajo cuyas caricias
lo escucharás gemir.

Seré música,
seré arrullo,
llámame mía
y oirás la armonía
del alma mía
en un himno triunfal . . .

It is a sensual poem, with a rhythm that reproduces a throbbing need to be engulfed, rocked, filled. The choice of the sea as her lover enriches the poem's eroticism with its implications of self-love and self-longing. The watery expanse is both her self and her desired other. The poem suggests that while she herself is the source of her inspiration, she is not in control of her own depths. She is an instrument that longs to be played, confident that her music will be poetry. She believes that the right man will be able to pluck the right strings, because—especially in these years when she is young and attractive and energetic—beauty, desire, poetry, and love are indistinguishable to her. Yet she chooses the sea in her poem, rather than a specific man, or even men in general, unaware of the implications of this choice—that only she can truly satisfy herself. Of course it is possible also to read this poem as a scarcely veiled seduction, her poetry a pretext through which she could publicize her desire. For those who might prefer that poetry be reserved for loftier purposes, this poem and this poet were scandalous.

She spent many years searching for the man who was also the sea, the man who could open her to herself, in whose loving embrace her poetry would spill out and speak to the world. But her imagination was wild, and her standards were high. Perhaps in those years she saw every man as a possible Adonis, a potential Zeus. She displayed her feathers, she preened in the hope of attracting her god. In her photo album are snapshots of a woman in her twenties. Clementina in a long, dark, velvet dress sitting sideways to the camera, her head tilted subtly forward, her eyes rolled slightly back, her mouth a knowing half smile. The background is as dark as her velvet dress; only her small, soft hands and her sphinxlike face are clear in the night of the photograph. Clementina leaning in a sunlit doorway in a dusty courtyard, her slim body slouched inside oversized workman's overalls, looking appealingly fragile. Clementina in shorts and a halter top. And Clementina draped in a flowing tunic on which some artist friends had painted bright, swirling designs for her to wear for a poetry recital. The following hopeful poem addresses her dream companion-lover:

We Two

Give me your strong hand and let us
embark on life's long road,
in our journey we may encounter
harm, a smile or pain.

It is sad to walk aimlessly
in the desert, with no goal or direction,
but our longing will uncover the door
that will flood our way with light.

I know you will sweeten my sorrows
with the honey of your word, and the road
will be paved with flowers, not thorns,
and in the evening birds will sing.

My eyes, red from weeping,
will drink joy from yours,
and when day melts into memory,
my life will burst into light for you.

My soul at every step will count off
the rosary of its dreams

and when the setting sun glows in the distance,
will recite to you its prayers.

Night will blanket us and the moon will be our lamp
and there will be peace and silence in our lives
and our souls will sleep
as one.

The earth in holy tenderness will take us in her arms
and we will forget at last our anger,
nights and twilights will end
with starlight kisses.

———

Los dos

Dame tu mano fuerte y emprendamos
el largo camino de la vida,
quizá en la peregrinación nos encontramos
con un dolor, una risa o una herida.

Es triste caminar por el desierto
sin rumbo, sin fin y sin oriente,
pero nuestras ansias descubrirán el puerto,
que llenará de luces nuestra frente.

Yo sé que tú darás a mis dolores,
la miel de tu palabra, y el camino
en vez de espinas, se cubrirá de flores,
y habrá de tarde en tarde un suave trino.

Mis ojos que el llanto ha enrojecido,
beberán en los tuyos la alegría,
y cuando el día se funda en el olvido,
reventará en luz, para tí, la vida mía.

Mi alma irá desgranando a cada paso
el rosario de sus ensoñaciones
y cuando brille a lo lejos el ocaso,
te dirá también sus oraciones.

Nos cobijará la noche y alumbrará la luna
y habrá calma y silencio en nuestras vidas
y nuestras almas, cual si fueran una
solo alma, se quedarán dormidas.

La tierra, santa en ternuras nos abrirá sus brazos
y olvidaremos por fin nuestras querellas,
se acabarán las noches los ocasos
con los besos de la luz de las estrellas.

If "he" will take her hand and be her love, they can be fellow travelers on life's difficult road. She asks a lot: that his hands be strong, his words sweet, his eyes joyful, and that he be willing to lose himself in union with her. But she promises much in return for his devotion and inspiration: their path will be filled with flowers, she will be his light, she will pray to him, and in their union they will be at peace with nature. Men must certainly have sensed her calling to them. But so many must have disappointed her.

In his prologue to *Bleeding Heart,* Alfonso Guillén Zelaya notices that "like her life, Clementina's poetry is a poetry without restrictions, resonating with a deeply felt sorrow, and in which glows, with spontaneous purity and true vigor, an authentic talent." He predicts that subsequent volumes will be even better, when her (now immature) pain and passions have entered fully life's depths, have plumbed the infinite mysteries and found the "Sacred Fountain." Clementina calls these early poems "ingenuous." She doesn't reject them, however, nor indeed anything she has written, because she sees them as representing a stage in her life, and every moment has its own expression. So it is important to treat these poems not merely as steps that lead somewhere else, but as creations from a time in her life that was as real as any other while she lived it, and to accord them the significance they had for her when she wrote them.

Disappointment is a major theme in *Bleeding Heart,* odd though it might seem for a young woman with so much of life ahead of her. Of the many postures in this collection of poems, the predominant one is that of looking back longingly, remembering an earlier lightness of spirit that evades her in the present. In the opening lines of the dedication she presents herself as a lugubrious romantic heroine who longs to articulate a reality of light and warmth and joy, but whose allegiance to truth demands that she express instead her sadness and despair.

> These lines are my soul crying out from the deep loneliness of my nights: sad flowerings that burst beneath the heat of twilight, flight of crystal larks shaking out their wings in the shadows, or birds tired of flying that stayed behind sadly contemplating the sky.
>
> I would have liked them to be bits of crystal kissed by the white light of dawn; lilies of joy, opening slowly to the sun's caresses; serene afternoons, asleep beneath a turquoise sky; pools of green water on which the moon reposes; open windows that sunrays pass through; but if this was my wish, something painfully tragic diverted the first impulses and instead of splendid and proud lilies, or roses red with life, I have left behind only imperceptible murmurs, wilted petals, rocked softly by the breezes of sighs.
>
> They are, nonetheless, my life's most honest expression and my soul's harp vibrates in these lines with all its sadness.
>
> I have not wanted to stifle my pain: I have let it spring forth, as a stream springs from the heart of a thoughtful mountain; have let it sing with arpeggios that the day is dying; let it beseech with folded hands and tearful eyes; let it raise itself toward the sky, as the subtle mist rises from dry lakes or as the echo of willows resounds beside sad rivers that in other times have felt the voices of its waters chattering and gay.
>
> These lines are like a backward glance that the soul passes through to comfort itself in its anguish; like solitary walks through fading gardens; like slow pilgrimages toward deserted beaches; like painful visits to the empty house that once heard our laughter.

The painfully tragic occurence she alludes to may have been the loss of her father or of a lover—or of her privileged childhood. She surely had no idea how difficult it would be to get by in a society that had no mechanism for absorbing a young single woman with a romantic imagination and a will to be free. She survived, but her early poetry bears witness to the emotional struggle involved in her transition from one reality to another. In "Melancolía" (Melancholy) the poet addresses her lugubrious muse:

> Mother or sister, taciturn and distant,
> you have illuminated your sad solitude,
> softened the plaint and quieted the rage
> and offer the despondent the shade of your compassion.

Oh that you would take me in your shadowy vessel
through unknown seas where all is still,
where night reigns and joy has departed,
to the vast domains ruled by death.

Open your arms, oh great melancholy!
and let my life be wrapped in your sadness,
so our great sorrows, arm in arm,
may give birth to new clarities.

Let me rest my tired head
on your peaceful and holy lap,
forgetting everything, absorbed by nothingness,
let me lose myself in your great solitude.

Let me embrace your tranquil shadows,
lose myself in your breast and explore your mysteries,
let my hungry eyes be satiated with silence
and my trembling hands with soft caresses.

Show me the melancholy path, sister,
that leads to silences and renunciations,
that leads us to that distant and mysterious land
where sad hearts find peace and calm.

———

Madre o hermana mía, taciturna y huraña
que has hecho luminosa tu pobre soledad
que suavizaste el quejido y acallaste la saña
y ofreces a los tristes tu sombra de piedad.

Quiero que me lleves en tu barca sombría
por los mares ignotos donde todo es inerte
donde reina la noche y muere la alegría
a los vastos dominios donde impera la muerte.

Abre tus brazos -Oh gran melancolía!
y deja que mi vida se envuelva en tus saudades,
así tu gran tristeza del brazo con la mía
puede ser que den vida a nuevas claridades.

Deje que recueste mi cabeza cansada
sobre tu regazo de paz y santidad,
que me olvide de todo, que me absorba la nada
que se esfume mi vida en tu gran soledad.

Deja que me abrace a tus sombras tranquilas,
que me pierda en tu seno y explore tus arcanos
que me sacien de silencio mis hambrientas pupilas
y de suavidades mis temblorosas manos.

Enséñame la senda melancólica hermana
que va hacia los silencios y las renunciaciones
que nos lleva a esa tierra misteriosa y lejana
do hallan paz y sosiego los tristes corazones.

Melancholy here is not exactly sadness or sorrow, but rather that *melancolía* that we do not have in English, that state of being, at once mental and physical, that takes hold of one but that one also embraces. It is sweet pain and bitter pleasure, a seductive languishing. In English we scoff at those who wallow in their sorrows, drown in their tears, or moon about. The Spanish language treats this state more kindly, celebrates it in fact, and in this poem melancholy is a protector, a nurturer, a psychological state through which one returns to the mother to find respite from life's troubles. It is a sanctuary where death reigns, dark and quiet. Melancholy rocks us; we float in her waters until we are ready to face again the light of day and be reborn. Again and again Clementina dips into the waters of melancholy, surfacing with poems like talismans to hold back despair.

At times she fears her despair will drive her mad; at times she longs for madness as escape from the cruel disappointments of reality. "Ansias" (Anxieties) presents the poet as dreamer, as one whose misfortune was to have been born with a soul that wanted too much, that foolishly thought dreams could become reality.

I have dreamed so much that at times I have wanted
to breathe on those dreams and make them flower,
to melt into their fragrances, lose myself in their oblivion,
and become liquid among the waves of a soft sunset.

Let my life be like the sweet rhythm
of a melody stillborn,
like a soft sigh, a gentle longing
for a dream that wanted to be but never was.

Aching desire to lose myself in the void
and return from its caverns with wounded soul . . .
Madness to be lost within myself,

to remain as always, without direction, lost,
without knowing what we are, with delirious eyes
fixed firmly on the edge of an abyss.

He soñado tanto que a veces he querido
soplar sobre esos sueños y hacerlos florecer,
fundirme en sus fragancias, perderme entre su
olvido, y diluirme entre las ondas de un suave atardecer.

Que sea esta mi vida como un dulce latido
de nota melodiosa que se apagó al nacer,
como un suave suspiro, como un tenue quejido
de ilusión que quiso haber sido y nunca logró ser.

Ansia dolorosa de hundirme entre la nada
y volver de sus antros con alma lacerada . . .
Locura de perderse dentro de uno mismo

para quedar como siempre, sin rumbo, sin oriente,
sin saber lo que somos, con ojos de demente
clavados con fijeza al borde de un abismo.

The dreamer feels too deeply and so longs to be lost within herself to avoid the world. She claims to desire nothingness, but her images belie this wish, for her desires are in fact sensual—to melt into fragrances, become liquid among the waves of a soft sunset. She wishes life could be a caress, a sigh, a rhythm, but instead she confronts nothingness. She does not leap into the abyss but contemplates herself staring fixedly at the edge of the void. Yet she stops herself in time, as she did that day in Juticalpa.

She turns most often to nature in her search for tenderness and acceptance. In "Imploraciones" (Beseeching) she approaches in turn a river, the sea, a tree, flowers and fruits, plains, jungles, and mountains, asking them to share their gifts. She is overwhelmed by the richness with which nature surrounds her, while her own soul writhes in melancholy, wrapped in shadow.

She also evokes nature to recreate that golden past in which she remembers herself as a fluttering butterfly, her hair loose, her cheeks rosy from the sun. One of the longest poems in *Bleeding Heart,* "Mi vida era como . . ." (My Life Was Like . . .), is a litany to lost innocence in which she compares her past to a clear, enchanting pool, a singing brook, the clear light of day, a high mountain, the blue sky. Her despair comes from her inability to communicate her real self, to be natural. Her rhythm is off, something has gone wrong, she is not being understood. She is so anxious to live fully, but at every turn she encounters prejudice, distrust, criticism. Who will understand her real self and appreciate that she is a poet and not subject to the social restrictions of lesser mortals? "Mi luminosa soledad" (My Luminous Solitude) bears witness to her loneliness.

> Drop by drop sadness falls
> on the deep silence of my life,
> and my broken, bloody and dying soul
> loses itself in the misty
> depths of silence . . .
>
> Who can plumb my anguish?
>
> The mirror of my hope is broken,
> the golden chrysalis is gone
> and in my vacant heart the immense shadow
> of my solitude, like a macabre wail
> dances sombrely . . .
>
> If the shouts of my heart could only
> shake the night with their clamor,
> what tender flowers would bud!
> What richness of lights, what flood of laughter
> would flow from the darkness! . . .

and I would flaunt all this, for those who
unknowingly have hurt me;
but I will not beg,
I will wander and wander,
leaving a trail,
like the lily
her perfume
in the wind,
of this longing to live that consumes me.

———

Va cayendo gota a gota
sobre el hondo silencio de mi vida, la tristeza
y mi alma, rota, sangrante y moribunda
va esfumándose en la profunda
neblina del silencio . . .

Quién en mis tremendas inquietudes
pudiera penetrar? . . .

Se rompió el cristal de mi esperanza,
voló quién sabe a dónde la crisálida de oro
y quedó mi corazón vacío, en donde danza
macabra y dantesca, como un lloro,
la inmensa sombra de mi soledad . . .

Si los gritos de mi corazón pudieran
con su fragor extremecer la noche,
¡Cuántas flores de ternura florecieran!
¡Qué riqueza de luces, qué derroche
de risas brotara de sus sombras! . . .

todo eso lo exhibiría, para que lo vean
los que inconcientemente me golpean;
pero yo no quiero pedir
pero sí rodar, rodar, rodar,
para dejar,
como el lirio,

en el viento
al expirar,
el perfume
de esta ansia de vivir que me consume.

Solitude haunts much of Clementina's poetry. The Spanish of solitude, *soledad*, carries the same ambiguity as its English counterpart. It can be painful aloneness or peaceful reclusion. Clementina's loneliness has been that of the woman whose life's quest does not coincide with the roles assigned to her gender in patriarchal societies, of the pioneer who finds herself continually swimming upstream. But her loneliness also has had another face: it is the solitude of the little girl alone with her books, the young woman alone with the sea, the poet alone with the blank page. Clementina once commented, "*Life is an apprenticeship in loneliness.*" Even in these first books of poetry she has recognized the potential of solitude, although she struggles with it, approaching it more as an adversary than a helpmate. One of her poetic tasks has been to learn to experience solitude as a fruitful moment, a creative space.

Clementina stayed briefly in Trujillo with relatives from her mother's family, working as a clerk in her uncle's store, then moved on to La Ceiba, another town on Honduras's Caribbean coast, 242 kilometers to the west. In La Ceiba she stayed in the home of her maternal aunt, Lola de Calix, and worked in a commissary. She sent poems and short prose pieces to the local newspaper and thought of herself as a writer. But there was no literary movement to her liking in La Ceiba, no group of writers with whom to associate, so, now that she had tasted the pleasures (as well as the inconveniences) of moving on, she packed up and went to live with her uncle Felipe Zelaya, doña Amelia's brother, in San Pedro, where she worked as a receptionist in a government office. San Pedro, the center of Honduran business and industry, is a steamy tropical town a short distance inland from Tela, one of the important shipping ports of the United Fruit Company. She also spent time in Tela, where her half-sister María Luisa Munguía lived. Clementina stayed with María Luisa for a few months, during which time she set up a business buying and selling used books.

Her life on the North Coast was full of plans and projects, fresh starts and false starts. She was on her own but still deeply tied to her past and to her family. She felt responsible for her mother and younger sisters in Juticalpa, although just how much she contributed to their financial needs is not clear. She sent packages home on an irregular basis with clothes and gifts, especially for her youngest sister, Graciela, the sweet little blond with the jovial and easygoing personality. But this interlude on the North Coast was more than anything heady with self-involvement. Clementina was doing what no self-respecting young Honduran woman of her social class would have dreamed of—she was acting as if she were in control of her own life. And while she never forgot that she was a daughter of the ruling class, she continued the custom begun in childhood of associating freely across class lines.

She began to establish a pattern of behavior that would continue throughout her life. Driven by an insistent restlessness, she lived in at least four different towns on the North Coast in a period of less than two years. She was always moving on—to find new friends, to visit old ones, to seek a new lover, to leave an old one behind—looking for some unrealized part of herself. Her father was gone, but she never stopped mourning his absence, searching among the new faces at parties, in cafés, at gatherings in foreign cities for the man who could fill in her the hungry, empty space created by Luis Suárez's death. "If you weren't my daughter, you would be my girlfriend." With her father she had not been alone, because he accepted her difference.

Clementina dedicated her first book of poetry to her mother, and the theme of a mother's unconditional love and acceptance, as well as musings on the complex mother-daughter bond, form a subcorpus within her body of work. When asked why her father never appears in her poetry, if in fact it is true that he taught her so much and was instrumental in her formation and that she loved and admired him so deeply, she answered that indeed he does appear in her poetry, although not explicitly. She once stated in an interview, "*I had a communication of inestimable worth with my father, of whom I have a clear and persistent memory, in fact I sometimes even think I am expressing myself with his voice.*"[1] At times when she felt depressed or lonely, she would pray to the spirit of her father. A number of her early poems project a religious, quasi-mystical devotion. The poet addresses the male divinity to ask for help in her pain or sorrow. She always speaks to him in a personal way, telling him that she knows he can help her, if only he would accompany her, light her way, ease her despair. When asked if she considered herself to be a religious person, she answered that she did, but that she is not interested in any organized religion. She believes in God, her God, a power capable of consoling her. The memory of her father had blended with an image of a supreme being to become her spiritual interlocutor.

"This Nubile Candor"

Filling Clementina's father's shoes would not be an easy task for any man charmed by Clementina's small feet, delicate hands, flirtatious walk, intense eyes, and fleshy mouth. She must have been hard to resist, although opinions vary widely regarding her appearance. Some remember her as beautiful, others recall her as "a rather ugly woman."[2] But somewhere beyond superficial description lies the insistence of attraction. To call Clementina beautiful one must deny or overlook the Eurocentric aesthetic standards that influenced the judgments of many of her contemporaries and that are implicit in the many caricatures of her that emphasize the expansive forehead, the large mouth, the wide nostrils. To call her not beautiful one must ignore the vitality and the strength of character that over time came to reside in the lines of her face.

She has a collection of 110 portraits that various artists have drawn or painted or sculpted of her, and she once said that her face is not beautiful, but it is interesting, that most artists are not inclined to search for beautiful models, they would rather paint a face that attracts them for other reasons. It is ironic that a woman so involved in knowing herself should be so willing to accept multiple visions and definitions from outside sources, yet she delights in seeing herself as others see her, indeed thrives on basking in reflections of herself.

It is 1991, and Clementina lives in Barrio La Hoya, one of Tegucigalpa's oldest neighborhoods, a time-worn labyrinth of crumbling stucco and slow memories. Behind her house is the República del Paraguay Elementary School, a busy, noisy, overcrowded institution full of little wooden desks and active children screaming and playing in the patio during recess. There is an odor of time and decay in the air. The sun bakes the candy wrappers and fruit peels in the gutters, and the Choluteca River, which once flowed clean and abundant, is a fetid sewer that during the dry season wafts its pestilence into the neighborhood. Poverty is all-pervasive in this capital city that provides little or no public assistance to its least fortunate citizens. Many survive on very little. There are supermarkets now in Tegucigalpa, even a mall with multiple cinemas, but in Barrio La Hoya Clementina gets by without recourse to them. Street vendors still offer their wares from house to house, and one can buy a single roll or a penny candy or a half liter of milk at the numerous *pulperías* or neighborhood grocery stores. There is a plaque on her front door that reads "Galería Clementina Suárez." She bought this house in 1975 and filled it with the icons of a long life devoted to herself, to art, to poetry and to politics.

When I walk in that front door I enter a hallway hung with artists' renderings of Clementina. To my left is an enormous canvas by Honduran painter Julio Vizquerra, an almost life-size Queen Clementina sitting fleshy and naked on a tipsy throne, wearing nothing but a crown and incongruously delicate little squat-heeled, pointy-toed, lace-up boots. Her breasts and belly sag and the expression on her face is dionysiac. It is a lovingly humorous portrait of the bohemian dowager queen in all her glorious debauchery.

I turn off the hallway into the kitchen. I sit across from Clementina at the small round table and drink strong black coffee prepared on the three-burner Tropigas stove. Mountains of plants soak up the sparse rays of sunlight from the barred kitchen window. As I drink my coffee I cannot help staring at the images of Clementina that cover every available inch of the kitchen walls. In one she is a young woman with shoulder-length curls, a kewpie-doll mouth and a sweet expression. In a caricature by Guatemalan Augusto Monterroso she looks like a twenties cabaret dancer with small, pointed breasts, bare shoulders, and Josephine Baker–style slicked-down hair. Esteban Valderrama of Cuba painted her with a serene smile on a mouth too small to be recognizable as hers. Soft curls frame an angelic face with a narrow forehead. The portrait looks nothing like her. In a sketch by her husband, Salvadoran painter José Mejía Vides, her hair is parted in the center and pulled back tightly from her face, arranged atop her head in a traditional woven Central American Indian headdress. Above the window is a watercolor by nine-year-old Suyapa Carías that captures her characteristically wide mouth, nostrils, and forehead with innocent accuracy. On the wall leading from the kitchen to her bedroom is a haunting portrait by Cuban artist Gelasio that shows a painfully introspective middle-aged woman studying her reflection in a mirror, a transparent gauze wrap scarcely concealing her bare breasts.

Most of the space in her bedroom, an exaggeratedly cluttered space, is taken up by her large bed. Here Clementina sits or reclines amid cushions and pillows when she is tired or not feeling well. And here she greets her visitors and holds court. At the head of the bed is a sixties-looking painting in bright colors by Migloressi of Paraguay. It is Clementina in a gossamer pink dress with blossoms in her hair and around her neck. She reclines demurely in a verdant, flowery field with dreamlike mountains behind her that seem to float atop a pale blue lake. On the opposite wall hangs Honduran painter Aníbal's version of a revolutionary Clementina holding a rifle with stern vigilance. Francisco Amighetti of Costa Rica paints and sketches her sitting opposite him at a table, looking like the next-door neighbor who stopped by midmorning for a cup of coffee and some gossip. In the portraits by Luis Angel Salinas of El Salvador she is an angel of redemption, a goddess with flaming hair and chiseled features gazing fearlessly into the future.

A veritable gallery of faces/facets, of characters that have come into being through a blend of assertiveness and passivity. The comments that some of the artists have made when questioned about their portraits of her are revealing. Dante Lazzaroni, for instance, said he painted her as a goblet from which one drinks of life. Gelasio has executed more than seven portraits of her because he claims she is the perfect model, she allows you to paint anything. She would make a painter feel confident that whatever he did was all right; she inspired an enthusiam to paint her. He sees her as somehow enclosed within herself, able to sit for hours, completely happy to be posing.

Luis H. Padilla admits that his portrait of her is really of himself. She did not pose for it; he painted it from memory, adding a few final touches from life. He says the clear, empty space in the background is the desert of himself, and the sadness in her face is his own sadness.

While the artist may see her quiet and empty, waiting to be brought to life on his canvas, she finds her own satisfaction in modeling. "*Posing for them I have felt revealed, as if they were uncovering me from the inside out.*"[3] She has been a mirror in which people have seen themselves reflected. All those portraits are Clementina, but they are also a document of the techniques, personalities, and obsessions of the artists who painted them.

Critics as well as other poets have also described her poetry in ways that are more a reflection of their own sensibilities than of the poetry itself. In his prologue to *The Last of My Saturdays,* Hernán Robleto establishes a relationship between one's natural environment and one's poetic expression, which he claims to find in this book. "In Clementina's poetry and prose burns the sun of the Tropics. . . . Her youth is explosive, with a Creole luminosity. It has the force of an arrow directed at the Sun and her aspiration is a burning thirst, a multiple intoxication, as are all the earth's fruits. In the prose of *The Last of My Saturdays* one observes this nubile candor" (ii–vii).

Viewed from the context of the multiple portraits, "this nubile candor" looks like just one more of the many dimensions of Clementina and her writing. But it was the characteristic most cherished by the male critics or poets or writers of prologues and semblanzas who, as they read her verses, were reading her body with the caresses of their critical desire. Clementina's poems were indeed expressions of the flesh as much as of the soul. She learned about herself by offering her poems and other masks, and watching for the reaction they caused.

She also learned about herself through the eyes of the artists who painted or sculpted her likeness. But not in a literal way, for, as demonstrated in the comments of Lazzaroni and Padilla, it was not always the essence of Clementina that was portrayed. It was rather the attention focused upon her that she needed in order to be able to see herself. In *The Last of My Saturdays* she has a short piece entitled "Píntame pintor" (Paint Me Painter) that suggests the symbiotic dimension of her quest for self-knowledge. "Paint me with the face you divine, with pomaded hair and blood-red cheek. Paint me with a woman's body, sun-drenched and fragrant. Paint my eyes like pools of water, with the depth of your seas and the blackness of your nights. Especially paint that look that rises from my heart full of tenderness. . . . You tell me I am ugly. I do not believe it, I cannot, for when you look into my eyes I feel beautiful from head to foot" (77–78).

Hard to resist indeed. Nor did Clementina resist the attentions of the numerous men who were drawn to her complex femininity. She once said,

"I have loved being a woman. When I was young I adored having men fall in love with me. I have been vain about my body and my life-style. I have had no complexes whatsoever, nor prejudices of any kind. So you see I have lived to the fullest my life as a woman. . . . I have always been in love with love, and not with the person himself. The proof is that I have been able to leave them, to put them to one side of my life. I have been a lover of love rather than of any individual. I have loved deeply, but I have come to understand that more than the person, what I have loved is love itself."[4]

But Clementina expressed this perception in 1982, at eighty years of age. Certainly when she left the North Coast to try out life in Tegucigalpa, she was still in search of the one, the right, the perfect man who would sweep her off her feet, the man to whom she could offer the unmitigated richness of her femininity. She thought she had found that man in the person of Antonio Rosa.

"Tegucigalpa, City of Memories"

After the North Coast, the next and most obvious move for a young woman of literary pretensions was of course the capital. Clementina remembered Tegucigalpa from her time as a student at the private academy of the Saravia sisters and from her visits to the home of her uncle when she accompanied her father when he attended the annual sessions of Congress as a representative from Olancho. But in 1915 she was "a schoolgirl wearing a uniform that covered a young body somewhere between chlorotic and frail; in short, an adolescent of no great importance."[5] When she returned a decade later she had shed her schoolgirl uniform and began causing a stir with her daring appearance and behavior. She painted her nails and lips bright red and never tried to hide the delight she took in makeup, hairstyles, and spirited and individualistic fashion. She moved in with her uncle Pío Suárez's family but did not feel comfortable in the household, an extended family of fourteen that shared a large house near the center of town. Perhaps among so many people she was unable to attract the attention she craved, or find a space to enjoy her increasingly beloved solitude.

Clementina quickly became an attraction in this small capital city. Tegucigalpa has historically been an isolated community, a situation dictated by its geography, economy, and politics. Jorge Fidel Durón, a contemporary of Clementina's, remembers that in the twenties "the only road that led out of the country was the Southern Highway, a route that required several days. It was not until the administration of General Rafael López Gutiérrez [1920] that the road heading north was completed as far as Comayagua. I recall that before then one made the journey on muleback, and it took over a week. Getting to the North Coast was a daunting undertaking."[6]

Tegucigalpa is located in the central mountainous region of Honduras on a plateau at thirty-two hundred feet above sea level. It is so hilly that in several locations streets of stairs connect one level with another. It boasts of being the only Central American capital that has never been destroyed by an earthquake, and consequently many of its central streets retain the same narrow, circuitous configuration as when they were first built. The old sections of the city give the impression of having evolved in a dense, organic fashion. Streets branch off from the central plaza with its cathedral, banks, and stores to wind their serpentine way over and around hills and rivers that divide the city into sections and neighborhoods, creating blocks of internal isolation, just as the city they comprise seems to live a life of seclusion. Messengers filter through from the outside world, the locals leave to visit other metropoli, but Tegucigalpa's isolation is tenacious and binds its victims in ways they may scarcely realize. María Guadalupe Carías, born in Tegucigalpa at the beginning of this century, reconstructs the solidarity of her old neighborhood with a heavy dose of nostalgia, but in a way that calls attention to a closeness that can be intrusive as well as supportive. "Life was simple but beautiful. Families were close and family members treated one another with respect, an attitude which was reflected in the way people treated their servants. There was great solidarity within neighborhoods. The sorrows and joys of one were the sorrows and joys of all. That is how those of us from La Merced and El Olvido were brought up, in complete brotherhood. At six in the afternoon the church bells tolled the Angelus; everyone blessed themselves. By eight o'clock it was night. The bugles from the barracks sounded the curfew. The family would pray together and the grandmother would tell stories and give out advice, passing the tradition down from one generation to the next."[7]

In 1944 Argentina Díaz Lozano, one of Honduras's few women novelists, published an autobiographical novel, *Peregrinaje* (Pilgrimage), about growing up in Honduras. In it she describes the social structure of Tegucigalpa in 1921:

> There were three social classes in Tegucigalpa. The aristocracy, made up of the old family names and some of the recently wealthy, who had worked their way into politics. This class danced at the Tegucigalpa Club or at the Presidential Palace . . . they entertained themselves at gatherings where their acquaintances (of the same social standing) were picked apart or elevated, where the young ladies played the piano and sang romantic ballads and the men courted them in verse and song. The middle class was composed of government employees, small businessmen and employees of banks and businesses. They amused themselves at the movies, in outings in the country to El Hatillo or La Granja, at the concerts in Central Park . . . and in trying to figure out a way to be able one day to dance in the virtually inaccessible Tegucigalpa Club. The lower class, backbone of any city, in the Honduran capital is made up of workers of all kinds: the janitors in government offices, the market women, the long-suffering wives of masons, carpenters, shoemakers, etc. They also attend the concerts in the Central Park, have outings in La Leona Park and La Concordia Park, dance at Christmastime and eat tamales and *torrejas* [fritters] on December nights. . . . But the soul of Tegucigalpa is the intellectual and university class. In its quiet streets, beneath gentle sunsets, poets and romantic and exalted writers of prose weave their dreams; journalists dash off their chronicles and commentaries; scholars of literature discuss Byron, Hugo and Zola. In 1921 the notables were Alberto Uclés, Luis Andrés Zúñiga, Froylán Turcios, Lucila Gamero de Medina and many other "wandering poets" of lost gaze and absent gesture. Tegucigalpa is the Athens of the Republic, where the literati and students of law and medicine discuss with vigor the latest world problems, the latest book or the recent extravagant behavior of some Continental celebrity. Women of 1921 allowed themselves to be serenaded and courted like queens, they dressed up to spend afternoons on balconies adorned with the most Spanish of ironwork, they attended mass on Sundays perfumed and graced with elegant

> black mantillas, they loved Bertini's movies, played stylish and sad-cadenced tangos on their pianos and gossiped about the latest love affairs and upcoming marriages.[8]

The city was green and cool, surrounded by forests of fragrant pine. La Leona Park, located a short walk up a steep slope from the Central Plaza, was then the edge of the city. Young boys would climb to the park and amuse themselves looking out over the city, waiting for cars to pass by, trying to guess who was out driving. One estimate is that there were between fifteen and twenty privately owned cars in Tegucigalpa in 1925, although various transport companies, such as Gómez y Estrada, rented their vehicles for outings. But horses remained the principal means of locomotion as well as a favorite diversion. Various stables rented horses, and at numerous locations throughout the city one could purchase hay and fodder. Young men paraded through the streets on steeds and demonstrated their virility on the race track.

One of the handsomest and most conspicuous of the young horsemen was Antonio Rosa. He was an expert equestrian, and when he wasn't strolling through Central Park in a white linen suit imported from London or New Orleans, he was either with his horses or participating in one of the local sporting activities. There were baseball and soccer teams, bicycling was very popular, and skating in La Leona Park was a favorite of the younger crowd. Antonio Rosa was a decent all-around athlete who excelled in discus throwing and weight lifting as well as equitation. His mother, Rosa de Rosa, owned a successful commercial establishment, a kind of grocery and department store near Los Dolores Church, and doted on her handsome son. She was able to provide him with the opportunity to travel abroad, where he immersed himself in the fads and fashions of the times and returned to open a store on the Central Plaza that specialized in providing elegant imported clothing, fine perfumes, and tobaccos for his wealthy clientele. He called the store La de Moda (In Style). It was a great success because of its central location, its select merchandise, and the popularity of its owner, but also because Antonio Rosa was a shrewd businessman. His friends would affectionately chide him for offering an item for nineteen pesos and ninety-eight cents rather than for twenty pesos, to make it appear a bargain.

Antonio Rosa was the quintessential man-about-town, the handsome don Juan that all the young ladies dreamed of catching and taming. He loved this role and took advantage of his reputation as a good catch by playing with the affections of numerous young ladies. Clementina probably should have known better.

In later years Antonio Rosa became involved in politics and fell victim to the intrigues that characterize governments run by nepotism, influence, and favoritism. He spent some time in jail, where the long hours of confinement offered him the opportunity to reflect and remember. Upon his release he led a more settled life and devoted a good deal of time to painting and writing. He subsequently published several novels of local customs as well as memoirs of his youth and young manhood. In one of these delightful memoirs, *Tegucigalpa, ciudad de remembranzas* (Tegucigalpa, City of Memories), he devotes an entire chapter to a lively description of a masquerade ball on 17 February 1926.[9] The chapter is replete with names, faces, and colorful details that evoke the social scene of the elite of Tegucigalpa society. Squarely at the center of the action is the narrator himself.

The ball was held in the meticulously scrubbed and extravagantly decorated hall of the International Club, the recently inaugurated social center of a group of young men from the capital. Antonio Rosa was one of the ringleaders of the group, which included the writers Guillermo Bustillo Reina and Arturo Martínez Galindo (both of whom later figure importantly in Clementina's life) and the journalist and caricaturist Augusto Monterroso. The hall was lit with hundreds of colored lights, and a band composed of a marimba, a saxophone, and an accordion played popular waltzes such as "Alejandra," indigenous melodies such as "Tecúm Umán," and even "San Luis Blues." A large crowd formed in the park and outside the door of the club to inspect the masqueraders as they arrived and try to guess their identities. Guests spared neither imagination nor expense to produce authentic-looking costumes of "queens, princesses, Spanish dancers, Egyptians, Gypsies, Arabs, dolls, nurses and God only knows what else; accompanied by princes, gauchos, harlequins, Pierrots, Apaches, soldiers" (139). But even among such splendid displays of finery, one person stood out from the crowd, at least in the mind of the narrator: "And without bragging I will say that my unforgettable mother, who was a businesswoman, sent to California for a genuine Roman toga—the kind that were used in the filming of *Ben Hur*—so that her 'spoiled son,' the peacock of the family, would shine at that year's carnival ball, the merriest and most splendid masquerade party ever in the social history of Tegucigalpa. . . . It would have been around ten at night when I appeared in the streets around Central Park in a luxurious Roman centurion's outfit, astride a white steed. The throng that filled the southern end of the park crowded together to see better. I soon dismounted and made my entry into the International Club while the numerous onlookers applauded" (137–38).

He goes on to describe with great flourish and obvious admiration the charms of the young ladies at the ball. His language is florid and self-assured, his comments those of a man utterly absorbed in the game of romance. The women are all flowers, heavenly visions, implacable seductresses who tear open a man's heart. But it's worth it! He and his friends sit around a table drinking cognac and ginger ale, waxing poetic at the sight of the masked beauties before them. They treat each one as the most beautiful woman present, then turn their appreciative gaze to the next, and so on throughout the night and the chapter. "Among them all, as if wrapped in a magic vision, we watched dumbfounded the ever so sweet Rosinda Fortín, disguised as a woman from Seville. Bewitching Sevillana whose eyes burn with a flame that captivates the soul. Ah! Who could hope to capture that elusive heart of gold . . . the most beautiful Aída Valenzuela, dark-skinned regent who would later occupy the throne as Honduras' beauty queen . . . the most lovely Delfina Barrientos who, in the guise of a Siamese queen, went around breaking hearts. Her rosy skin and graceful body made her a treasure of enchantment . . . the hypnotizing Estelita Reyes, already judged to be the prettiest doll in the store of dreams established in this capital city . . . Lolita [Fortín] is one of the most beautiful ladies who adorn our small but select social world" (139–42).

The literary bachelors drinking cognac and ginger ale are clearly as much impressed with themselves and their literary flair as with the women by whose charms they purport to be imprisoned. It is a gallant and flirtatious game, seemingly harmless were it not for the vulnerability of the females, whose reputations and futures depend on their being desirable but untouched. Males and females bill and coo, they dance and dress and write verses for one another, but they are not allowed to couple unless their union follows the rules of the patriarchy, more precisely, the rules of "our small but select social world." The rules are as follows: women must be attractive in a public way while they are single, so that all men can see and appreciate their charms, in order to help them make their selection. They are the objects for sale in "the store of dreams established in this capital city," but appreciation is not to go beyond the visual. While a woman must be attractive and chaste, a man's desirability is derived from qualities other than appearance, among which chastity is not a priority. Indeed, a man who has overcome a woman's resistance may be esteemed as more virile by his fellow bachelors and even by the very women who have so much to lose if they themselves were to succumb to prenuptial seduction.

Antonio Rosa climaxes his recollection of that grand ball with a description of his flirtation with Maruca Reyes Noyola. His previous mention of her, although flattering in the extreme ("but there is none other like Maruca Reyes Noyola, who is so rhythmic and graceful in the art of dance; no one enjoys such popularity and goodwill as she," 143) is essentially indistinguishable from the complimentary panegyrics that populate his narrative. So one is taken somewhat by surprise when he reveals that he is so impressed by María (Maruca) that he rips up her already full dance card and insists she be his dance partner for the rest of the evening. Not only that, but "the contract with María was not only for the rest of that unforgettable evening, it was a sweet contract for life" (150).

In February 1926, when Antonio Rosa was busy decorating the International Club, parading as a Roman centurion, and courting the woman he was to marry, he was also deeply involved in a relationship with Clementina Suárez, and possibly with other young women in Tegucigalpa as well. Clementina soon set up house in an apartment in Barrio Abajo that Antonio paid for. He continued to live in his mother's house and to carry on as a bachelor-about-town, but he visited Clementina in her apartment on a regular basis. She did not work at this time, nor did she find it necessary, for Antonio was not only wealthy but generous, and she lacked for nothing. She became pregnant and in April 1928 gave birth to her first daughter, Alba. The following year Silvia was born. Clementina and Antonio never married, and they did not hide their relationship. For him this most likely presented only minimal difficulty, for it is not at all unusual in Tegucigalpa, even today, for a man to have a mistress. The difficulty accrues rather to the mistress.

Clementina could easily have been one of the young ladies courted and flattered at that ball—in fact she probably was. But it would have been unseemly for Antonio Rosa, an elderly gentleman reminiscing about his youth in print, to publicize his affair with a woman he never married. So we know to some extent the importance of Antonio Rosa in Clementina's life, but we can only surmise what she meant to him. When I asked her why she and Antonio did not marry, especially when she became pregnant, she answered in what I came to recognize as her typically evasive manner.

JNG: You two never married, did you?
CS: No.
JNG: Why did you decide not to get married?
CS: Well, because in that sense I have always been very free. I don't think marriage is necessary in a union of love between two responsible individuals. Now, for irresponsible people it is a security, but I haven't needed it.
JNG: Did Antonio feel the same way about it?
CS: I don't know if he shared my thoughts on this or if he took advantage of the situation. But it was a union that I soon determined to dissolve, because it was completely incompatible with my way of being and with my ambitions.

Clementina was swept off her feet by the dashing Antonio Rosa. Who, in fact, could have come closer to being Tegucigalpa's answer to Prince Charming? Even as an old woman, in exalted moments of recollection, Clementina has referred to him as "an Adonis." She recalls him as handsome, rich, virile, and well dressed. Besides, she wanted desperately to get out of her uncle's house and have a space of her own. A densely patriarchal society offers few possibilities to the woman who wants something more from life than a man. But the one option always available to women who are sufficiently attractive and astute is to get by, or get ahead, through a man. So, in those early days of testing the waters, Clementina, in love with love and self-assured enough to defy society, became a kept woman. And while she always would be a daughter of the aristocracy, by choosing so boldly to violate that most fundamental rule of the patriarchy, by defying and thereby denying the primacy of the marriage contract, she set herself in opposition to her own social group.

One of the most popular stories in the Clementina legend is the tale of the clever way she circumvented the question of her daughters' paternity. Tegucigalpans chuckle as they call attention to the fact that "Rosa" is both a woman's name and a last name. So, whether Antonio Rosa liked it or not, Clementina's two daughters acquired his last name. In the Hispanic tradition of naming, children take their father's paternal family name, followed by their mother's paternal family name. So Alba Rosa Suárez and Silvia Rosa Suárez were both named for the queen of flowers and also for Antonio Rosa.

As one elderly Tegucigalpan explained, the prevailing morality did not allow for the relationship that Clementina had with Antonio Rosa. It was a cause for criticism, but many people admired her precisely because she ignored the social standard of the times. The criticism must have been fierce, for commenting on one's neighbors' activities is inevitably a popular pastime in small, isolated communities. Alejandro Castro, the editor of a long-lived and popular Tegucigalpa weekly, devoted more than one editorial to the phenomenon of gossip. He authored a regular column in his *Revista Tegucigalpa* (Tegucigalpa Magazine) called "Cartas al terruño" (Letters to the Homeland), in which a fictional "Pedro" addresses letters to "Juan." The letters are ruminations on everything from cock fights to women's fashions to the shortage of affordable housing in the capital, in which Castro criticizes in a paternalistic yet neighborly style. On several occasions "Pedro" informs "Juan" of the damage that can be caused by gossips. "The vice of gossip is fashionable in Tegucigalpa. Manly behavior and womanly honor are frequently under attack in tongue-wagging sessions in the street as well as in intimate family gatherings." It seems it is primarily women who participate in this sport: "Young girls start out, in conversations that seem quite harmless, criticizing the manner of dress of their friends; trying to figure out where the money comes from to pay the seamstress. . . . They soon go on, with biting commentary and a deliciously ironic style, to attribute horrid physical defects to the friend in question. . . . They then dig deeper, and facile and loose tongues begin to embellish almost infantile untruths, that in the course of the conversation begin to take shape, with a mean joke or a *double entendre,* until it becomes the hundred-headed monster of traitorous calumny. And it is then, when they feel protected by the impunity of 'they say,' that the most obnoxious inventions and hurtful insults are heaped on the lustre of immaculate reputations."[10]

Of course Clementina's reputation was not spotless, so she gave the gossips more than ample fuel for their fires, and the talk has not stopped yet. Alejandro Castro's tone is severely critical in this and other letters to "Juan," in which he elaborates on the methods and consequences of gossip. What he does not discern, or at any rate does not touch on in his letters, is the female reality in Tegucigalpan society that prompts this practice. In the 1920s, upper-class women had to care very much about their own appearance, as well as the appearance of their competitors. The number of middle- and upper-class women who worked outside the home or had professional careers was negligible. A woman's career was to attract a man, marry him, and then serve him. Society offered women access to politics, the arts, or money through wealthy and successful men, making them a commodity vied for openly. Participation in the status quo typically does not lead to analysis and criticism of the system, and the women of Tegucigalpa gossiped about Clementina because they were immersed in the conventions of their social class. If a woman has always obeyed the rules in order to earn her expected and respected place in society, it simply is not fair for some other woman openly to disregard those same rules and get away with it—worse still, to reap from her defiance the very rewards that the obedient hoped to win by being dull.

One of the consequences of gossip is to exclude the transgressor from the group. So little by little Clementina became an outsider among her own class and sex. Certainly she suffered from the gossip and ostracism, although it is also true that she was excluded from circles and gatherings in which she had little desire to participate anyway. It is hard to imagine her longing to join, for instance, "a group of gay young women who are toying with the project of organizing a club devoted to marriage propaganda, in opposition to the bachelors' club, which was founded here a short while ago and which has as its object, according to our sources, not only to discourage marriage among its members, but also to exclude from its ranks those who have not yet indulged in a love affair" (57).

Except for a handful of old-timers from Juticalpa who remember Clementina as an ordinary young girl, friendly although studious and often solitary, most people have an image of her as irascible, sharp-tongued, and opinionated, capable of vulgarity, even in public, and willing to insult anyone she thinks deserves it. Stories abound of dignitaries quaking in their boots when Clementina is invited to address a gathering, fearful lest she strip them of their pretensions and expose their not so dignified selves. There is the anecdote, for example, of the party in San Pedro Sula where Clementina found herself surrounded by a group of catty women who began baiting her, asking her how many men she had slept with. She replied that she didn't know the number, but she could assure them first of all that she had slept with all of their husbands. And she reminded them that they were all whores; the only difference between her and them was that they were provincial sluts, whereas she was international, and her tastes were more refined. There is also the story about when Clementina was invited to a luncheon meeting of a local women's group because she was to be given an award by the group for her literary accomplishments, after she had won national recognition in 1970 with the Ramón Rosa National Award for Literature. When she was asked to say a few words to the ladies, she told them that she knew they were probably expecting her to thank them, but that she had nothing to be grateful to them for, that anything she had achieved in life had been hard won, that she had had to struggle against people like themselves all her life, and that what she knew of life she had learned in the street. She said she knew that they had chosen to honor her only because she had received the national literary award, that there were women in the audience who in the past had been instrumental in denying her entry into the very club where they were now having lunch, and that they were a bunch of hypocrites.

These anecdotes about Clementina, even though most of them are impossible to verify, are a part of her community's folklore and reveal as much about Tegucigalpa as they do about Clementina—or perhaps more accurately, they reveal much about the relationship of the collective to its unusual, rebellious, or disruptive members, to its artists and writers especially. It has been suggested that gossip is a form of voyeurism whose excitement includes "the heady experience of imaginative control: gossip claims other people's experience by interpreting it into story."[11] The strange irony of gossip is that it excludes while at the same time allowing the gossipers to appropriate its stories as part of its own identity. So Clementina will remain a vital part of the life and self-image of Tegucigalpa in part because she was once excluded. Tegucigalpans can participate in her antisocial behavior by retelling the stories of her rebelliousness. Honduras dearly loves its artists, its poets, and its eccentrics, but it doesn't want to have to take them so seriously as to be obliged to support them, so it appreciates them vicariously, using stories about them as entertainments, morality plays, and communal celebrations of a shared identity.

As a young woman in Tegucigalpa, Clementina was sensitive to criticism and exclusion, and it hurt her, but her stubbornness always won out, and she learned to ignore the criticism of those she considered morally or intellectually inferior. In self-defense she learned to fight back, and revenge has been sweet. Now that she is an old woman, she feels immune to attack. One of her survival strategies has been to accumulate the approbation of famous people, so that the local know-it-alls will be too intimidated to contradict their assessment of her. This may in part explain the enormous satisfaction she derives from her large collection of portraits. She began collecting respectable approbation when Alfonso Guillén Zelaya wrote the prologue to *Bleeding Heart* and encouraged her to continue with her poetry. She is very proud of her acquaintance with Pablo Neruda and of the words of praise she received from another friend, Miguel Angel Asturias. She certainly had closer friends, and friendships that lasted longer and were more important to her, but she shrewdly capitalizes on her acquaintance with these superstars as a way of shielding herself from criticism.

The "New Woman" in Honduras

The twenties was the decade of the "New Woman" in the United States, a time of superficial as well as profound changes in women's lives, when everyone who could afford it, from flappers to suffragettes, participated in some form of outrageous behavior. These currents of rebellion and innovation caused ripples even in the staid waters of Tegucigalpa society.

On 9 January 1927, two articles in the same issue of *Tegucigalpa Magazine* reveal this rippling as well as society's efforts to calm the waters and return to normalcy. An article by Delia Becerra argues that the schools of Tegucigalpa place too much emphasis on teaching young girls embroidery and should instead spend more time on the culinary, that is, the more practical arts. On the following page a news item reports, "The Pope declared that today's women's fashions 'do violence in every way against human and Christian dignity.'" The pope goes on to urge "that heads of family restrain the irreverence and corruption of their daughters and wives as expressed in their immodest clothing."

But another article in the same magazine the very next year, on 10 March 1928, reminds parents that they must be "genuinely understanding and intelligent in order to be able to educate their daughters in this time of transition for women." Writing under the name Aurora Boreal, the author of "Charlas para Mujeres" (Talks for Women) reminds us that "the time has passed when young girls spent their time embroidering endless monograms on batiste handkerchiefs, or making interminable lace for daddy's birthday, with no other dreams than those their parents permitted them and with no other future than the fiancé imposed on them. Girls have escaped from this lukewarm atmosphere into the world of sports, universities and businesses. Dressed in near-masculine attire, free during the day to act as they please out in the street, they worry the poor old people who have no idea how to control the youthful enthusiasm of their daughters." The point of the article, ironically, is that, with all the masculine activities women are pursuing, it is important for mothers not to neglect to instruct them also in the domestic arts.

A photograph a few pages later shows the women's basketball team, Club Helios. They had defeated their rival the previous Sunday and are posing in their "masculine" sportswear, which consists of white short-sleeved blouses, plaid skirts that reach just below the knee, white pumps, and scarves tied around their heads with large white bows over their right ears. They are displaying two banners for the photographer that read not "Club Helios" or "United in Victory" or something equally sporty and appropriate to the moment, but rather "Union" and "Peace." It seems that active women were not limiting their energies to sports and typing but were taking an interest in politics as well.

Many women in fact have played an active though largely unrecorded role in society and politics in Honduras. Indeed, in the early decades of the twentieth century, one of the most persistent and vocal public figures was the educator and journalist Visitación Padilla. From a humble beginning as a provincial schoolteacher from Talanga, she moved to Tegucigalpa and developed into an outspoken and influential member of the Liberal Party.

She remained single her whole life, devoting herself with great energy and commitment to various causes, including anti-imperialism, temperance, and women's education. She lived with her mother, who is remembered as being possessive and somewhat tyrannical. Whenever her daughter went out, which must have been frequently, she became angry and complaining. It is said that she locked the doors of her house at 6:00 P.M., after which no one was allowed to enter or leave. It is ironic that one of the few Honduran women who established an enduring public fame should have had such a structured and restricted private life. Perhaps those long evenings behind locked doors offered her the time she needed to prepare her lectures at the Escuela Normal para Señoritas and to write the numerous stories and articles that appeared in the local press. As a vigorous and emotional intellectual, capable of combining her commitments with action, she was not above taking to the streets to call attention to a public issue or to garner support for civic action. She was, in fact, one of the figures at the center of the public protest surrounding the occupation of Tegucigalpa by the U.S. Marines in 1924.

Since the nineteenth century, the United States has intervened frequently in the internal affairs of the Central American nations. Justifications have included failure of the countries to repay their foreign debts, protection of U.S. interests, safeguarding the lives and property of U.S. citizens, and protecting Central American citizens from the chaos and violence caused by internal power struggles. In 1923 three candidates vied for the presidency of Honduras: Policarpo Bonilla, Juan Angel Arias, and Tiburcio Carías Andino—and two banana companies vied for control of the country and its president: the United Fruit Company and the Cuyamel Fruit Company. A chaotic situation developed when no one of the three candidates achieved a majority of the vote in popular elections. Franklin Morales, U.S. ambassador to Honduras, called for military aid to protect U.S. citizens from the dangers of civil war. Two hundred marines entered the Honduran capital on 19 March 1924 and installed themselves in the U.S. embassy, just one block off Central Park. Although there was no large-scale military confrontation during their stay of over a month, their presence caused deep resentment among Hondurans of all political persuasions, who felt it was an insult to their sovereignty.[12]

Froylán Turcios, who at the time was involved in the publication of two literary magazines, *Ateneo de Honduras* (Honduran Atheneum) and *Hispanoamérica* (Spanish America), and was serving as president of the Honduran Atheneum, of the Ibero-American Association, and of the Committee for Peace, reacted with unbridled ire and patriotism to this affront to his country's dignity; he immediately began publishing a daily paper called *Boletín de la defensa nacional* (National Defense Bulletin).[13] He financed the printing himself, wrote many of the articles, and solicited articles from prominent intellectual leaders. He initiated a "protest book" in which citizens signed their names to register their disapproval of the U.S. military presence in their city. Turcios claims that more than nine thousand names appeared in this book, a significant number considering that the population of the city was approximately thirty thousand.

One of the most frequent and virulent contributors to the *Bulletin* was Visitación Padilla. In her almost daily articles she calls on the citizens of Tegucigalpa to sign the protest book and to make known their patriotism by demonstrating against the presence of the marines. She employs a variety of strategies in her rhetoric: she praises, cajoles, exhorts, and illustrates her point through stories and dramatizations of imaginary conversations. In a voice of righteous indignation she appeals to Honduran national pride, and for those unmoved by this plea she resorts to criticism and insults, reminding the gentlemen that many women have demonstrated greater bravery and commitment than they. "I am aware that we all protest, but it is better to do so as have the worthy matrons and young women of Comayagüela, as have the distinguished Central American professor Miss María Luisa Herradora and the women and young ladies of this capital, who have honorably added their signatures to the book of our national honor, to serve as an example to the men who are afraid of the gentleman Minister from the United States."[14]

Earlier in the same article she quotes from a text by María Herradora that had appeared in the *Bulletin* the previous day, referring to it as "so lovely and sincere." She praises Herradora for refusing to remain silent and hopes that "certain ladies of Tegucigalpa whose daughters Miss Herradora teaches will take note of her beautiful words, especially the following: 'Although I count myself among those who consider that a woman's center of activity should be the home and the school, from whence she can make her influence felt, just as men do in their parliaments and other places which correspond to them, I am unable to remain silent now, owing to my Honduran-Nicaraguan origin, when an immense pain is renewed in my heart due to the arrival of North American troops in this capital city" (59–60).

Visitación Padilla is often referred to as a feminist in Honduras, even though her outspokenness and her involvement in public issues mask an essential conservatism. Like María Herradora, she envisioned a society firmly grounded in a traditional division of labor, but one in which women are well educated, the better to instill virtues in their children and to influence their husbands in moral issues. Like many other crusading women whose projects took them away from home and into the streets, or who were able to be activists because they did not have the responsibilities of motherhood or because they could afford household help, she did not address the contradictions inherent in urging other women to be both wives and mothers as well as publicly active.

Clementina also is referred to as a feminist in Honduras, but how different the contours of these two women's lives! Perhaps the paucity of women whose names or works have managed to survive the amnesia of time inspires those who do remember to recall their strength, or that unique quality that made them memorable, and to equate strength or uniqueness with feminism. Indeed, perhaps the truest feminist is not she who articulates the clearest and most correct theoretical construct, but she whose life is itself a feminist construct. If that is the case, then Clementina is a feminist, even though she may not fit every feminist's criteria, for she wears makeup and loves to flirt and seduce men, is sometimes cruel to other women, and often used powerful and influential men to attain some desired goal. I call her a feminist even though she does not care for the word, preferring to think of herself as a free woman and a realized woman. She associates the word *feminist* with man-hater and complainer. In 1985 she said: "*I am not a feminist. I don't like women's groups. It's not that I am against women, it's that I feel I have gone beyond those problems and I don't want to be debating them any more. I have been independent all my life. I don't have to go around fighting for the liberation of women, because I am a liberated woman.*"[15]

There have been other women who are bright lights in the cultural firmament of Honduras, but their stories have not yet been told. As I pursued my research on Clementina I came across various references to Honduran women who lived unique or creative or productive or eccentric or politically committed lives. The information was usually minimal and therefore all the more tantalizing. I have often since mused on how wonderful it would be to be able to walk into the National Library in Tegucigalpa and find on a shelf a row of biographies of Honduran women. There would of course be a biography of Visitación Padilla that described her childhood in Talanga, that explained why she moved to Tegucigalpa and why she never married, but raised an adopted son. It would tell me what she looked like, how she spoke, what her philosophy was. I would learn why the temperance movement was so important to her, and whether she ever defied her mother and sneaked out of the house after 6:00 P.M. Did her contemporaries admire her, or did they think she was too bold, too masculine, too outspoken? Did she ever travel? Did she die a fulfilled woman?

There would be a biography of Guadalupe Gallardo, born in Danlí in 1853. What was it about that anatomy class at the University of Guatemala that made her decide to abandon her medical studies? What was her life like, and her personality, described as "consummately bohemian . . . dark and wandering, but of great literary significance . . . devoted to freedom and to the more economically favored classes"?[16] She was a poet and an actress. What had happened to her that she would write such despairing lines as these?

> Why does the soul not break
> the prison of this wretched body,
> and follow its path
> with those birds of the sky?
> Why prolong this life if only to taste
> the bitterness
> of waking from that dream?
> Ay! from that fortunate age
> I look around and have nothing!
>
> ———
>
> ¿Por qué la carcel no rompe
> de este miserable cuerpo,
> y sigue el alma su ruta
> con esas aves del cielo?

¿Por qué prolongar la vida si todos probamos luego
que es amargo despertar
de aquel sueño?
¡Ay! de esa edad venturosa
¡miro en torno y nada tengo![17]

Twenty years later, in the same small town in eastern Honduras, Lucila Gamero was born. She grew up favored by her father, who shared with her his knowledge of science and medicine. She never earned a degree to become a professional practitioner of medicine, but it is said that her healing powers were in great demand in Danlí and that she was known to have performed eye surgery and blood transfusions. She belonged to numerous scientific and literary associations and referred to herself as a feminist. She was a prolific novelist, arguably the author of the first Honduran novel.[18] Is it true that she was excommunicated from the Catholic Church for the publication of *Blanca Olmedo,* a romantic novel of decidedly anticlerical bent? How did she find the time to write nine novels, raise a family, and attend international congresses? Was her husband supportive of her career?

One biography that would be difficult to write, but worth the effort, is that of Teresa Fortín—difficult because much of the life story will have to be gleaned with imagination and sensitivity from her paintings, especially those created when she was an old woman whose health and memory were failing. The forty paintings, collectively titled "My Life," were exhibited in 1980 when Teresa was eighty-four years old. Her biographer would have to track down those paintings and read from them the interior narrative of this woman whose life looks lonely and timid from the outside, but whose inner beauty brought forth the poignant "The Wedding I Did Not Have"; "The Future, a Happy People," her innocent vision of human possibility; and a haunting Chagall-like self-portrait entitled "History of My Life."[19]

And Mercedes Agurcia, the tall, bony woman who taught and inspired the young poets and dancers of Tegucigalpa in the thirties. And Siriyaca Ruiz, an illiterate woman from Olancho who came and went in the presidential palace as if she owned the place. And the women still alive whose lives and accomplishments deserve to be recorded: Emma Moya Posas, journalist and self-styled anthropologist; Leticia de Oyuela, historian and scholar who nourishes the cultural life of Tegucigalpa; Juana Pavón, street poet.[20]

But for all their color, intelligence, creativity, dedication, or talent, none of these women has possessed or nurtured two essential elements to the degree that Clementina Suárez has: the unmitigated conviction of her vocation as a poet coupled with a practical astuteness that helped her discern the path to poetness. She wanted it all. She wanted not only to be inspired and to write poetry; she wanted to live the life-style she considered poetic and to be recognized as a poet. She wanted to be a poet among poets. When she moved to Tegucigalpa she started doing just that, but she soon realized that being a woman presented obstacles that her male colleagues did not have to overcome. As she explained, "*There are no longer people like myself who devote their lives to poetry, they are almost all gone. Not because they haven't the ability or the vocation, but because they believe there are more practical things, more productive and easier things they can do with their lives. Because without a doubt, devoting oneself to a calling entails great sacrifice. I don't think I'm the only one with a calling, but I'm the only one who has given her whole life to it. I gave up my family. They think you're crazy, out of it, on some other wavelength, that you're lazy, that you're incapable of managing a household. I have been married, I lived with a man, I had my daughters, nonetheless I had to leave him [Antonio Rosa], because I couldn't adjust. I'm not one to be cooking three meals a day for a man, I can't do it. I simply cannot get concerned with everyday tasks. Between reading a book and writing my poetry and cooking a meal, I prefer my poetry and my book. But my husbands didn't like that. . . . Besides, one has to be a bit of a Quixote to live in these circumstances, because one never has any money. Women today don't want to make these sacrifices. They want a financially secure life. I don't think I'm the only one with a calling, there must be many, but the sacrifice I have made for my vocation, that is what they are lacking. They start off with a bang, they publish a few poems and then they stop publishing. One has to keep studying her whole life, and one must live a life for poetry; it's not just one day. Some day there'll be another.*"[21]

When Clementina started giving poetry recitals in 1931 as a way to promote her work as well as to earn money, she would come out onto the stage of the National Theatre barefoot, dressed in flowing tunics, often black, sometimes diaphanous. Her hair was loose on her shoulders as she moved her arms, her head, her whole body, adding physical substance to her verses. As for that story about Clementina appearing in a recital "dressed only in her chaste nakedness," she denies it, insisting that she often wore a flesh-colored leotard under a flowing, gauzy robe, which may have given the impression of nudity. Whatever she wore, she was a woman trying to be as free as Isadora Duncan in a community both shocked and tantalized by the increasingly visible "New Woman." International performing artists such as Ruth St. Denis, Josephine Baker, and, of course, Isadora Duncan personified this openness to the body that was expressed and perceived as both exotic and natural. Women took to the stage and took to the road in much-publicized exploits and adventures. In Latin America it was the golden age of the great *declamadoras,* when the Argentine Berta Singerman crossed the continent reciting the best-loved poems of the Spanish language to appreciative audiences, and Eusebia Cosme popularized the exciting new *poesía negra* fashionable in Cuba. Amelia Earhart did not visit Tegucigalpa as did her famous male counterpart, Charles Lindbergh, but the local papers and magazines carried stories of her deeds as well as those of other adventure and publicity seekers such as Ruth Elder and Thea Rasche. Much editorial comment accompanied photographs of women with short skirts, short hair, bare arms, rouge, and lipstick, women on stage, women wearing pants, women flying airplanes, women dancing the Charleston. In New York or Paris Clementina would have been a lot like many other young women experimenting with their identity, breaking rules, and exploring new territory. But in Tegucigalpa she was unique, which for one thing meant that there were few if any women with whom she could discuss these things. The Honduran capital was for the most part not ready for her liberated behavior. Had it accepted her difference, she wouldn't have been noticed. In "Compréndeme" (Understand Me), from *Temples of Fire,* she explains what makes her so special:

> Understand, understand,
> poor man who judges
> according to human laws.
>
> The Arcanum has elected
> that I glorify the World,
> my smile a rose

in the cross of the kiss.
My frivolity
is the exalted ardor
of the cardinal directions,
the lyrical wail
of fire, of water,
of wind, of earth,
stellar serpents
that mythify me.

Ay! Do not judge me
according to your human laws.
I am the golden key
with which you will open the sublime
doors of true
and eternal life,
without the dirty corpse
of social posture your mind creates.
. . . .
if you want to know the reasons,
if you desire to know the arcane
and magnificent organism of All,
climb to the grotto where the divine star,
beautiful spider spins her web;
descend to the dark and wonderful end;
or walk then, unknowing, fearless
along the very fine white thread
of a sigh that trembles on my lips
and return and explain the heights,
the common ground of the grotto,
and loudly proclaim if it is more solemn,
stronger, deeper and more sacred
than the cause of my vanity,
wisp of intangible smoke that resides
beyond the crystal of my soul . . .

———

Comprende, comprende,
pobre hombre que juzgas
conforme a tus leyes humanas.

El Arcano ha querido
que glorifique al Mundo,
riente como rosa
en la cruz del beso.
Lo frívolo mío
es el ardor mirífico
de los cuatro Puntos;
es el gemido lírico
del fuego, del agua,
del viento y la tierra,
boas estelares
que me vuelven mítica.

Vaya! No me juzgues
conforme a tus leyes humanas.
Yo soy la llave de oro
con que abrirás las puertas
sublimes de la vida
verdadera y eterna,
sin la carroña sucia
de las poses sociales
creadas por tu mente. . . .

si pretendes saber las razones,
si ambicionas saber el arcano
y estupendo organismo del Todo,
sube al antro en que el astro divino,
bella araña entreteje su maya;
baja al fondo tremendo y obscuro;
o anda luego, ignorante, sin miedo
por el hilo muy fino y muy niveo
del suspiro que tiembla en mis labios,
y regresa y explica la altura

el asiento pedestre del antro,
y di a gritos si aquello es más grave,
y más fuerte, y más hondo, y más sacro
que la causa de mi vanidad,
copo de humo intangible que se halla
más allá del cristal de mi alma . . .

Besides having to contend with her society's expectations of what a woman should want and how she should behave, Clementina was faced with the challenge of creating a life-style for herself in this society of male poets with whom she identified, for she had no role models. The only Honduran women who wrote poetry during the twenties and thirties were those who wrote but secreted their poems away for fear of ridicule, or those who sang a few sweet verses before getting married and having families.[22] *Tegucigalpa Magazine* is sprinkled with rosy poems by languishing lasses, such as "El rosal y la Chorcha" (The rose arbor and the woodcock), by Rosario Iris (probably a pseudonym). These few verses published in *Tegucigalpa Magazine* on 24 March 1928 indicate the technique and sentiment typical of these women:

Beneath the green bower
of the Normal School garden,
hangs a coy cage
by the rose in flower.

A treasure to behold,
a pretty little bird,
yellow, yellow bird,
that seems made all of gold.

———

Bajo la verde glorieta
del jardín de la Normal,
cuelga de un lindo rosal
una jaula muy coqueta.

En la jaula, su tesoro,
hay una linda avecilla,

es amarilla, amarilla,
y parece que es de oro. (9)

These were the *poetisas,* women who knew their place, who wrote child-like poems that the male literary establishment of Tegucigalpa patronizingly found charming. There is a streak of *poetisa* in the early Clementina. In a few of the poems from *Bleeding Heart* the lyric voice is a butterfly, a drop of water, a little girl, a cloud. But these innocent flutterings are minimal, overshadowed by the darker, more brooding side of her romanticism. The male poets referred to her with affectionate admiration as "*nuestra poetisa*" (our poetess), but Clementina bridled at being associated with what she considered dilettante dabbling in verse and insisted that she was a poet, not a poetess.

Literary Life in Tegucigalpa

In keeping with this self-image, Clementina worked her way into the literary circles of the capital. For, while she was being criticized by the watchful citizens of Tegucigalpa, and the select world of the Tegucigalpa Club did not welcome her, she was being protected by those who saw in her behavior and attitude cause for admiration, who not only welcomed her but treated her royally. It was mostly the intellectuals, and mostly men, who found themselves intrigued, impressed, or enchanted. Clementina knows whom she likes and pursues their acquaintance with directness. She sensed that other writers, particularly those who responded to her femininity or were of bohemian tendencies, would be her closest friends and allies.

There were three major circles, distinguished by age, social and economic class, and ideology, although the fact that Tegucigalpa was such a small (approximately 30,000 inhabitants) and introverted community meant that members of the various circles saw each other regularly, and there was much exchange and comaraderie, as well as competition and antagonism, among the groups. In one circle were the established writers, the respectable men of letters such as Alejandro Castro, editor of *Tegucigalpa Magazine,* and Alfonso Guillén Zelaya, well-known poet and director of the newspaper *El Cronista* (The Chronicler). A second group was the well-dressed set, young men of literary inclinations, although not necessarily dedicated exclusively to this pursuit, such as Antonio Rosa and his pals Arturo Martínez Galindo and Guillermo Bustillo Reina. These gents tended also to be dashing and handsome, sophisticated and international, and their writing reflects their savoir faire. The third and youngest group were the self-styled bohemian writers, poets such as Daniel Laínez, Marcos Carías Reyes, Claudio Barrera, and Ramón Padilla Coello. Some of these young men later became established, known and respected for their writing, and in retrospect have come to be classified as the Generation of '35.[23]

THE RESPECTABLE GENTS

Clementina fostered relationships with all of these circles, but each responded to her differently. She was the first group's darling. These venerable gentlemen found her young, attractive and intelligent and enjoyed her company at their *tertulias* in the Café de Paris and the Jardín de Italia. She in turn took advantage of these gatherings to further her literary education. She never returned to school after the Academy of the Saravia sisters closed, but she discovered that she could learn what was important to her by associating with learned and articulate individuals. A contemporary of Clementina's recalls, "I remember that Clementina used to participate in those tertulias. It wasn't that she sought them out, but that she attracted the tertulias of Tegucigalpa. This concern of hers to be around these people was a substitute for book learning, because I don't think she spent too much time reading. The great intellectuals of the time—Alejandro Castro, Alfonso Guillén Zelaya, Arturo Martínez Galindo, José Rodríguez Cerna—there they would be talking and telling jokes with Clementina. She would spend hours and hours sitting there listening. They were the kind of tertulias that don't exist anymore. Now if you go into the Jardín de Italia, all you hear are discussions about soccer. It used to be that someone like Ramón Padilla Coello would show up and recite his poetry, things of that nature. There were no other women at those tertulias, that's what set Clementina apart. The other women were afraid, but she took part. The men looked upon her as an intellectual."

THE WELL-DRESSED SET

Her relationship to the second group was more complex, richer in romance, gossip, and narrative detail. The members of the well-dressed literary set were closer to her own age and more predisposed to see her as a potential mistress, muse, or femme fatale. Indeed, the father of her two daughters, Antonio Rosa, and her first husband, Guillermo Bustillo Reina, were both part of this circle. Stories abound of her literary links with various of these gallants, with literature figuring not only as a topic of conversation at tertulias, but as a cultural medium in which Clementina played a literal as well as a figurative role.

One of these tales, which concerns a link that Clementina established between herself, Antonio Rosa, and literature, is told in "The Last of My Saturdays," a short story in Clementina's book of the same title, a collection of fifteen short prose pieces. A woman awaits her lover's visit. He always comes on Saturdays, and this Saturday, as usual, she has prepared her house for him. "My house was decorated festively that day. The lace tablecloth where his breakfast awaited him was strewn with violets, I had dusted carefully the better for the light to stream in, and flowers everywhere would grace his steps. A white bed, white and perfumed as an oriental divan reflected the glorious multicolored sky. On the cushioned carpet over which his feet would tread, a path of blossoms" (3).

She waits and waits, but he does not appear. She confesses, "To me he was everything, my one, adored, beloved, idolized, brother and friend . . . my Lord, my all. Consciously and unconsciously I had been directing all my actions to him, all my thoughts, all my dreams. I had sacrificed everything for him, given everything, lavished all on him, cheerfully, wantonly, madly" (4).

When he finally shows up, days later, he tells her their relationship cannot continue because it is causing him problems. He leaves, and she does some soul-searching. "I took the key to my heart and opened it: it was a chapel, a silken sanctuary hung with velvet and carpeted with my soul, and my supplications rose to the altar, to the image of my living God, who had just entered my sanctuary only to rend it. . . . And suddenly I realized, for the first time, that my intense love had never been understood" (7).

But from her pain and disappointment she has gained strength. "Since then I have returned many times, but I no longer wait for him, for that was the last of my Saturdays" (9).

The blank page is Clementina's stage, where she is free to create herself as she would have liked to have been or as she perceived herself. "The Last of My Saturdays" is an example of how Clementina has contributed to the formation of her own legend. She does not identify herself as the woman or Antonio as the lover, but there are enough tantalizing similarities that local readers would have been tempted to read the tale as autobiography, forming an image of her that is perhaps larger than life. Or is it? A resident of Tegucigalpa remembers as a teenager in the thirties reading "The Last of My Saturdays" over and over again, crying over the woman whose lover abandoned her. She had to hide the book under her pillow because her mother had forbidden her to read such trash by that whore who called herself a poet. But to her, Clementina was a romantic heroine.

Clementina sometimes tells the story another way. She says it was Antonio's birthday, and she had prepared an intimate celebration. She bought dozens of roses at the market and made a path of rose petals from the door to the bedroom and scattered petals over the bed. When he finally arrived, late, he was drunk from celebrating with the guys. He stumbled into the apartment and fell onto the bed complaining about the mess of flowers all over the floor and on the bed. She decided he was hopelessly insensitive and ended their relationship then and there.

However the teller chooses to embellish the tale, not long after the birth of her second daughter, perhaps even earlier, Clementina realized that she had made a big mistake by falling so passionately in love with Antonio Rosa. She had attributed to him the qualities of her dream lover and ideal mate, but he was in fact far from being the godlike male who would love her completely and make her life a romantic poem. He was unfaithful, a merchant not a poet, and, rather than doting on her, he expected her to wait on him as his mother always had. Little Silvia was scarcely seven months old when Clementina packed up and left.

Who can explain the mystery of attraction or the power of illusion? When Antonio Rosa died in 1983 he had accumulated a healthy collection of diplomatic and literary awards. He had written six novels and fathered at least eleven children. In a photograph taken at a family gathering he looks benevolent and balding. Maybe it was just the photograph, but he didn't seem very dashing. I had a hard time imagining him as Clementina's Adonis in a white linen suit or a Roman tunic or galloping on a handsome steed. I only know that that photograph will never be the real Antonio Rosa for me. The image Clementina has bequeathed him is stronger and clearer than literalness.

Clementina has also entered other literary dimensions, not of her own composition but as the flesh-and-blood person who inspired the creation of fictional characters. Or so many Honduran readers believe. People say, for example, that the title character of Antonio Bermúdez's novel *Ester la cortesana* (Esther the Cortesan) is based on Clementina. Bermúdez was, like Antonio Rosa, one of this second group of literary gentlemen, a debonair man about town with literary and diplomatic ambitions. It is said that Clementina and the novelist were lovers, that they became estranged, and that he in revenge wrote this tale of a woman who wantonly destroyed men, literally. The opening chapter, "Se trata de una mujer" (About a Woman), describes the woman to whom Bermúdez refers as the "heroine" of the story, although the fictional Ester never surfaces convincingly, figuring in the background as a powerful force in the lives of five men who are each in turn fascinated to the point of obsession by this woman who plays the roles of prostitute, femme fatale, avenging bitch, witch, and seductress. She manages to ruin the lives of all five men, as indicated by the various chapter titles, such as "El patético caso de Adolfo" (The Moving Case of Adolfo)—Adolfo ends up committing suicide—"La lamentable aventura de Isaac" (Isaac's Unfortunate Adventure), and "El castigo de Valderramos" (Valderramos's Punishment). All these men are seduced by her charms, although she is described as not beautiful: "Her face has no delicate features that particularly attract one's attention, aside from her burning eyes and her moist, fleshy and provocative mouth. But she has a winning and suggestive way and the rhythm of her walk awakens a frenetic rush of desires."

Unable to explain whence this woman's power of seduction, "the popular imagination amuses itself by attributing supernatural influences to this woman's life" (15–18). Belying the novel's title, the real focus is the five men whose lives are destroyed by this woman. Ester merely walks down the street and in her wake leaves a trail of panting males desiring her, bewitched. Ester lies on her bed tantalizing men, who become insatiable in her arms. These men, and their friends who observe their obsession and offer advice, are confounded by her power over them and hate her for it. They become ill, distracted; they lose interest in work and friends; they despair to the point of suicide. The message is clear: a woman can ruin a man's life, so it is best to avoid those women whom men cannot control.

Clementina of course denies any resemblance to Ester. She did have a friendship with Antonio Bermúdez, but she says she remembers him fondly and does not think he had her in mind when he conceived the tale of the cortesan. This literary link nonetheless calls attention to a particularity of Clementina's that permeates much of her poetry, her early publications as well as her more mature work: a sexuality that is electric, voluptuous, and mystical. She began to fashion her sexuality in *Temples of Fire,* where the female lyric voice is passionate, powerful, even divine. One poem from this book, baldly titled "Sexo" (Sex), is short, simple, and to the point. It begins:

Sex,
flesh-rose,
lust-flower
where my youth exults.

———

Sexo,
encarnada rosa,
flor de lujuria
por donde salta mi juventud.

Her sex, the physical locus of pleasure, is exalted to religious or at least ceremonial status by the use of metaphors such as: "amphora replete / with sensations and vibrations" (anfora llena / de sensaciones y vibraciones); "harp vibrating . . . voluptuousness" (arpa que vibra . . . voluptuosidades); "lily burning / on the altar of fire" (lirio encendido / en el altar de fuego); "wondrous grotto" (gruta maravillosa). It is the shrine where she offers "the divine flower / of life and love" (la divina flor / de vida y amor). In "Explicaciones" (Explanations), from the same book, she enlarges the parameters of this divine locus to include her entire female self. She calls on her lover, "Sidereal animal / my beautiful beloved "(Animal sidereo /

bello amado mío), to pay homage to her. She invites him to enter her realm, if he would aspire to know the deepest meaning of things:

> The World is a Thousand and One Mysteries
> ethereal,
> subtle,
> divine,
> that require feminine eyes.
>
> ———
>
> El Mundo es los Mil y un Misterios
> etéreos,
> sutiles,
> divinos,
> que requieren ojos femeninos.

She explains:

> I am Scherezade
> who knows all,
> you the great King
> who knows nothing.
> My spirit is the key
> that opens all doors,
> that opens all the magic boxes
> that hold the fragrance of the stars
> and the jewels of all suns,
> all things beautiful.
> . . . .
> My knowledge
> is the fragrance
> of the rose of my ignorance.
> My science is the science
> of the lily:
> to live,
> to perfume,
> to glow,
> to love

the rocks, the birds,
the blue sky,
magnificent nest
of pale and marvelous constellations. . . .

Your wisdom
is melancholy,
your science
a mere skeleton,
your art is a lake
that mirrors the stars' trembling,
the snowy lily,
the seer;
but it is not the star,
nor the lily,
nor the seer.

———

Yo soy Scherezada
que lo sabe todo,
tú el Rey tremendo
que no sabe nada.
Mi espíritu es llave
que abre todas las puertas,
que abre todas las cajas
milagrosas que guardan
el perfume de las estrellas
y las gemas de los soles,
todas las cosas bellas. . . .

Mi sabiduría
es la fragancia
de la rosa de mi ignorancia.
Mi ciencia
es la ciencia del lirio:
vivir,
perfumar,

lucir,
amar
las piedras, las aves,
el cielo azul,
nido magnífico
de las pálidas constelaciones miríficas. . . .

Tu sabiduría
es melancolía,
tu ciencia un completo
esqueleto,
tu arte es un lago
que copia el temblor de la estrella,
el nevado lirio,
el hada;
pero no es la estrella,
pero no es el lirio,
pero no es el hada.

It is not only knowledge and ecstasy that she holds within herself. Her very poetry is inseparably linked with her physical, female self.

My art
is rooted
in the rhythmic restlessness
of my weak being
and verses flower
red as kisses
crystaline flourishes,
fountains of life.

El arte mío
tiene sus raíces
en la undívaga inquietud
de mi débil ser
y florece versos

con el rojo de los besos,
pompas cristalinas,
fuentes de la vida.

The flowering of her poetic sexuality occurred sometime during or after her first trip to Mexico in 1930, when her world opened up, her stage became larger, and she saw the possibility for a more explicit honesty in her poetry. Mexico had long been associated in her mind with freedom and culture, and that first visit was momentous. It has been impossible to ascertain with any certainty exactly what she did or how long she stayed in Mexico, because everyone, including Clementina, has taken all the subsequent Mexico stories and mixed them up into a hopeless confusion of chronology. Clementina loved Mexico more than any other place she has lived, with the possible exception of El Salvador, so it is a temptation to imagine that her initial contact with Mexico was like an awakening that gave her the courage to return to Tegucigalpa, publish her first book of poetry and expand her public appearances from intimate recitals in cantinas and at parties to a glamorous production at the National Theatre. There are stories about her meeting Diego Rivera that tell of the master being inspired by her sincere and expressive face. It is said that he painted two portraits of her, that her face appears in one of his murals, that he taught her to love and appreciate the beauty of her body, and that she returned home inspired to share her newfound delight in pure and natural sensuality, knowing that Tegucigalpa was probably not ready for her message but determined to be a pioneer.

There are also stories about how she managed to afford that first trip to Mexico. To raise the money she got a job working as a waitress in the Jardín de Italia, one of the centrally located cafés frequented by many of the city's politicians, businessmen, and intellectuals, a newsworthy event in a community as class-conscious as Tegucigalpa in the thirties. She labored just like any of the other waitresses, serving food and drinks and working for tips. What distinguished her from the other waitresses was the fact that she was Clementina Suárez, already a friend of many of the café's patrons. Customers conversed and joked with her, invited her to sit down and have a drink with them. She wore a fancy apron that Toñita Fuentes, an excellent seamstress who had studied her craft in Paris before opening an elite dressmaking shop in Tegucigalpa, had made especially for her. Across the pocket she had embroidered "PROPINAS" (tips), and the charmed customers gladly contributed to Clementina's travel fund. Arturo Martínez Galindo was one of the most generous, gallantly inserting hundred-*lempira* notes into the pretty pocket.

This particular arrangement of the facts makes for good narrative progression, which is probably why it has evolved this way in the collective folklore of Tegucigalpa. But the following articles from *Tegucigalpa Magazine* offer contradictory details. One of the popular letters from Pedro to Juan, this one from 1934, comments that Clementina, "a restless woman of the avant garde possessing the most interesting qualities, one never knows what to expect from this very original temperment . . . was working in one of the city's cafés." This is such a singular and curious thing for her to do, even though she may be "a self-declared penniless aristocrat," that the author feels compelled to ponder her possible motives, concluding, "I do not know how to determine the amount of frivolity or tragedy in the poetess's attitude . . . only she can tell us the whole truth."[24] She portrays it now as one of numerous times in her life when she has had to work for a living, proving that she is one of the people. Whatever her motive, she surely needed the money, because she was receiving no financial help from her family, and, besides wanting to travel, she had two little girls to provide for. At any rate, it seems it was not 1930 when she collected tips at the Jardín de Italia, but 1934, probably in preparation for a trip somewhere, although not that first one to Mexico.

As for just what she did or whom she met in Mexico, another letter from Pedro to Juan discusses Clementina's first big recital in the National Theatre in 1931. The author praises her for having overcome the many obstacles that a place as small-minded as Tegucigalpa presents to the realization of "spiritual works." He calls her "that fine writer and sweet little woman, cruelly persecuted by the biting tongues of provincial hypocrisy and small-town ignorance unable to appreciate the purity of love when it sings freely in flight." Despite these difficulties, she has been able to "command respect for her person, her talent and her prestige as a strong woman despite her apparent fragility." He reminds his readers that she "had the wisdom to travel, if briefly, and receive first from foreign audiences the acclaim which she now establishes in her own country" (164). If Alejandro Castro, who amiably hid his identity behind Pedro's signature, was correct, and he probably was, as he was one of Clementina's good friends, her visit to Mexico was brief. As to whether she met Diego Rivera and he painted her portrait, it is not improbable, given Rivera's reputation for being a tireless womanizer who frequently found his way into women's hearts and beds by honoring them with a portrait. And in fact some of the female faces in his famous murals were his wives or women with whom he had friendships or love affairs.[25]

Clementina claims that two of the portraits in her collection were executed by Diego Rivera. What actually hang framed on her wall are black-and-white photocopies of two paintings that show neither date nor signature. She says the two Riveras were among the approximately forty paintings that "disappeared" from the Mexican embassy in Tegucigalpa in 1969. Some people claim they have seen those portraits; others insist they never existed. Rather than argue that one version or another is the true one, I prefer to ponder the moral of the story. I too was impressed when I first heard the stories about Diego Rivera; it somehow added legitimacy to my developing image of Clementina to think that an artist as famous as Rivera also found her interesting—which merely reveals our penchant to make judgments through the eyes of authority. The stories also reveal Clementina's awareness of that proclivity as she contributed to the contours of her own legend.

But for all her newfound worldliness and her exalted sense of her femininity, she still did not have the kind of love and comprehension she longed for, even from the gallant and handsome young men of the well-dressed literary set. In "Yo fui Leda" (I Was Leda), from *Temples of Fire,* she explains that she cannot be satisfied with any ordinary man (and it seems that even the extraordinary ones turn out to be ordinary): she has been spoiled by a love affair with a god.

> I have known the Olympian kiss of Zeus;
> have felt his roseate bill
> rising perfectly up my thighs,
> to my egg-white belly with its navel
> like a blind eye, to my lavish breasts,

lifting and white,
to my delicate neck, my mouth . . .
Zeus is so beautiful as a swan!

I have felt his wings enclosing me
and his soft and warm semen
seed in my burning flesh.
Later . . . the world was sweet,
and I was happy as never before,
with the sad smile of she who was unwell
and returns to life, knowing
I bore the seed of the father of the gods.

How beautiful to be the lover of an Olympian!

My womb conceived and two white eggs,
his flesh, my flesh, from my secret
were born, sweet and glorious
to burst open like roses
of pure white radiance.

I was the mother of children so sublime
they filled the world with their song.

How beautiful to bear the children of immortals!

My flesh is so nostalgic today,
perversely reduced to human;
how I long to feel the soft pink beak
sliding up my body
of whiteness of bark of the great forest.
How I long to feel his snowy wing
on my lifting breasts trembling
with sidereal delight, beside the oak.

I think only of Olympian snows!

And you mock my fall from grace,
you who want to hold me
in your long snake arms
and excite me with your very human mouth.

Respect for this widow, if you please,
go away and tell your poor soul
that its lover, a nymph in other days,
dreams of two wings embracing her.

After Zeus, to have a mere man is unworthy.

———

Yo sé del beso olímpico de Zeus;
su pico sonrosado lo he sentido
idealmente subiendo por mis muslos,
por mi vientre de alburas cuyo ombligo
parece un ojo ciego, por mis senos
en demasía túrgidos y blancos,
por mi cuello delgado, por mi boca . . .

Que bello es Zeus cuando se hace cisne!

He sentido sus alas envolviéndome
y sus suaves y tibias poluciones
germinar en mi entraña hecha de fuego.
Después . . . he visto al mundo tan amable,
sintiéndome dichosa como nunca
con la sonrisa triste de la enferma
que vuelve a ver la vida, por saberme
fecundada del padre de los Dioses.

Que bello es ser la hembra de un Olímpico!

Mi útero gestó y dos huevos blancos,
carne de él, carne mía, de mi arcano
salieron a la luz dulce y gloriosa
a reventar como si fueran rosas
de blancura impoluta y refulgente.

Fui madre de unos hijos tan excelsos
que llenaron al mundo como un canto.

Que bello es tener hijos de inmortales!

Grande es hoy la nostalgia de mi carne

porque maldita degeneró en humana;
como ansío sentir el suave pico
sonrosado subiendo por mi cuerpo
de alburas de cortezas del gran bosque.
Como ansío sentir su ala de nieve
sobre mis senos túrgidos temblando
por el goce sidéreo, junto al roble.

Sólo pienso en las nieves del Olímpico!

Y crees mi desgracia una ironía
para tí que deseas estrecharme
entre tus brazos largos como boas
y arderme con tu boca muy humana.

Respeta mi viudez, hazme el favor,
vete lejos y dile a tu pobre alma
que su amada una ninfa en otros tiempos
sueña con el abrazo de dos alas.

Después de Zeus es inicuo un hombre.

One might guess that she was referring to Antonio Rosa in this poem, especially because of the reference to two children who are roses. Or she may have been writing about no man in particular, but about her fantasy, the divine male to complement her divine female. Once, when asked who had been her best lover, she answered, "*The current one is always the best. If the previous one had been better, I'd still be with him.*" Perhaps what she should have said was that the lover she had not yet had would be the best.

The first man she legally married was Guillermo Bustillo Reina. This time she chose a man who was literary as well as handsome. He wrote poetry, taught English, and worked in journalism.[26] But their marriage lasted only a matter of months and was punctuated by outbursts of jealousy so violent that she feared for her safety. In her poetry recitals she exhibited not only her artistic talent but also her sexuality, a transgression of traditional marital expectations that did not go unnoticed by her new husband, whose normally volatile character was often pushed beyond his limits of control. One story which Clementina herself corroborates is that when she was to give a joint recital at the National Theatre with Guatemalan poet Humberto Hernández Cobos, Guillermo's possessiveness got the better of him, and he asked her not to perform. When she refused, he arrived at the theatre brandishing a pistol, threatening to shoot her as well as her Guatemalan costar. The police stationed themselves at the entrance to the theatre, and the show went on.

But Clementina quickly realized that, just as it had not been enough that Antonio was handsome and rich, neither was it enough that Guillermo was handsome and literary. He proved himself to be controlled by the same passions and prejudices as most of the men she knew. He may have loved her in private, but he could not accept the public Clementina. He wanted their lives to center around him, which meant that she would have to give up her poetry. Not that he asked her to stop writing, but he did not want her to promote herself, to give recitals, to be a café poet, hanging out drinking and talking with the other (male) writers. For her part, Clementina seems to have been unwilling to compromise if it meant modifying her behavior or giving up the life-style she had come to see as her own. She was used to being generous with her affection, staying up late, and not spending a lot of time at home, and she wasn't about to change just because she had gotten married. Friends and relatives remember Guillermo frequently packing a pistol as he went out looking for his wife who was supposed to have been home hours before. Clementina tells of being in the hotel room of an Argentine actor who was visiting Tegucigalpa. She says she was interviewing him for the newspaper when Guillermo broke down the door and started shooting. A bullet lodged in the wall above her head. She knew then that she had to leave him or risk being in his line of fire the next time.

Guillermo Bustillo Reina never remarried, although he does have a son. Some people recall him as emotionally unstable, prone to violence and melancholy, while many who were his students describe him as an intelligent and dedicated teacher who easily won their respect and affection. A few years before he died in 1964, some friends went to visit him on Christmas eve. He was alone, sitting in his wheelchair, with a bottle of whiskey and a photograph of Clementina in front of him. "You know," he told them, "the one thing I regret in my life is having lost Clementina." Her friends of course told her what he said, and she often muses on his words and on the numerous lovers who have passed through her life. She has loved much, but she has never been able successfully and happily to live with a man for very long. She of course blames it on the men.

THE BOHEMIANS

The third group of literary men with whom Clementina associated in Tegucigalpa in the thirties, those who came to be known as the Generation of '35, was comprised of those who were neither proven and respected nor debonair and upwardly mobile. This was a result in part of their age (most of them were five or ten years younger than Clementina) and in part of their class (most of them either were not from the ruling classes or disregarded or rejected class as a determinant of their self-concept). In the thirties they were youthful, idealistic, and talented. And while separately concerned with individual expression and the passions of their souls, collectively they have left an impression of having been a group with a distinct personality. Claudio Barrera, one of the most productive of these writers, became the speaker for and anthologizer of the group. He describes them as "young men alienated from their surroundings by their waste of time and energy; they lacked patrons and readers; in spite of this, they were full of enthusiasm and of unshakeable faith in their own poetic sensibility."[27]

These young men saw themselves as *bohemios,* a term that has meant different things in different cultural contexts. In Tegucigalpa in the late twenties and early thirties, according to an elderly resident of Tegucigalpa, bohemio was defined as "he who does not desire wealth or comfort, who lives from the affection of those around him, who wants to be accepted for what he is. He is not attached to anything material, longing only for the satisfaction of writing verses." These bohemios saw themselves as different from the rest of their society, driven by nobler ideals. They were young rebels without a cause whose greatest need and desire was to create, but who often dissipated their energies in the cantinas of the poorer sections of town. Marcos Carías Reyes calls this group of artists a "brotherhood." In an article entitled "Bohemio" in the 13 June 1928 issue of *Tegucigalpa Magazine,* he describes them as young students, artists, writers, and composers. They are all "imaginative, visionaries, dreamers, disdained and disdaining. They all have a flicker of genius. They all love illusion, utopia, glory" (11). They are all poor, their genius as yet unrecognized. They are followers of Rodó, the Uruguayan essayist who inflamed the youth of Spanish America with his call to idealism and his warnings against the barbarity of materialism. Carías Reyes continues, "We are all bohemians who live in a perennial state of heightened sensitivity, who long to reach a zenith, who struggle to give life to that 'something' that keeps us awake at night, who exist in a fever of beauty, of blue, of truth. . . . The youth who stays awake wanting to express in verse his first dreams. The student who heroically attempts to possess the mysterious secret of the codices. The painter who imbibes twilight's deliquescence. The musician who captures fleeting emotion on the staff. The beautiful friend who one day set off for the tentacular metropolis, chasing fame" (12).

Marcos Carías Reyes may have been thinking of Clementina in his reference to the "beautiful friend," for they were very close, some say lovers. When he killed himself in 1949, just a few doors away from where Clementina was staying in Barrio La Ronda, she heard the shot and ran to find him—too late to help the sensitive man who once had counted himself among the idealistic youth, but whose position as personal secretary to his uncle, General Tiburcio Carías Andino, the dictator who ruled Honduras from 1933 to 1948, caused him to be the target of cruel and perhaps unfair criticism. Many remember that he used his authority and access to the ruler to promote the arts and was often able to intercede on behalf of indiscreet or incautious intellectuals, but others felt he had sold out by accepting a position in the government and could not forgive him. Some say this ostracism was the cause of his suicide.

His article "Bohemia" takes us through a night in the company of this group of young men at the "wretched tavern" of Niña Pancha. They listen to "Mi cielo azul" (My Blue Sky) on Niña Pancha's gramophone as they drink round after round and philosophize on the nature of their specialness. They criticize each other's work, discuss cubism, recite poetry. A frequent topic of conversation, as well as of their writing, is women. They pour out verses to the chimera of femininity. "The bohemian heart bled in exalted sensitivity. Strange apparitions floated in the clouds of smoke and in the evocation there appeared, shining with promises, the sweet semblance of the absent sweetheart." This talking about women is an important cement in male bonding, and it necessarily must take place in the absence of the discussed. In fact, it is precisely the female absence that makes the poetry more poignant and the solidarity more masculine. This brings up the question of Clementina's role in this coterie, because she was not only a literary comrade but a physical presence at many of these gatherings in cafés and taverns and in her own apartment. Was she one of the brotherhood, one of the guys? Was she their quintessential Woman, their chimera in the flesh? Were they able to ignore her gender? Did she even want them to?

As dawn approaches the bohemios mourn the death of their magazine, a beloved enterprise that offered them their only chance for publication. Yet it could hardly have been successful, for to devote one's time to the practicalities of publication was demeaning, to say nothing of unfamiliar. To expect to earn one's living by one's art was unbefitting for sensitive souls committed to Beauty and Truth. Book publishing for profit as we know it today did not exist; one would normally finance the publication of one's own work. The more fortunate might have a protector who helped out financially; in some instances, if one knew the right people, government funds might be available. One then gave the book away to friends, relatives, and other writers, inscribed with the author's sentiments, signed, and dated. Many considered it either inappropriate or amusing that Clementina offered her books for sale. She sold them at her recitals, and she peddled them to bookstores, always carrying a supply when she went out on the road. She even gave a recital and sold books in Juticalpa. People attended more out of curiosity than admiration; her relatives were embarrassed, and the gossips had something to discuss for weeks. No one from her hometown took her seriously as a poet or thought she would "make it." (Not until she received the national award for literature in 1970 did teachers from Juticalpa even think to mention her in their literature classes. And not until 1987 did the city publicly honor her literary achievements.)

Besides Niña Pancha's tavern, another favorite bohemian hangout was Mamá Yaca's *estanco,* the term used to describe the watering holes in the poor sections of town that sold the local moonshine, known as *guaro.* Mamá Yaca was the name the bohemian poets bestowed on Siriyaca Ruiz because of the maternal affection she showered on them, giving them food and drink on credit, getting them out of jail, listening appreciatively to their new poetic compositions. Siriyaca, an activist in the Liberal Party known for her boundless energy and generosity, was fifty-one years old when she decided to leave Olancho and take up residence in Tegucigalpa. For many years she administered the Liberal Party soup kitchens in Juticalpa, seeing to it that the voters who arrived in the provincial capital during elections were properly fed. She supervised the preparation of hundreds of tortillas and entire beef cows while watching over the cooking of enormous quantities of black beans, the staple of Honduran nutrition, and the roasting of pigs. Besides her political work, Siriyaca earned a living working in the kitchens of some of the wealthiest families of Juticalpa society. She was known for her outstanding culinary skills, so her services were sought when the Becerras or the Cernas or the Zelayas entertained their neighbors or fancied her *nacatamales* or her *sopa de mondongo* (tripe soup) on Saturdays. It was customary for the ladies of the aristocracy to keep to their beds for an extended period of time after childbirth, resting and eating only a special Olancho cheese that Siriyaca made superbly, so she always had plenty of work.

Siriyaca was originally from Jutiquile and worked in the Zelaya household, and when doña Amelia married Luis Suárez, she continued to work for her. As was the custom in Olancho, entire families formed alliances in the exchange of human services. A few of Siriyaca's nine children died during infancy, but the survivors all knew the Zelaya family and often worked in the Zelaya house or on the hacienda. Siriyaca was eighteen when doña Amelia's first daughter was born, and, besides cooking for the family, she also became Clementina's nanny. One of her sons, Servando, became quite attached to the young Clementina, and often his only duty was to watch over her as she played.

Perhaps it was this relationship of service, in which human beings share their lives, but with a clear understanding of class differences, that produced a lifelong friendship between Clementina and Siriyaca and her family, a friendship based on serving and being served, but not a servile relationship. Siriyaca understood Clementina's class superiority. But she had lived in her house, knew her mother's idiosyncracies, had observed her father's drunkenness, had changed Clementina's diapers—in short, knew her on a level of intimacy where pretensions become transparent. So service was often rendered with affection, and class differences tempered by the demystification that cohabitation fostered. When Clementina was eighty-six years old, Servando came to visit her in Tegucigalpa after having lost touch with her for many years, surprising her when he walked into her room reciting one of her first poems. Siriyaca's daughter Olivia lives just a few blocks from Clementina in Barrio La Hoya. She wasn't in the habit of visiting her much, but when she heard that Clementina was ill in 1987, she began to stop in regularly to check on her.

Siriyaca moved to Tegucigalpa when General Tiburcio Carías Andino came to power in January 1933. His foremost goal was pacification, a euphemism for saying that he was tired of the efforts of the Liberal Party to wrest power from him. With the conviction that the only good Liberal was a dead one, a silent one, or an absent one, the soldiers of his National Party entered cities and towns routing out the opposition. His political style came cynically to be referred to as "entierro—encierro—destierro" (burial—jail—exile), so Siriyaca, being a highly visible member of the Liberal Party, thought it prudent to retire to the big city, where her reputation was less well-known. But it was not her personality to be inactive, and her home in Tegucigalpa soon became a refuge for people from Olancho who came to the capital in search of work or education. When she arrived, one of the first people she looked for was Clementina. When Luis Suárez was alive, Siriyaca knew she could always go to him if she needed help, and she may have thought that this relationship would continue with Clementina. In fact, it was Clementina's good fortune to be loved by this extraordinary woman, who was always there to help when she needed it.

She was illiterate, strong willed, and extremely generous. Everyone knew and loved her, from the drunks who came to her estanco to the officials who worked in the presidential palace. She was the kind of woman who would stride into the office of the minister of education and say, "Look, there's this young man who wants very much to study and become a doctor, but he has no money. What a waste of talent it would be if the government didn't help him out. So what do you say?" When a poor laborer would arrive from Olancho looking for work, with only the shirt on his back, she would literally make him give her the clothes he was wearing so she could wash and iron them so he could look presentable as he went job hunting. Sometimes there were so many people sleeping at her house that her own children complained, but she would abide no mean spiritedness and continued to help anyone she could.

Her estanco served typical working-class food and cheap liquor. The bohemian poets frequented her establishment because she loved young people, she loved poetry, and she gave them lots of credit. They were all poor in those days, so poor that they would often not have the five cents to buy a cigarette, but Mamá Yaca never turned them away. Sometimes they would recite their poetry to her in payment. She was indeed a mother to them all, especially to Clementina, who was of course her favorite because she had cared for her since she was a baby.

A Unique Life-Style

Clementina was the only woman at those gatherings at Mamá Yaca's. These friends were like her family, now that she had so little contact with her own, and she spent a lot of time with them. Besides the bohemian poets, a number of other interesting men found Mamá Yaca's working-class establishment more to their liking than the more elite cafés in the center of town: the painter Max Euceda; Pablo Zelaya Sierra, considered Honduras's best and most cosmopolitan artist of his time; Abel Cuenca, political exile from El Salvador; Enrique de la Flor, a Peruvian who had ended up in Honduras via El Salvador; Medardo Mejía, lawyer, journalist, and Marxist.

She of course was criticized by her neighbors, who saw the way she took care of Alba and Silvia. She did not prepare meals at regular hours, and often the girls would be out playing in the street when other children were napping or being bathed. Doña Leonor, a widow who lived across the street from Clementina in Barrio La Ronda, did not approve of Clementina's life-style. She thought a mother should stay at home, which Clementina rarely did. And she thought it wasn't good for the girls that Clementina had so many male visitors. So it began that when Leonor noticed Alba and Silvia out playing, looking unkempt, she would take them to her house and bathe and feed them. They gradually spent more and more time with Leonor.

Clementina recognized a good thing when she saw it, so the next time she wanted to take a trip, she asked Leonor if she would look after the girls. Leonor had several children of her own, but the two who were closest in age to Alba and Silvia were Francisco and Carlota. Alba and Silvia were soon living in Leonor's home, and the four children grew up thinking of themselves as one family. Alba and Silvia still think of Leonor as their second mother, with as much affection as they feel for Clementina. When they were young they were hurt by their mother's absences, and they resented not having a more normal, nurturing mother. On the other hand, they felt special because their mother was a poet. They may not have understood what that meant, but they adored her glamour whenever she came home. Sometimes when Clementina gave recitals at the National Theatre she dressed Alba, Silvia, and Carlota as pages, and they felt important and glamourous themselves handing out programs.

When Clementina was in town she stayed at Leonor's, except when she had enough money to set up an apartment of her own. Her living quarters, unusual for Tegucigalpa, sound now like hippie apartments from the sixties. She furnished them imaginatively with her limited funds, covering packing crates with colorful fabrics and making her own pillows and curtains. She covered the floors with woven straw mats from the market and decorated the walls with the art that she loved to collect and with whatever she found appealing, such as gourds and baskets. She loved dolls and had many of them: a tall black one named Farina, a Chinese doll she called Li-Tai-Po, and lots of rag dolls with long, dangly legs.

She was rather cavalier regarding her maternal responsibilities, preferring the occasional grandiose gesture to the monotony of daily maintenance. Once her daughters were ensconced in Leonor's house she traveled more freely, sending money when she could, but there were times when she couldn't or didn't. She would bring them all presents when she came home, and if she couldn't get home for a holiday she always sent a box of gifts. And just as Leonor treated Alba and Silvia no differently from her own children, so Clementina, to the extent that she provided for her children, always included Leonor's children in her attentions.

Antonio Rosa, for his part, never denied that Alba and Silvia were his daughters and dutifully gave each girl five lempiras every Saturday when they visited him at his store in the center of town. Sometimes Clementina's friends would contribute financially also. Tegucigalpa was (and is) a poor city; even its wealthiest were not the super rich such as one finds in El Salvador or Guatemala. But there was a tradition of sharing, especially among the less well off, so, though it may have been difficult for Alba and Silvia to grow up in such a nontraditional way, they were always cushioned by the warmth and support of friends.

It may be that time heals old wounds, and that as we age we learn to appreciate our families in ways we couldn't when we were young. This is true for Clementina as well as for her daughters. One senses a truce among them now, although resentments and antagonisms continue to simmer below the surface. It must have been difficult for Clementina to deal with her maternal responsibilities, and equally difficult to have had her for a mother.

For Clementina the years 1930–36 were a time of relatively carefree and self-centered existence. The publication in rapid succession of her first four books legitimized her life-style, at least in her own eyes. She expanded her range of familiar territory with visits to Panama, Costa Rica, Nicaragua, Guatemala, El Salvador, and Mexico that were often lengthy stays during which she gave poetry recitals, visited with friends, appeared at public gatherings and ceremonies, had love affairs, fostered friendships with artists and writers, and generally thrived on being an anomaly. Working as her own agent, she cultivated relationships with everyone from ambassadors and high officials in the military and government to bankers, businessmen, and prominent intellectuals. She sent letters to the Tegucigalpa papers detailing her more significant activities, and her poems and lyrical prose pieces appeared in newspapers and literary journals throughout the region. She even published a magazine she called *Mujer* (Woman). Her presence was sought at highbrow cultural events sponsored by embassies and official culture institutes. Local papers often carried photographs of her in one of her flowing tunics or captured in various sultry or sophisticated poses. Sometimes a studio portrait accompanied the publication of a poem. Although she is often smiling in informal pictures taken by friends, in her formal photographic portraits from the thirties her characteristic expression is brooding, at times seductive, at times melodramatic.

Her magazine *Woman* remains a mystery to me, as I was unable to locate any extant copies of it. She founded it in late 1933 or early 1934 in Tegucigalpa. She remembers having published six issues, and that it cost three lempiras per issue. She appears on the front cover of the 4 March 1934 issue of *Tegucigalpa Magazine* wearing a feminine version of a bellhop's uniform, offering her magazine for sale. Although it is a posed studio photograph, she did indeed take to the streets to publicize and sell *Woman,* not only in the capital but in the cities on the North Coast as well. The magazine was literary, although she included diverse articles of general cultural interest, some written by herself, others by the various local writers who were by now her good friends. Its name leads one to believe that the articles may have had a feminist orientation, but she insists that this was not the case, that she called it "Woman" because she was a woman and she was doing all the work, and she simply wanted to advertise the fact that a woman could publish a magazine.[28]

Her next volume of poetry, *Engranajes* (Gears), appeared in San José, Costa Rica, in 1935.[29] This was a unique book for her. While her first four books were all miniature handfuls, measuring between twelve and fifteen centimeters in width and featuring almost unreadably small print, *Gears* measured twenty-five centimeters and was printed on rough brown paper, with fifty-three poems of varying length, but none more than a page. Some have long, run-on verses; others are elliptical, haiku-like creations of four lines. The love poems are no longer tragic, desperate, and melancholic, but exude a sense of voluptuous plenitude. Besides these poems of a sexuality in bloom there are poetic statements on womanhood, such as "Resúmen" (Summary Statement), which can be read as a declaration of female independence, a challenge to society, and a rejection of traditional values.

> So pretty . . . I would like her as my betrothed!
> So good . . . I would like her as my wife!
> So interesting . . . So pretty and so good . . .
> I would like her as my lover!

> Qué bonita . . . ¡Para que fuera mi novia!
> Qué buena . . . ¡Para que fuera mi esposa!
> Qué interesante . . . ¡Qué bonita y qué buena . . .
> Para que fuera mi amante!

"Mujer" (Woman), on the other hand, is a clear-eyed statement of acceptance of her womanhood in a male-identified society:

> A girl! said the doctor at my birth.
> A girl! said my mother when she kissed me.
> And he, too, called me Woman.

I hardly knew the first,
the second I left behind,
the third I followed . . .
Bad choice, they told me later! . . .
But it was the one determined
by my name, Woman.

———

Mujer! dijo la obstétrica que me vio nacer.
Mujer! mi madre al besarme.
Y ¡Mujer! él, para llamarme.
A la primera, apenas la conocí,
a la segunda, la abandoné,
sólo al tercero seguí . . .
Mal camino, me dijeron después! . . .
Pero fue el que me señaló,
mi nombre de Mujer.

Gender consciousness is a central component in Clementina's sense of her own identity. But it has never been an anguished or introspective questioning as to the true nature of femininity. Just as she has always taken it for granted that she had the right to live in accordance with her own standards, she seems to have accepted her particular femininity. Rather than analysis that might have led to self-doubt or to efforts to modify her behavior, she stands firmly grounded in her gender, surrounded by herself, as it were, taking it for granted that she is female. A paradox flowers from this enviable sense of self. Her deep centeredness and self-assurance confront her need to interact with her social environment, and from the ensuing struggle poems are created. Poems as brave as "Understand Me" and "Explanations," and others as frightened as "Yo" (I), a terse, simple, eight-line poem from *Temples of Fire* in which the poet is herself an indecipherable poem, a being without a home:

Song of sadness,
emblem no one could decipher,
dark dream,
sad thoughts,

in a stormy sea I live my life
directionless,
with wings outspread
always toward the setting sun.

———

Canción de pena,
lema que nadie descifrar pudiera,
ensueño obscuro,
mente entristecida,
en un proceloso mar vivo la vida
bogando sin oriente,
con las alas abiertas
siempre para el poniente.

This is the dark, painful side of the "New Woman." Her movement follows the sun, she marches forward, but she is ultimately without direction unless she can draw guidance from within herself, because she has stepped outside of the rules—the loneliness of the pioneer.

With the publication of *Gears,* Clementina seems to have reached a plateau. As the title suggests, all the gears are working, and they mesh just fine. Her lyric voice comes across as centered and in control, in love with love and with life. She has lived in Mexico and all the capitals of Central America. Her daughters are being looked after. She is applauded and admired and has lots of friends. For many people this state would be an invitation to continue the pattern that had produced such success. But Clementina found this a good time to move on again. She went to the North Coast, where an old friend in the military secured her free passage on a ship sailing for New York. It was 1936, and Clementina was off to conquer new worlds.

CHAPTER THREE

"Ever Widening Horizons"

New York

Until Clementina boarded that United Fruit Company ship in Puerto Cortés bound for New York, every new city she had ever visited had welcomed her. But all the cities where Clementina found friends and admirers were Central American, except for Mexico City, yet even in Mexico it was mostly members of the Central American expatriot community who formed her circle of friends. The proportions varied and the names were different, but the common interpersonal dynamics—how groups form, the ways people meet each other, the assumptions individuals make about one another and about strangers, and, perhaps of greatest importance, the common language—were recognizable and expected.

New York presented problems new to her because of the language, the climate, the city's size, and cultural differences. She resisted learning English, she hated the cold, and she associated mainly with other Spanish speakers. Her experience was not unlike that of many Hispanic artists and intellectuals, among them Federico García Lorca, the young poet and playwright from Spain who was both fascinated and repelled (mostly repelled) by the materialism, the extremes of wealth and poverty, the racism, and what he perceived and experienced as the isolation and alienation of the individual.[1] He spent almost a year (1929–30) living in a student dormitory at Columbia University, writing poems about solitude, Harlem, and the inhumanity of the northern metropolis. The last two sections of his volume of poetry that records with surrealistic imagery and intensity this period of existential anguish, *Poeta en Nueva York* (The Poet in New York) are entitled "Huida de Nueva York, Dos valses hacia la civilización" (Flight from New York, Two Waltzes toward Civilization), followed by "El poeta llega a La Habana" (The Poet Arrives in Havana). Upon leaving New York, the poet, in life as in his poem, went to Cuba, where he basked in the tropical heat and dispelled his loneliness with Spanish conversation.

Like García Lorca, who registered in a class of English for foreigners but withdrew after the first week, "convinced of his incapacity for learning a foreign language," Clementina made little or no effort to learn English. Consequently, she had difficulty breaking into the established literary circles of New York. She made some contacts with the Hispanic intellectual community, whose patriarch at the time was Federico de Onís, chair of the Department of Spanish and Portuguese at Columbia University and founder of the Casa Hispánica there, a favorite gathering place for Hispanists from the United States as well as students, professors, and writers from Spanish-speaking countries. She recalls participating in a poetry reading with Cuban poet Eugenio Florit on Forty-second Street and working for the Spanish-language magazine *Democracia.* She earned some money by caring for the handicapped daughter of a wealthy Central American living in New York. She also worked in a factory for a while, and she sold stockings.[2]

But no one in New York would notice that Clementina Suárez, Luis Suárez's daughter, protégée of Alfonso Guillén Zelaya, darling of Tegucigalpa's literary circles, was working as a day laborer; no one would think to write newspaper articles describing her charming egalitarianism.[3] With no well-known connections to bring her into the limelight, she floundered on the sidelines. An additional obstacle to her success at penetrating this foreign culture was the fact that Honduras was not fashionable in the United States. When Clementina arrived in New York, the Hispanics who were the center of sympathy and curiosity were Mexicans and Spanish. The Mexican mural movement, led by Diego Rivera, José Clemente Orozco, and David Alfaro Siqueiros, all three colorful and controversial personalities, had made a tremendous impact on the international art scene. It was a very strong movement, "frankly political, frankly leftist, but like a breath of fresh air in opening up the parameters of art to a new and sweeping art form that made easel painting look precious and overrefined." All three of these artists had been invited to the United States to paint murals, and numerous U.S. artists such as Jackson Pollock, Ben Shahn, and Louise Nevelson admired them and studied with them, while other Mexican artists were being fussed over and promoted by wealthy or influential New Yorkers. Mexican art was trendy and supported by dealers and art critics such as Francis Flynn Payne and Alma Reed; even the Rockefellers joined in when they commissioned Diego Rivera to execute a mural at Rockefeller Center. Even more numerous were the writers, artists, anthropologists, and the merely curious who flocked to Mexico during the twenties and thirties, attracted by the Mexican Revolution and the ensuing social reforms and cultural renaissance.[4]

Spain at this time also captured the imagination and sympathies of many Americans. The upheaval occasioned by the end of the dictatorship of José Antonio Primo de Rivera, the birth of the Spanish Republic and the subsequent civil war were followed with great interest by leftist groups in the United States. They saw the Republic as a great hope for mankind. The heroes and martyrs of the Republic became their heroes, and they raised funds, wrote speeches, and volunteered to fight fascism with the Republican forces in Spain.

But Clementina was a poet, not a mural painter or a freedom fighter, and she was from Honduras, a country that has yet to inflame the North American imagination. She brought with her no aura of ancient civilizations, revolutionary leftist politics, or colorful folk culture. Until the 1970s, when Nicaragua's Sandinista revolution managed to excite the political consciousness and romantic idealism of the West, being Central American has not been an entrée into the hearts of intellectuals, North or South American.

Cuba and Revolutionary Inspiration

Clementina had soon had enough of New York. She heard that the place to be was Cuba, so, like García Lorca before her, she set sail for the Caribbean. "*I saw that I was wasting my time in New York. It's very difficult to connect with what's happening in the United States. They're very isolated there; people don't participate, and I wasn't about to go searching out those isolated groups. I could have studied the language, it wasn't that, it was the people themselves I couldn't get used to. Nothing interests them: they eat, sleep, work; eat, sleep, work. It's only a minority, an elite, that takes part in world affairs. So I moved on to Cuba, because I was attracted by the Cuban intellectuals, brilliant men, well-known throughout Latin America.*"

Clementina's stay in Cuba was not long, but it was important to her. Surrounded by the images and activities of a decadent Havana, she could easily have been seduced by this world of night clubs and casinos, of teas at the Havana Yacht Club, of Fords and Hollywood stars such as Claudette Colbert, Joan Crawford, and the Lewis Sisters. But while Hemingway was catching big fish and drinking daiquiris in La Floridita Bar accompanied by Greta Garbo, another, more autochthonous Havana was also flourishing. Eusebia Cosme, for example, known for her dramatic renditions of the newly popular poesía negra, entertained audiences with such poems as "Lavandera con negrito" (Washer woman with little black boy), by Emilio Ballagas, and "Sensemayá," by Nicolás Guillén. And Clemencia Martínez Alonso was directing a play entitled *Emancipada* (Liberated), described in a Havana magazine, *Carteles,* on 22 July 1934 as "a revolutionary work written by women and for men."

When Clementina arrived in Cuba she experienced both exhilaration and relief. A Mexican friend had given her a letter of introduction to Juan Marinello, the Cuban poet and revolutionary leader, so she was soon connected with intellectual and political circles in Havana. Her life resumed the style she had developed as a cultural vagabond in Mexico and Central America. When asked how she managed to support herself, she answered, "*I've always been able to get by, I've always had a very simple life-style, one always finds a way. I lived with a Salvadoran family, and then, with odd jobs here and there, with a magazine or whatever, I earned enough to make ends meet.*"

The poetry she wrote during her stay in Cuba is strikingly different thematically from her previous work. In 1937 she published in Havana a collection of thirty poems that she called *Veleros* (Sails). These poems are like her previous ones in that they are fundamentally autobiographical in the sense of being self-defining, for they are the poet's conversations with herself as she struggles to incorporate a new vision into a redetermination of her poetic voice. But what distinguishes *Sails* from *Bleeding Heart* or from *Gears* is that we see the social and political realities of her world making themselves felt in her expression. One can read *Bleeding Heart* and glean not the faintest idea of the Honduran environment that surrounded the romantic and suffering female lyric voice, which is not disembodied, for it is firmly grounded in her sensuality, but which claims no identification with any social or political reality. Who would ever guess that in the years when Clementina was mourning the loss of her butterfly youth or weeping over love unrequited, thousands of peasants were being massacred in El Salvador, U.S. Marines were invading Nicaragua, and Honduras, El Salvador, Guatemala, and Nicaragua were suffering under repressive dictatorships.

It is difficult to imagine that Clementina was unaware of her political environment. Her travels, her well-informed acquaintances, and her talent for perceiving what was important or timely or fashionable were factors that would certainly have led her to react to the events of enormous magnitude that were happening all around her. It is especially perplexing to picture her as unconcerned if one has had the opportunity to know her in her old age. She regularly reads at least two of Tegucigalpa's four daily papers, she receives publications from Cuba and Nicaragua, she is informed and opinionated as to the comings and goings of local politicians, she attends peace conferences throughout Central America, and she speaks out on every possible occasion against U.S. imperialism. But just as she grew up in Juticalpa without being deeply affected by the political events of her youth, and as she lived out her twenties absorbed in her own growth and development and expression, so too she seems to have drifted through the first half of her thirties concerned mostly with her sexuality, her notoriety, and her personal struggle for recognition as a poet.

But something changed in her in New York. Unlike García Lorca, who drew on his horror and isolation in the cold and hostile world of New York City to create some of his most interesting and troubling poetry, Clementina's difficulties produced no poetry in her. Rather, she simply moved on, looking toward a different and more hospitable space where she could continue to search for herself in the response of others to her. She was shaken to the core of her self-perception in New York, experiencing herself as small and insignificant in this intimidating city. The consequent self-doubt and need to recapture her old sense of self-importance was the fertile inner soil that, when mixed with the political reality she encountered in Cuba, produced the conditions that resulted in her ability to perceive the larger drama around her and to incorporate it into herself and into her poetry.

Since the early years of the twentieth century, Cuban politics have been precocious in defining and working toward social reform. In the early 1920s virtually all sectors of society were united in opposition to the corrupt Zayas regime and in favor of fundamental reforms. Trade and labor unions, women's groups, students, and intellectuals joined with commerce, industry, finance, and the professions to demand change. Writers and artists assumed a vocal and committed role. "At the Café Martí near Central Park in Havana, writers and artists under the leadership of Rubén Martínez Villena engaged in passionate discussions on the essential form and function of national literature. The debate on form would persist unresolved for another decade, but on the matter of function, the consensus was striking and immediate. More than advocates of cultural revival, writers assumed for themselves the role of agents of national rejuvenation."[5]

Cuban women were more active than their counterparts in Central America. "By 1919, more than one-quarter of the ranks of the professions were filled by women" (238) and numerous feminist organizations had formed to agitate for the right to vote, for equality of educational opportunity and improved employment prospects and conditions.

As early as 1920 the Radical Socialist Party called for the socialization of property and the construction of public housing. In 1925 the Cuban Communist Party applied for membership in the Comintern and rapidly gained members and notoriety. So by the time Clementina arrived in Cuba in 1937, Cuban workers, students, and intellectuals had a history of political organizing and activism. The Veterans and Patriots movement in 1923 to oust Zayas; the sustained opposition during the Machado regime carried out by a vast clandestine network that culminated in Machado's overthrow in 1933; the revolution of September 1933 that replaced Céspedes, the provisional head of state, with a revolutionary junta—all these plus an implacable resistance to U.S. intervention were the accomplishments of a society that took politics seriously.

Clementina recalls the political climate of Cuba: "*I saw that there was a revolutionary fervor there. Everyone who was anyone—in journalism, in art, in everything—was a revolutionary. Juan Marinello, Alejo Carpentier, Nicolás Guillén, Serafina Núñez. And women, lots of women. But most importantly, the majority of the workers already had a different consciousness—mechanics, anyone you would talk to. Everybody was talking about a change, they were prepared.*

There were no demonstrations; it was an underground movement, but very strong."

The clandestine nature of the activities of the Cuban Left in 1937 was the result of U.S. support for Batista and the colonel's subsequent elimination of all visible opposition. Of the members of the resistance who survived Batista's repression, many left Cuba, some to participate in the struggle in Spain. Their frustration with the situation at home led them to support the Republic with an extra measure of militancy and conviction. There is no question that Republican Spain was a powerful symbol on an international level. As one critic has noted, "While the 1930s was a decade of political and artistic confusion, there was one event, at least, that helped to bring things into perspective: the war in Spain. It was precisely the kind of black and white situation everyone was looking for."[6] There was initially no doubt in the minds of most supporters that it was a contest between good and evil and that good would triumph.

The ideological support and active participation of intellectuals in struggles for social justice have given rise to what is perhaps the most polemical and emotional debate in Latin American literature of this century: the question of the writer's responsibility to popular movements. In the early 1930s, when poets such as César Vallejo and Pablo Neruda joined the Communist Party, the debate over the nature of revolutionary art and the role of the poet was intense. The poetry of the numerous writers who were concerned with their contribution to a changing society is striking in its variety: their themes range from the bald listing of inequalities and injustices to reflections on the role of the poet and his or her relation to society and social transformation. In their efforts to reconcile the form of their poetry to its message, some opted for clarity and simplicity, while others experimented with rupturing sound and sense as if they were the very tools of the ruling class.[7]

In Central America, the 1930s was a time of right-wing dictatorships and their attendant censorship, so writers were drawn, sometimes unwillingly, into this debate, knowing that the side one chose might well have more than theoretical consequences. In 1935, for example, the year Clementina published *Gears* in Costa Rica, Carmen Lyra, one of Costa Rica's most distinguished writers, lost her teaching job because of an article she wrote entitled "¿Qué caminos tomarán los escritores latinoamericanos ante la situación actual del mundo?" (What Paths Will Latin American Writers

Take in the Present World Situation?). In answer to her own question, she advocated a revolutionary literature for Latin America and urged all writers to take a political stand.

The primary concerns of revolutionary writers of the isthmus were imperialism and nationalism. These concerns found expression in poems that celebrated regional color, traditional values, and indigenous heroes and cultures, or in poems that attempted to confer heroic status on anti-imperialist leaders such as Augusto César Sandino of Nicaragua or Farabundo Martí of El Salvador.

The *Reportorio Americano* (American Repertory), probably the most prestigious and certainly the most long-lived Central American periodical devoted to literature and ideas, is an excellent measure of the tastes and concerns of educated Central Americans from 1919 to 1959, the years of its publication under the direction of Joaquín García Monge in Costa Rica. A survey of the journal from the 1930s shows the contributions of such distinguished and various figures as Alfonso Reyes, Stephen Spender, Waldo Frank, Pío Baroja, Unamuno, Juan Marinello, Salarrué, and José Santos Chocano. Female voices were few but impressive, including Gabriela Mistral, Claudia Lars, Magda Portal, and the Chilean educator Amanda Labarca.

As the war in Spain continued, the *American Repertory* carried, besides the expected essays and poems by openly declared leftists such as Pablo Neruda and León Felipe, an increasing number of articles that addressed the issue of the responsibility of non-Spanish citizens in this war. In 1937 there appeared an open letter from Chilean writers in which Vicente Huidobro, Luis Alberto Sánchez, Marta Brunet, and 95 others publicly lent their support to the Spanish people. Shortly thereafter the *Repertory* published a similar letter signed by 116 Mexican intellectuals, including Enrique González Martínez, Miguel Covarrubias, Agustín Yáñez, and Juan O'Gorman. In the following issue, 68 members of the Union of Writers and Artists of Ecuador publicized their solidarity with the Spanish people. Solidarity was in the air. How could Clementina not have been swept up in the glorious cause?

Back in Tegucigalpa, even those same young men who gathered in Mamá Yaca's estanco to drink the night away and talk about true love and poetry found themselves affected by social concerns. In an interview with

Nicolás Guillén, Honduran poet Luis Alemán (a pseudonym of Claudio Barrera) confessed to the Cuban poet, "It was a book of yours—*Cantos para soldados y sones para turistas* [Songs for Soldiers and Rhythms for Tourists] that had such a powerful influence in my country, Honduras, that an entire generation of poets—the Generation of '37—turned their attention toward social concerns as the central motif of their poetry."[8]

Turning their attention to social concerns meant different things to different poets. Many of the poets of Honduras tried their hand at the poesía negra that Guillén and others had popularized, certainly an appropriate experiment for Honduras, which has a sizable black population on the North Coast.[9] Daniel Laínez (1914–59) became known for his poems of country life and values, and he, Claudio Barrera (1912–71), and Jacobo Cárcamo (1916–59) often used their poetry as a vehicle for explicit condemnation of social injustices and even, on occasion, of specific political figures. All of these poets questioned the nature of poetry and developed the theme of the poet as a member of society. Many of them also expressed a consciousness of the revolutionary, or at least rebellious, possibilities of poetry by experimenting with the techniques offered by the various movements and manifestos that collectively came to be called the *vanguardia.* But none of them have left a record of their struggle to redefine and reposition themselves as poets in society so clear or impassioned as that of Clementina.

Sails is Clementina's first incursion into revolutionary poetry. While not all the poems in this volume are explicit expressions of a revolutionary consciousness, they are all the result of the poet's attempt to come to terms with and to articulate a new sense of herself and a new understanding of poetry. It has been said that "for many of the poets of this period [the thirties] the conversion to communism would be retold in terms of a personal myth of transformation."[10] Although Clementina never converted to communism as a specific ideology, she did experience an awakening that made her question her assumption that life centered on her own needs and passions and that her poetry's main purpose was to express those emotions.

Sails, then, was Clementina's most exciting work so far, although one would not guess it from reading the prologue, where we find once again the curious but not uncommon masculine perception of the poet and her poetry. The author of the prologue, Alfonso Cravioto, devotes most of his laudatory lyrical prose to a description of Clementina's personality, her spirit, and her body. He describes her "emotional restlessness" and her "emotional electricity." He asserts that "her joie de vivre is at once the sadistic pleasure of pain." He claims that she is "self-absorbed and silent; in a word, intense." He tells us that "her blood is Dionysian . . . and her body is like a cauldron of effervescent wonders." He then extrapolates from his own effusiveness that, because of her vibrant spirit and body, she has been able to create "poems unique in literature written in Spanish, that seem composed by an angelic bacchant or a seraphic fauness." Cravioto clearly found Clementina to be an interesting and sexually attractive woman. His comments on her poetry, however, seem based on a reading of her works previous to *Sails,* for he fails to mention the confusion, the emptiness, the militancy, and the search for a new lyric voice to express the lessons perceived by an awakening consciousness. One has only to read Clementina's dedication: "To the morning /—in you, Alba, in you, Silvia—/ and to everyone's morning" (Al mañana que hay /—en tí Alba, en tí Silvia—/ y al mañana de todos) to realize that something is happening in this collection of poems that goes beyond Cravioto's perception of Clementina's creative carnality, beyond his appraisal that "she has cleansed sex of all its hypocritical viscosity and made it shine again, in pagan splendor, with the sacred glow of creation. This is her moral and also her aesthetic value."

The fact that Clementina allowed this incongruous prologue to precede her thirty poems (for certainly she had control over its inclusion) testifies to the powerful role that sexual attractiveness plays in a woman's ability to penetrate the traditionally male literary establishment. In the real world of flesh-and-blood human beings, a woman's smile, her walk, her habit of taking your hand when she sits beside you, of running her hand along a man's back as she talks to him, are natural and affectionate gestures that also serve to create sensual bonds between poet and reader, poet and critic. When Clementina says she loves being a woman, she means she enjoys being seductive, that she likes it when men admire and desire her.

The following reading of *Sails* foregrounds the transformation of the poet's consciousness and finds that her stylistic and thematic choices evolve in a progressive fashion, as illustrated by the first five poems. The opening poem, "Estrella, árbol y pájaro" (Star, Tree, and Bird), harks back to the style and concerns of *Bleeding Heart.* The poet is alone, a lonely star in the night sky. She is a tree that casts no shadow. She is a solitary bird that sings an ancient song. Even the form is reminiscent of her earlier poems—carefully crafted eight-syllable lines divided into quatrains.

She expands on the theme of the solitary voice in the next poem, "Canción" (Song), but to the metaphors of solitude she adds the anguish of the poet who has lost touch with the source of her inspiration as she struggles to give shape to her song. The meter is less rigid, and the shape of the poem on the page is more urgent. She illustrates her loss for words with metaphors of broken anchors and distant harbors. In the first poem she calls herself a solitary star, but here she berates her lyric voice for being neither high nor low. She is adrift in waters she cannot comprehend.

In the third poem, "Diálogo con el viento" (Dialogue with the Wind), she turns to the wind, archetypal element of poetic inspiration, and begs it to fill her voice. Here, for the first time, she uses symbols of revolution: flags, posters, the color red. She asks the wind to sever her ties to the past so she can participate in this new force.

In the next poem, "En brazos del nuevo viento" (Embraced by the New Wind) she has taken the first step out of herself (or, more accurately, out of her old self) and begins the experiment of speaking with the voice of one who would be many. The following poem represents her desire for poetic rebirth. It is both a declaration and a plea.

Multiplied

Before I wanted to be,
I wanted to be
me.

Now I want to be,
I want to be
everyone.

Constricted throat!
Blind eye!

Before I wanted to be,
I wanted to be
me.

Now I want to be,
I want to be
everyone.

———

Multiplicada

Antes quería ser,
quería ser
yo.

Ahora quiero ser,
quiero ser
todos.

¡La garganta oprimida!
¡La mirada ciega!

Antes quería ser,
quería ser
yo.

Ahora quiero ser,
quiero ser
todos.

In *Sails,* Clementina believes in salvation through revolutionary commitment, but this optimism will be tempered over time, for she must resolve the contradiction between the pull of freedom and solitude, and the responsibilities that come with sharing and social consciousness. Can the individual remain autonomous while absorbed in the collective? Can the self-styled woman who has made a career of (and by) defying society's rules transform her voice to speak even for those who might reject her difference? Who makes up the *pueblo* (people) she wants to incorporate into herself, or for whom she wants to speak?

The nature of her self-proclaimed commitment has been the subject of debate in literary and political circles in Honduras. Those who look for an expression of ideological purity are disappointed. Those who expect that the life and the poetry are sister texts that can be read side by side, and that both should offer up the same meaning, are frustrated by contradictory messages. I suspect that what Clementina found so compelling about revolutionary transformation was the passionate idea of revolution itself. Just as she would come to recognize that she loved love as much as any particular loved one, it seems probable that she loved the revolutionary fight as much as she loved the "masses." Indeed, her life became a battleground where the personal and the political fused. Rather than adherence to a revolutionary ideology, her relationship to the fight has been a practical, even vital one. As she explained, "*I would not have survived were it not for my fighting spirit and my determination to get where I wanted to be. Sometimes it seems like a miracle that I've made it; win or die has been my motto. Now the fight itself holds as much satisfaction for me as victory. . . . From the beginning I was resolved to be prepared for anything, that nothing would scare me, nothing would surprise me. Being independent has its price. One has to be ready to defend herself. . . . I was born a rebel and I have protested through my life and through my work against the absurd laws that limit human beings. . . . I move heaven and earth to get what's mine and I know I'm right to do so. One must be tenacious to get ahead. I decided to forge my destiny as I pleased and not to please others.*"[11]

Most of the remaining twenty-five poems of *Sails* are variations on and explorations of the themes presented in the first five. The elements that recur with a rhythmic insistence are the wind, the sea, and the scream or battle cry. She moves between being adrift and being connected and multiple. She articulates her new vision, or she laments her inability to see and say the new. In "Esa ya no es mi sombra" (This Is No Longer My Shadow) she mourns the loss of the past.

I had it all
and lost it all.
A hammer and sickle
beheaded my dream.
I have just torn three centuries from my eyes!

From what long and dark prison
have I escaped
that I don't even know
my own age?

I have fled from within,
fled from without!
Though you reach out
you will not touch me.
The shadow left behind
is no longer mine.

Todo lo tuve
y todo lo he perdido.
Una hoz y un martillo
decapitaron mi ensueño.
¡Acabo de arrancarme tres siglos de los ojos!

¿De qué larga y oscura prisión
he podido escaparme
que no puedo precisar
ni la edad que tengo?

¡Me he fugado de adentro!
¡Me he fugado de afuera!
Aunque extiendan los brazos
no podrán alcanzarme.
¡La sombra que se queda,
esa ya no es mi sombra!

But in "El grito" (The Cry) she applauds change and rejoices in the promise of the future.

Firm in the ranks,
I await the hour
that will free all obstacles
and hurl me into the sea of struggle

with the joyful will
of one who defying death
conquers life!

I was
a desperate butterfly
imprisoned in the walls
of useless hours.
But the new battle cry
has finally reached my ears
and I have opened my arms to it
as to a horizon of light
that shows me the way
to hope's only harbor! . . .

———

Enfilada y firme,
espero la hora
que desamarre todos los obstáculos
y me aviente a los mares de la lucha
con la alegre capacidad
del que desafiando la muerte
vence a la vida!

Yo era
una desesperada mariposa
aprisionada en las paredes
de las horas inútiles.
Pero el nuevo grito
llegó por fin a mis oídos
y yo le he abierto los brazos
como a un horizonte de luz
que me señalara
el único puerto de esperanza! . . .

A number of the poems in *Sails* are also love poems. In "Duda" (Doubt) we see the Clementina of *Bleeding Heart* and *The Last of My Saturdays:* weepy, languid, longing, hurt by the lover who has deserted her. In "Amor salvaje" (Savage Love) it is the Clementina of *Gears:* sensual, strong, seductive, happy to be a female in love. But we also see a new Clementina in love in poems such as "Los arados" (The Plows), where she discovers the possibilities for love and for poetry in the word *compañero.*

The paths have separated
and the plows are left behind.
I have begun to call you "comrade"
and have sewn my poverty to yours.
I one stitch, you another . . .

———

Se han bifurcado las sendas
y van atrás los arados.
He comenzado a llamarte "compañero"
y he cosido mi pobreza a tu pobreza.
Yo un punto, tú otro punto . . .

Some of the themes and motifs that appear for the first time in *Sails* will prove fruitful in subsequent works, such as the combining of sexual and revolutionary love, while others, such as her flirtation with socialist realism, will thankfully die on *Sails*'s vine. In "De eslabón a eslabón" (Link to Link), for example, she unsuccessfully mixes comradely love with motors and factories: "Our hands, entangled in motors / will be clasped, / and the factory's smoke / will proclaim our union" (Enredados en los motores / se apretarán nuestras manos, / y será el humo de la fábrica / el que anunciará nuestra unión). Metaphors such as the wind, the sea, and solitude, that have been integral to her poetry from the beginning retain their primordial significance but expand, contract, or metamorphose. It is revealing to compare that first sea poem from *Beginnings,* "My Poem to the Sea," with one from *Sails,* "Canción marina sin espuma" (Sea Poem without Spray). In the earlier poem the lyric voice establishes a sensual relationship with the sea, singing to it, seducing it, inviting it to inspire her. She finds jewels, colors, and textures in the sea; it is a cornucopia of poetry. But the sea does not always give up its treasures, so in "Sea Poem without Spray" it is reduced to a black river. Pearls and sapphires, murmurs and tenderness are replaced by cowardly mirrors and bloody nails.

Today,
if by chance the sea exists
it would be a black river.
Today when I say sea
it is as if I were saying blood.
Knotted at my throat
are necklaces of salt.
The waves know that my cry
went down to the sea.
High tide waters
galloping through the air.
Clear, transparent water,
if only you would wash away my pain!
All my landscapes
are breaking on your back.
Cowardly mirrors
reflecting my dark stars.
How I want to
bury myself in your tides!
Pull bloody nails
from the back of the sea.

———

Hoy,
si acaso el mar existiera
el mar sería un río negro.
Hoy cuando yo digo mar
es como si dijera sangre.
Anudados a mi garganta
tengo collares de sal.
Ya todas las olas saben
que mi llanto bajó al mar.
Aguas en mareas altas
galopando por los aires.
Aguas claras, claras aguas,
si me lavaran el mal!

Quebrándose en tus espaldas
están todos mis paisajes.
Copiándome estrellas negras
están espejos cobardes.
¡Ay! Cómo bien quisiera
hundirme en tu pleamar!
Arrancar clavos de sangre
en una espalda del mar.

"Canción del futuro cierto" (Song of the Certain Future) is one of the two poems in this work whose context is other than the inner battleground of personal transformation. As a meditation on the mother-daughter bond, it draws our attention back to the book's dedication. Her long separation from her daughters, first in New York, then in Havana, caused her nostalgia, loneliness, perhaps guilt, but the child-rearing philosophy implicit in the poem—to encourage independence and watch from a distance as one's children grow and experiment with life and find their own paths—was an attitude that came naturally to a woman so involved in personal freedom and self-determination.

With my back to life I will watch you pass
—you, Alba, you Silvia—
testing your sails
heady with distance, enamored of the sea!

In a swing of clouds
I will watch them pass,
in their journey through cities
toward sunflower days.

The wind clearing a path
for the whims of their wings.
Their two parallel desires
furrowing the quiet waters.

Ships sailing
with your swing—my arms—

you Alba, you Silvia—
on other paths now.

———

De espaldas a la vida miraré pasar
—tú Alba, tú Silvia—
estrenando veleros
ebrios de distancia, locos de mar!

En un balanceo de nubes
las miraré pasar,
en itinerario de ciudades
para sus días tornasoles.

El viento abriendo caminos
para el afán de sus alas.
Surcando por aguas mansas
sus dos ansias paralelas.

Barcos en que navegan
con su columpio—mis brazos—
tú Alba, tú Silvia—
en otros caminos ya.

The thirty poems of *Sails* paint a picture of a woman torn and tossed about in a dialectic of hope and purpose versus despair and inactivity. Cuba had shaken her out of her complacency and given her life a new purpose. It was time to move on again.

CHAPTER FOUR

Bohemian Revolutionary

Mexico

When Clementina left Cuba she continued the life-style she had developed of traveling, staying with friends, dabbling in journalism, giving poetry recitals. An article from a Guatemalan newspaper indicates that she has distinguished herself as unique and professional in the world of poetry: "Clementina Suárez demonstrated last night what a simple, profound and satisfying recital can be, without the theatrical ostentation so common among our performers." That same month an article in *El Pueblo,* a newspaper from Havana, calls attention to her growing fame: "Despite the cruel indifference there to anything regarding art, her personality is making itself known with increasing intensity in Honduran literature." The following month Nicaraguan Agenor Argüello, in an article in a Honduran paper, refers explicitly to her ideological orientation: "Clementina Suárez is, undeniably, the best avant-garde poetess in Central America; her woman's soul breaks with archaic molds and proclaims her liberty to the four winds . . . she has known how to turn life into a rainbow, to live life fully in all its permutations, to communicate her emotions in sincere verses. . . . Clementina is a socialist. Her poetry cannot help but echo her ideological concerns."[1]

The making of the myth has had many phases. With the publication of her new, revolutionary poetry, the dimensions of her legendary dark side and its counterpart, her reputation for spontaneous candor, expanded. Those who defended her youthful disregard of society's rules as pure, genuine, and refreshing could now stand by her current flailing at hypocrisy and injustice by naming it pure, genuine, and mature. Those who recoiled from her openness and purported licentiousness could now add communist to her list of faults. Her supporters wrote prologues to her books and semblanzas in newspapers and journals, they introduced her to new audiences with flowery, appreciative prose, and they composed poems dedicated to her. Her debunkers continued to talk behind her back, although during this time there was less criticism at home because Clementina spent relatively little time in Honduras, where her critics were of course most numerous. Her long absences helped people forget her past scandalous behavior, while rumors of her growing international fame persuaded many to judge her less harshly. At any rate, she chose to publish her next book, *De la desilusión a la esperanza* (From Disillusion to Hope) in Tegucigalpa, in 1944.

The introductory remarks to the work, by Alejandro Bermúdez, indicate that her public image as a poet has evolved away from that of creator of poems of spontaneous and nubile candor. Bermúdez calls her "A woman who has taken her task as poet absolutely seriously." He notes that she now faces squarely the realities of life and death and the problem of primary importance of the times, "justice for the dispossessed masses of the earth." He believes she occupies a singular position within feminine poetry. He clarifies, "When I say feminine, I do not mean to imply soft or excessively sweet. I mean only to refer to that poetry written by women. Clementina is forming singlehandedly an attack brigade. There are other illustrious women in our America, dedicated to similar tasks, in different latitudes. But none like her, with a delicate exterior appearance, but with an enviable interior strength, with a determined direction, with a beautiful loyalty to herself and to her personal time, yet without disregarding the exigencies of her historical epoch. No verbal scintillations. No deceiving sweetness. No false flattery. No illusory promises. Metaphors spring from her, burning coals bright with truth, naked and constructive beauty. Her literature is antiliterature. Her poetry is not simply poetry, but pure poetry. A new sap flows through her poetry. The blood of a humanity on the march, of a humanity whose supreme goal will be the creation of beauty on the ample pillars of justice."

To call Clementina a socialist or a communist is misleading (she herself disregards these designations, calling herself a revolutionary) and only clouds the central drama of her life, the internal struggle that informs her next three books: redrawing the boundaries between self and other. Her own pronouncements on this relationship are enlightening. Interviewers have often asked her to place her work within the context of literary trends or generations, but she invariably refuses to delimit the boundaries of her context. She quips that she has outlived most of the generations with whom she has been associated and furthermore that what characterizes her work is an attitude and a center or locus of inspiration rather than a technique or an ideology. "*I write everything with the same intensity. All my poems are a testimony of my attitudes, my anguish, my joys, and I do not turn my back on the tragedies suffered by humanity.*" She elaborates on this idea of being in touch with humanity's pain: "*The most important thing for me is to know that I have communicated with the people and that the people love me, the people who hear their own voice in that of the poet. And not just my people, but all the people of the world, any people.*" Reminiscing on the lessons she learned in Cuba, she said, "*It was in Cuba that I learned that poetry has another mission besides singing for the sake of singing. It is inconceivable that an authentic poet not have a message for her people, and even intimate poetry can have a message. I realized that I was a part of my people, a part of humanity, and it was then that I realized that nothing was foreign to me.*"[2]

Clementina summed up her poetry in this way in 1972, but from 1937 to 1959, the years during which she wrote *Sails, From Disillusion to Hope, Creciendo con la hierba* (Growing with the Grass), and *Canto a la encontrada patria y su héroe* (Song to the Found Fatherland and Its Hero), she wrote (and published) those books because, while she may have had a preverbal knowledge of this oneness with humanity, the poems were her way of making this understanding a real part of herself. Throughout her life Clementina has sought recognition of her worth as a poet. But to whom does one look for infallible judgments concerning the quality of expression? The public, the marketplace, the critics, other poets, one's self? At a crucial moment in her life, Clementina sought the judgment of someone she was able to accept as an authority.

León Felipe, the great Spanish poet of untarnished revolutionary principles and incessant wanderings, left Spain for the last time in 1938 and made Mexico his home until his death there in 1968. He was tremendously popular in Mexico, where he was a symbol of resistance and exile, a voice that expressed the human drama of a divided Spain. For a period of time between León Felipe's arrival in Mexico and the publication of *From Disillusion to Hope* in Tegucigalpa in 1944, Clementina spent many hours with the venerable poet, much as she had often done in Tegucigalpa in earlier years absorbing the conversation of men of letters over cups of coffee. She described him with admiration: "*You would have loved him. He was so effusive, so ardent! The theatre went wild when he recited his poetry, anti-Franco poetry. He was belligerent! He vowed never to return to Spain while Franco was there. We used to meet in a café in downtown Mexico City, 'El Papagayo.' He drank so much coffee, five, six cups. I would get sick, I'm not used to drinking so much coffee. It wasn't good for my stomach, but I would drink coffee just to be there with him, talking and listening. He was a fervent enemy of bad poetry. 'No, no, no,' he would say, 'either it's poetry, or it isn't.'*"

When asked to explain how he distinguished good from bad poetry or, rather, poetry from texts not worthy of the name, she said, "*The themes, the form in which it is developed. A poem is good or it isn't. Those who truly know about literature can distinguish.*"

We can see from her remarks that she was impressed and inspired by her friendship with León Felipe because she recognized him as a superior being, a poet who had achieved an uncommom depth of wisdom and love, that he was able to convey in his poetry and that endowed him with that superior vision that enabled him to determine quality in others' poetry. Her feelings about the Spanish poet reflect a characteristic disparagement of theory or overintellectualization. Clementina is impatient with literary criticism that is too analytical or technical, preferring, as do most people who are not literary critics, to evaluate poetry through emotion and intuitive response. She learned from him, but it must have been difficult to hear, from one whose opinion she valued so highly, that her early poetry was romantic, meaning self-indulgent, a horrible indictment at the time. Later in life she learned to accept all of her poetry as the expression of her self in its various stages of evolution, although she favors her work from *Sails* on. She was once asked in an interview which of her books she considers her best. She replied, "*The things I have not been able to say in a poem. I am always searching for the answer in the next one. It is as if I am always just beginning to find the authentic words in my poetry that will lead me to a universal expression, always allowing intuition to be my guide. So my best book will be the last one I write.*"[3]

She claims that, inspired by León Felipe's encouragement to start afresh, she burned a suitcase full of poetry that she considered unworthy. She says that before *Sails* she "hadn't found a style." What she means by "style" is an authentic voice that speaks to great numbers of people because it articulates not only her singular hope and despair, but that of many, specifically "*el pueblo,*" meaning no less than the oppressed masses. I write this with a dose of irony for two reasons: first, this ambition seems quaintly naïve given the history of the relationship of poetry to revolution in the twentieth century as well as Clementina's class background; second, I am not convinced that her poetry has had any resonance within this amorphous pueblo. I question in fact whether any of the poets who have strived for this authentic multiplicity have been successful. I think the answer to this question can finally be found only in the response of the reader or listener. In countries like Honduras, when even in the final decade of the twentieth century the illiteracy rate approaches 50 percent, it is clear that it is not literally the masses to whom Clementina or Roque Dalton or León Felipe have spoken. The poet will always speak only to those who care to or are able to hear. So while Dalton's poetry was probably most appreciated by other angry youths like himself rebelling against Salvadoran bourgeois society; and León Felipe likely appealed mostly to sensitive individuals like himself, committed to social justice and left hurt, angry, and alienated by the failures of revolutionary movements in Spain, Central America, and elsewhere; so Clementina's poetry will speak most clearly to women struggling to live and love and create in a world that is hostile and uncomprehending, but that also offers pleasures and recognition and relationships that they need and desire.

The dialectic between self and other is played out not only on the grand scale of self and humanity, but also in Clementina's relationship with her daughters. They lived together as a family only sporadically until 1947, when both girls had graduated from high school and she brought them to live with her in Mexico City. But despite, or perhaps because of, the absences and distances, her children and her motherhood are of central importance to her. As with romantic love and revolutionary commitment, part of what attracted Clementina was the idea of motherhood and its poetic possibilities. Five of the twenty-two poems of *From Disillusion to Hope* are about mothers and children. In "Canción de cuna para una hija" (Lullaby for a Daughter) she muses on time and the passing on of the word from generation to generation.

> But only your new mouth
> will know how to say the word.
> Even though I wanted to, daughter,
> I was full of the past.
>
> ———
>
> Más sólo tu boca nueva
> sabrá decir la palabra.
> Yo aunque lo quise, hija,
> en mi estaba el pasado.

The tone of the poem is one of rejoicing—that through her daughter she is reborn, that her body has created the future.

In "Dentro de la noche" (Within the Night) she envisions herself as a maternal guardian angel. "And I standing over your life / like a hand of snow / that guards your night" (Y yo en pie sobre su vida / como mano de nieve / que cuidara su noche). She hears the echo of her own footsteps in her daughter's, a daughter who walks, "holding my hand / like the fruit of the tree / that gave it life" (Tomada de la mano / como la fruta al árbol / que le dio vida). She imagines herself as a constant though not always conscious presence in her daughter's life, one that will ultimately be acknowledged.

> And she will say: someone speaks behind the moon
> with a voice from beneath my blood.
> I carry within me a shadow leaning
> like a sky that saves its stars for me.
>
> ———
>
> Y ella dirá: alguien detrás de la luna habla
> con voz que sale debajo de mi sangre.

Una sombra inclinada llevo dentro del pecho
como cielo que guarda para mí sus estrellas.

The most poignant of the maternal poems in this work is "Canción para dos niñas pobres" (Song for Two Impoverished Little Girls). It is a plea for forgiveness by a mother who explains that she has had to learn how to love her children. Nothing can be taken for granted by the woman who chooses to design her own life; even a mother's love must be viewed through the lens of poetry for the poet to understand it.

Now I know how to love you
tender flesh of my flesh.

But life had to destroy me
in its windstorms,
So I could give you
the pure chalice of my love.

———

Ahora sí sé quererte
carne tierna de la entraña

Pero fue preciso que la vida
me destrozara en sus arenales,
Para que entregarte pudiera
el cáliz puro del amor.

Not being with her daughters but not being able to forget them informs the other two poems that portray the mother-child relationship. They are among Clementina's finest work, in part because they are truly revolutionary in that they produce a vision of motherhood that departs radically from the traditional version of the selfless and long-suffering mother who sacrifices herself for her children. In "Contigo crece el mar" (With You Grows the Sea) the poet celebrates her daughter's difference and emphasizes her unique individuality:

You do not grow by my side
but you rise like a shaft of wheat,

all see you blossoming
with songs, doves and flowers.

———

No creces a mi lado
pero te levantas como espiga,
todos te ven florecida
de trinos, de palomas y de nardos.

In a society that requires that its women give themselves completely to the care and nurturing of their families, "Poema del paso desatado" (Poem of the Unfettered Step) may be read as a rationalization for abandoning one's responsibilities, but it can also be read as an expression of a love that allows the loved ones the freedom to be autonomous:

From my blood two little girls watch me
with eyes that pierce my empty body.
They enter and stand like complete worlds
suspended from their moon, their sun and their dream.
Covering your face I want to protect you,
light footstep that walks and returns on my path.
I have a mother's fear—yet I want you to leap—
to leap over my blood and not turn back to see me.

From my ageless mouth I tell you goodbye;
I have nothing to do with your stem, your flower and your tree,
you are unbound from me, enormous in your distance,
with your hands to the wind you went your own way,
without tears or pain, free now in the land. . . .

Your day has flowered and no longer fits in my hands,
while your body rises mine returns.
You will put pieces of your bread in my mouth
giving my death a bit of your life.

———

Desde mi sangre dos niñas me miran
con ojos que se clavan en mi cuerpo vacío.

Entran y están de pie como mundos completos
colgados de su luna, de su sol y su sueño.
Tapándote la cara quisiera defenderte
huella leve que andas y desandas mi camino.
Miedo de madre tengo—sin embargo quiero que saltes—
que saltes sobre mi sangre sin volver a verme.

Desde mi boca sin fecha yo misma te digo adiós;
nada tengo que ver con tu tallo, tu flor y tu árbol,
estás de mí desprendida, enorme en tu distancia,
con las manos al viento de mi vena te fuiste,
sin pañuelo ni pena, ya libre en el paisaje. . . .

No cabe ya en mis manos tu florecido día,
mientras tu cuerpo asciende ya estoy yo de regreso.
Pedazos de tu pan me darás en la boca
dándole así a mi muerte un poco de tu vida.

Most of the remaining poems of *From Disillusion to Hope* can be read as a thematic unit, a continuation of the effort begun in *Sails* to reposition the mirrors of her vision. The dialectic of inner and outer, self and other, is renewed and reaches a higher level of intensity, as evidenced in the powerful primordial metaphors, the honed language, the naked confusion and anger. In "Mis espejos rotos" (My Broken Mirrors) she creates a hallucination of blood, exhaustion, madness, and solitude. The setting is once again the sea.

Sea
—stagnant tomb—
green eye
where my sadness
is captured intact.

———

Mar
—remanso de ultratumba—
ojo verde

donde está intacta
retratada mi tristeza.

The sea, which had been her watery symbol of sensuality and inspiration until *Sails,* when she accused the sea of being a cowardly mirror, is now a cloudy mirror whose tormented waters are bloodstained. She tries to deny that it is she whose waters produce such images of suffering and despair: "No. No. No. / This is not my sea, / nor these my eyes" (No. No. No. / Este no es mi mar, / ni estos son mis ojos). But the litany that follows testifies to the persistent intrusion of failure and frustration. "My Broken Mirrors" is a nightmare, reminiscent of expressionism's scream of horror or surrealism's disinterment of phantoms from the unconscious.

Suicidal sea-eye,
sinister, human sea.
Dark-plumed bird, cold vastness,
in your six-month sleepless night
virgins are mutilated,
fish close their eyes
and angels have broken wings.

So you see,
I too am drowned.
Dismembered in your waters,
white bones broken
in the belly of your rotting God.

Shipwrecked impulse,
my spirit wounded
my laughter broken. . . .

———

Mar de pupila suicida,
mar siniestro, mar humano.
Pájaro de plumaje obscuro, mole fría,
en tu noche de desvelo de seis meses
las vírgenes están mutiladas,

los peces tienen la pupila cerrada
y los ángeles el ala rota.

Ya lo ves,
yo también estoy ahogada.
Hecha pedazos en tus aguas,
rotos los huesos blancos
en la barriga de tu Dios podrido.

Naufragado el impulso,
herido mi júbilo
rota mi risa. . . .

With this now broken mirror of her poetic vision she sees herself not multiple, but fragmented. So she dives ever deeper into the waters of self and memory, searching for the secret of wholeness. But the memory to which she looks for answers is no longer the nostalgic evocation of childhood innocence. In "Figuras en el agua" (Shapes in the Water) she attempts instead to reach into the collective memory of her gender.

If I were to remember
what I was taught
a hundred years ago.
The truth of the rose split
in the tender river.

I would speak of a sob,
of a child of blood
and even of a skeleton
that danced
in the air.

And making an effort,
I would arrive at the origin of the archangel,
his swallow-like reflection
his dagger-sharp vigil.
I would remember
the death I saw in a mirror,
and a stalk with its head broken

its hands
and eyes open.

Tell me. And I would tell you
the sad tread
of rushes in the snow.
The painful fingers
of the child who weaves
his cradle in the wind.

And shaking moss from my body
—shadows that watch over me—
I would tell you the story
of sheets that have names,
of shrouded women
who buried their secret
in the sea.

———

Si recordara,
lo que hace cien años
me habían enseñado.
Que verdad de rosa partida
en río tierno.

Hablaría de un sollozo,
de una niña de sangre
y hasta de un esqueleto
que bailaba
en el aire.

Y haciendo un esfuerzo,
llegaría al orígen del arcángel,
a su reflejo de golondrina
y a su vigilia de puñal.
Recordaría,
la muerte que vi en un espejo,
y un tallo de cabeza rota

que tenía las manos
y los ojos abiertos.

Dime. Y te diría,
el paso triste
del junco dentro de la nieve.
El daño que en los dedos tiene
el niño que teje
su cuna en el viento.

Y quitando musgo de mi cuerpo
—sombras que me hacen guardia—
la historia te contaría,
de sábanas que tienen nombre,
y de mujeres que amortajadas
en el mar enterraron
su secreto.

From Disillusion to Hope is not a success story, as its title suggests. It is rather a record of insights, attempts, but ultimately failures to attain a voice and a vision that are multiple. Instead of the desired knowledge and communication, her efforts bring her "Soledad multiplicada" (Solitude Multiplied):

The exalted word loses its meaning,
common language debases emotion.
The spirit wanders lost on rocky ground
and is ash in our hands. . . .
Rivers pour their waters into my veins
yet they fill me with a heavy silence.

———

Su sentido pierde la palabra exaltada
y un callejero idioma vulgariza la emoción.
El espíritu se extravía en terrestres guijarros
y en forma de ceniza nos queda entre las manos. . . .
En mis venas los ríos desembocan sus aguas
sin embargo me cargan de un pesado silencio.

And she resents that her best efforts have gone misunderstood or unappreciated. In a petulant gesture of dismissal in "La negada presencia" (The Presence Denied), which echoes Alfonsina Storni's "Hombre pequeñito" (Little Man), she blames the inferior beings (here, men) who have been unable to hear what she has tried to communicate.

> I always felt sorry for
> he who did not know how to love me . . .
> I was born to distant stars
> alone at dawn. . . .
>
> My wings are useless
> on earth's shores.
> You are a small man
> and cannot reach my flight.
>
> ———
>
> Yo siempre tuve pena
> del que no supo amarme . . .
> Nací en estrellas altas
> y al alba estuve sola. . . .
>
> Nada pueden mis alas
> en orillas de tierra.
> Eres hombre pequeño
> y no alcanzas mi vuelo.

It is telling that she chose to include at the end of this book two poems that had originally appeared in *Temples of Fire* in 1931, "Compréndeme" (Understand Me) and "El ruego" (The Plea), for both texts undertake to explain to uncomprehending readers that she is alive, electric, in tune with the music of the universe, one with the primary elements. Their inclusion is a reminder (to herself as well as to others) that she is the same woman who once unquestioningly celebrated her femaleness, and that she too is one of the superior beings.

Clementina's most successful revolutionary poems thus far are those that are also the most intimate, where we see that the freedom, justice, and struggle she espouses are necessary for her own survival. She has poems that superficially are about workers, hunger, bread, combat, revolutionary heroes—none of which have been her daily experience (although she has worked and probably has gone hungry on occasion). Yet the voice that speaks, for example, for the worker who has died, is clearly hers—demanding, uncompromising, and tough—although it could also be that of a union leader or a militant worker determined to win or go down fighting. This poem works because it is a felicitous convergence of an attitude that is genuinely the poet's, speaking through a mask or persona that is not hers, but that is appropriate to the attitude. Clementina's pride in her body is transferred to the worker, who wants to die whole and natural:

A Worker Dies

I will not go down like an old rag
not a single tooth has fallen from my mouth.
My flesh is intact
my head raised high above my supple form.

I will die, but with a fresh mouth
with a firm, clear voice I will answer the call.
I know life's minutes are numbered
that destiny never turns back.

I am not afraid to enter the shadow
let no one come to mourn my death,
the froth of my blood is used up like oil
for that moment I ask only for silence.

Once I am dead I do not want them to fix my hair
or cross my hands over my breast,
I want to be left as I fell
placed simply in the open earth.

Una obrera muerta

Yo no bajaré a la tumba convertida en harapo
ni un solo diente de mi boca se ha caído.
Las carnes en mi cuerpo tienen su forma intacta
y ágil en su tallo se yergue la cabeza.

Yo iré a la muerte pero con el labio fresco
con voz firme y clara responderé a la llamada.
Yo sé que están contados los minutos de la vida
y que jamás el destino su sentencia retrasa.

Sobresalto no tengo por entrar a la sombra
nadie quiero que venga por mi muerte a llorar,
la espuma de mi sangre como aceite se acaba
y para ese instante a todos sólo pido silencio.

No quiero que ya muerta peinen mi cabello
ni que las manos juntas pongan en mi pecho,
quiero que me dejen así como me quede
y así en la tierra abierta me vayan a dejar.

Having been hurt by hypocrisy, she rails against it:

I do not want them to dress me up, or to profane my death
by being present, those who never were in life.
Sincere comrades, those I've always had,
let only them bury me.

Nor do I want a tombstone or a cross,
I want nothing the poor do not have.
Even after death my fist will be clenched
and my name will be like a flag in the wind.

———

No quiero que me vistan, ni que me ultrajen muerta,
estando conmigo los que nunca estuvieron.
Compañeros sinceros, los que siempre tuve,
sólo esos que se encarguen de irme a enterrar.

Tampoco quiero seña, ni que una cruz me pongan,
no quiero para mí nada que los pobres no tengan.
Pues aún después de muerta, mi puño estará cerrado
y en el viento mi nombre será como bandera.

Clementina's revolutionary poetry does not conform to what has been the predominant aesthetic propounded by practitioners and critics of engagé literature in Central America. (While there is certainly no aesthetic that all can agree on, nor has there been a manifesto of common principles and prescribed practices, poetry that situates itself in combat or in the countryside, that is explicitly anti-imperialist or that criticizes bourgeois values and attempts to remove poets from their pedestals and put them in the street is the most highly regarded, perhaps in part because it is the most easily recognizable.) Neither is her life-style a manifestation of typical revolutionary principles, but it certainly has a "revolutionary" aesthetic all its own.

There were revolutionary contemporaries of hers whose lives mirrored a single-mindedness and a commitment to action, and it is illuminating to compare the shape of Clementina's life with the lives of other "workers" in the political or the cultural revolution. One of these individuals is Graciela García, born in El Salvador in 1896, who has devoted her life to revolutionary political movements throughout Central America. Her commitment has taken the form of leadership and active participation in the Communist Party and in countless congresses and demonstrations, as well as in organizing unions and founding schools. She was jailed in Tegucigalpa in 1944 after being arrested in a demonstration against the dictator Carías. In a section of her memoirs entitled "Momentos violentos en que me he encontrado" (Violence I Have Experienced) she mentions her participation in militant confrontations throughout Central America. "I have gone through various avatars, as I have participated actively in important demonstrations, defying the power of machine guns, risking my life, which was the case in Tegucigalpa in 1944. . . . In El Salvador, as a representative of the Women's Committee for the Candidacy of Dr. Arturo Romero, the candidate of the Salvadoran Communist Party . . . they attacked us with guns, bombs and stones. . . . And also in El Salvador, toward the end of 1944, . . . they tear-gassed us in the hopes of dispersing us. . . . And in Guatemala as well, defending the regime of Dr. Juan José Arévalo in 1945, there were numerous encounters between reactionary forces and revolutionaries. . . . I have suffered prison, exile, persecution and constant surveillance in Guatemala, El Salvador and particularly in Honduras."[4]

It is interesting to note that Graciela García's activities were not limited to a single country. As the publishers of her memoirs have noted, "Graciela A. García, Salvadoran by birth, is an active revolutionary who has made all of Mexico and Central America her home." Despite the isolation of the Central American republics due to typography and the lack of good roads and adequate public transportation, it was quite common for people to migrate back and forth throughout the isthmus. (The only railroad in Honduras, for example, is the one connecting the banana plantations with shipping ports on the North Coast, and the maintenance of some stretches of the Pan American Highway in Central America has been sorely neglected.) This movement was often the unwilling migration of individuals who found themselves on the losing side in political contests and fled their homeland seeking safety in a neighboring country. Others chafed under the censorship and surveillance of watchful dictators and chose temporarily to reside in whichever Central American country happened to be at the moment winning the good fight. Leftists fled Guatemala in large numbers in 1934, for example, because of brutal repression by Ubico and went mainly to Mexico and El Salvador. Active opposition to Ubico began in Guatemala in 1941, and his fall in 1944 prompted the return of political exiles, many of whom were influential in organizing labor unions, political factions, and leftist publications. Intellectuals and political activists from other nations also came into the country, and they too influenced the course of political development.

There were those who followed the revolution to organize, to demonstrate, to publish newspapers and books, and to teach in the working-class universities that were founded throughout the region. Many Central American writers were also activists, such as Miguel Angel Asturias, who had helped found the Universidad Popular de Guatemala (Guatemalan People's University) in 1922, which operated until Ubico closed it in 1932; and Carmen Lyra, who was instrumental in the opening of the Escuela Popular (People's School) in Costa Rica in 1937, followed by the Universidad Popular (People's University) in 1940. And there were those who followed the revolution because leftist governments tended to look favorably on growth and experimentation in the arts and lent their moral as well as financial support to the kinds of projects that so many artists and writers found appealing during these decades, such as open-air art schools, the painting of monumental murals in public buildings, art exhibits in public parks, mobile lending libraries, street theatre, and art inspired by folk and indigenous themes.

In 1945 the new president of Guatemala, Juan José Arévalo, a philosophy professor, inaugurated a political ideology he called "spiritual socialism," a doctrine of human liberation that rejected both liberalism and conservatism in favor of a psychological and moral liberation on a foundation of social reform and anti-imperialism. His successor, Jacobo Arbenz, carried this revolutionary movement even further, initiating such widespread reforms and siding with the Soviet Union to such an extent that the United States eventually backed a movement to overthrow his government in 1954. The purge of the Left that followed the coup put an end to this brief but intense period of social change and experimentation in Guatemala. Similar periods of euphoric cultural and political activity have characterized Central American life throughout this century. The battle between Left and Right, change and tradition, has been emotional and violent. The Left seldom stays in power for long, but they periodically reappear with a renewed energy to organize and fight. Right-wing dictatorships were notoriously long-lived in the twenties, thirties and forties, so it is easy to appreciate the sense of hope and expectation with which intellectuals and political activists congregated in support of leftist or even moderate governments. These intervals of optimism were cut short again and again by conservative regrouping, often aided by the United States.

Clementina fits into this picture of revolutionary idealism and cultural migration in a unique way. She was not at all a Graciela García, fighting in the trenches for socialism (one of Graciela García's memoirs is entitled: *En las trincheras de la lucha por el socialismo* [In the Trenches in the Fight for Socialism]), although she did spend time in Guatemala in the 1940s. Nor was she a Rafael Heliodoro Valle, a Honduran scholar who traveled extensively but spent most of his adult life in Mexico because he found there a fertile and receptive environment in which to carry on his bibliographical research and journalism.[5] Nor can she be likened to her compatriots of the Generation of '35, such as Jacobo Cárcamo or Claudio Barrera, who, having pledged allegiance to the bohemian life-style, upon leaving Honduras in search of greater appreciation soon drank their lives away and dissipated their talent. (Jacobo Cárcomo lived in Mexico from 1938 to 1959, where he died, penniless and alcoholic; Claudio Barrera was living in Madrid when he died from alcohol-related complications.) That Clementina did not suffer the same fate as so many of her hard-drinking fellow poets owes more to a sturdy constitution than to abstinence, for her drinking is notorious; even in her eighties she can put away several whiskey and sodas and be none the worse for it the next morning.

Clementina's role in or contribution to revolutionary culture or the culture of revolution is eccentric, but therein lies much of its value. It is also by and large ephemeral, for it is made of spaces that are lived in, moved out of, spaces full of people that come and go, replete with paintings and poetry, alive with projects that are accomplished or not. They are spaces that are a reflection of Clementina, mirrors the size of houses where she can surround herself with superior souls—artists, writers, revolutionaries. The word *salon* comes to mind to describe these spaces, but as she herself explained, it was never anything official, nothing formal enough to deserve that appellation. Bohemian salon? Clementina called the first of these spaces a gallery: Galería de Arte Centroamericano. The second she called a ranch: El Rancho del Artista. Art was to be the motivation that legitimized the creation of these cultural spaces.

She had been interested in art since her first visit to Mexico in 1930, when she began modeling for artists. She soon included artists in her lists of superior souls and sought their company with a particular fascination. She loved hanging around their studios, watching them paint and being painted by them. She acquired her art education in much the same way she learned about literature—by watching artists and listening to their opinions and theories.

It was 1946, and Clementina was also interested in her daughters. They were both attractive young women just out of high school, and perhaps Clementina thought that now that they were all a little more mature (and the girls no longer in need of daily and mundane maternal attentions), they would be able to live together as a family. But when the three women took up residence together in Mexico City, they had no history of stable family life on which to base their relationship. Alba had lived mostly with doña Leonor until she was about fourteen, when she was sent to a convent school in Nicaragua. She was strong willed and rebellious, and this move was made in the hope of quieting her down, or at least keeping her out of trouble for a while. She later returned to Tegucigalpa, enrolled in María Auxiliadora, the secondary school for girls, and graduated in 1946. Silvia, meanwhile, quieter and more obedient than her older sister, went to live with her Aunt Rosa, Clementina's sister, in San Pedro Sula. When both sisters had graduated from high school they went to Mexico, where they stayed briefly in the home of María de la Selva, sister of the Nicaraguan poet and diplomat Salomón de la Selva. María was a fiery and independent woman, a writer who published political essays under the pseudonym Aura Rostán. It was then that Clementina saw the need for a place to call her own where she could give her daughters a home, so she rented a large house in Colonia Roma. In order to meet her expenses, she rented rooms in her home, mostly to artists, writers, and Central Americans in exile in Mexico.

Alba's impression of their life in Mexico is that it was disorganized, in part because there were not sufficient funds to pay for official university studies for her and her sister, so their lives seemed to have no plan or schedule. They took a few courses at the Academia de San Carlos and had some good times, but neither girl responded to Mexico as their mother had, and within two years they had both decided to leave. Alba formed a romantic liaison with a young Nicaraguan with whom she returned to Honduras accompanied by Silvia.

Silvia went back to the North Coast to live with her Aunt Rosa. There she met her husband-to-be, an agricultural engineer from Mexico who was working for the United Fruit Company in Tela. They were married in 1949 and later went to Mexico, where they currently reside. She had children, took courses in languages and secretarial skills, worked as a secretary, likes to travel, and has never had any ambition to write. She dresses impeccably and projects dignity and discretion.

Alba, on the other hand, was very attractive and fun loving, much like her mother, a curious combination of wildness and self-discipline. She shares her mother's restless spirit, which has found expression in a variety of intellectual pursuits. She has studied languages, has degrees in social work and law, and is currently a magistrate in the appellate court of Tegucigalpa. For her law degree she wrote a thesis on the implications for women of the adultery law in Honduras. She considers herself a feminist and likes to write poetry. Even though she is a practicing lawyer, she feels more akin to poets and artists and counts many of the local talents among her friends. When she left Mexico and her mother she went to live with her young Nicaraguan lover in Costa Rica but soon left him and returned to Tegucigalpa. She married poet and journalist Héctor Bermúdez Milla but divorced him when she realized it was not in her to be at any man's beck and call. They have one son. She never remarried. Like her mother, she lives as she pleases and doesn't seem to care what anyone thinks about her life-style.

When asked to recall the time she spent in Mexico living in the large house that Clementina took to calling the Galería de Arte Centroamericano, Alba recalled that Costa Rican artist Francisco Amighetti stayed there and painted her portrait as well as Silvia's. She remembers that Mexican poet Pita Amor walked around the house barefoot and that Clementina gave lots of parties, at which she often recited her own poetry or that of Miguel Angel Asturias and others.

Silvia was particularly taken with Asturias. She often went with her mother to visit him. She remembers him as a sweet man who was living with his family in Mexico, a very large man, gentle and kind. She also has fond memories of Alfonso Guillén Zelaya and Rafael Heliodoro Valle, two distinguished Hondurans who spent many years in Mexico and whose homes were gathering places for Hondurans and other Central Americans. Nothing like Clementina's home, to be sure; they were more sedate gatherings of friends and admirers come to enjoy the wisdom and hospitality of the teacher. Alfonso Guillén Zelaya, the poet and journalist who wrote the prologue to Clementina's first book, was a Marxist and found it impossible to live in Honduras under Carías, while Rafael Heliodoro Valle, as mentioned, found the cultural climate of Mexico more stimulating and receptive to his scholarly endeavors.

So the home that Clementina set up for herself and her daughters in Mexico City soon evolved into a kind of pensión, but any boarders had to modify their expectations if they thought they were paying for privacy, solitude, quiet, and three meals a day. Quite the contrary. One guest, a Nicaraguan poet in exile working with the anti-Somoza movement, remembers that there were so many paintings around that he would sometimes have to move the canvasses that were blocking his doorway in order to get into his room. A Salvadoran intellectual and political activist, in exile with her husband, rented a small apartment in the pensión and was fascinated (and somewhat horrified) by the continual flow of visitors, the all-night gatherings, the mix of respectability and debauchery. "I observed Clementina's intense, agitated life. Clementina is fascinating, open, a bohemian artist, she lived in that kind of environment. And then there was her drinking. In the early morning hours she would still be drinking. She had her 'get-togethers.' There were two Clementinas: one very proper, and another who would suddenly, well—. . . All manner of Mexican intellectuals would gather there—Samuel Ramos's wife was her friend, and painters, Frida Kahlo for example. Clementina always loved painting, exhibits, in a way she brought together all the Central Americans in Mexico."

Clementina of course needed the money she collected from her boarders, as she had no other steady source of income, but clearly her motivation for choosing this particular way of making money was that she loved being surrounded by creative people. She was now in her forties, still very attractive, sexually appealing according to the accounts of men who knew her at the time, still wanting to be desired and admired, but now more and more interested in being supportive and nurturing to young talents. Numerous stories contribute to an image of her as a bohemian patron of the arts, an eccentric and seductive woman who would invite a young painter to her home, supply him with paints and brushes, let him sleep on the sofa after staying up all night drinking and talking with her, hang his paintings on the walls of her gallery-home, and help him sell his work. Many artists repaid her kindness and encouragement by giving her paintings or adding their contribution to her growing collection of portraits. Sometimes she simply did not return paintings left in her care.

Her participation in the art market was seen by some, including herself, as natural. Others found it suspect, perhaps more because of the way society viewed art and artists than of anything unethical about her dealings. The very concept of an art gallery was still a novelty, even in Mexico, where, despite the international prestige gained by the mural painters, the idea of a public willing to spend money on the work of Mexican artists was just beginning to take root. Wealthy Mexicans and Central Americans typically were willing to purchase European art or local reproductions of European paintings, because they viewed Europe as the center and standard of fine art. Coupled with this reluctance or blindness in the presence of their own artists was a profound mistrust of any equation that involved art and financial gain. Many artists refused to charge high prices for their work, hoping to maintain a certain moral integrity through poverty. Others insisted on making a good living from their art and suffered the suspicion and criticism of those who clung to the belief that the true artist must remain beyond the reach of material temptation.

The first art gallery in Mexico, Inés Amor's Galería de Arte Mexicano, opened in the basement of her family's home in 1935. It became the best-known and most influential gallery in a city that eventually came to recognize the worth of its own artists and began investing in their work with enthusiasm. By 1975 there were one hundred galleries in the Mexican capital, but in 1947, when Clementina started calling her living space a gallery, the Mexican art world, even the gallery of the proper and aristocratic Inés Amor, was characterized by the excitement, freedom, and idealism of a creative movement not yet marked by time and success. Passages from Inés Amor's memoirs suggest fun and energy combined with seriousness of purpose: "In those days when we would all get together in the Gallery and when everyone would critique each other's work in a candid and honest way, there was more of an opportunity to learn and improve. I believe that now, because of a lack of communication, many artists don't have the perspective they need to see themselves. I remember that before every new painter who came along was carefully scrutinized by the others. On Saturdays we would have a live model from four to eight in the afternoon and anyone could come: it was an opportunity for those just beginning to mix with the more accomplished artists. . . . We were always in a good mood, always ready to enjoy ourselves, parties galore, everything from get-togethers in the studios to dances in the Salón Leda."[6]

But while the Mexican art community may have been inspired by a sense of mission and newness, it was also plagued by an intense individualism and competition. A strident nationalism plus a desire to maintain his position of prominence led the influential Diego Rivera to the extreme of requesting that the Mexican government forbid the entry into the country of art by non-Mexicans. And he was not alone in his xenophobia. As Inés Amor observed, "There was enormous rejection by Mexican painters of foreign exiles. . . . On the other hand, the exiles were fascinated by the Mexican landscape and Mexican nature, by pre-Colombian and folk art, but I believe they were able to find very few residents of the city interested in befriending them. I have the impression they felt out of place, in fact they were, because Mexico never managed to understand them" (121).

One of the results of this combination of professional envy and incomprehension was that many of the foreign artists in Mexico, according to Amor, "led extremely bohemian life-styles, since they had no steady work . . . they lived rather like gypsies; besides the fact that they had arrived here with nothing" (120). It was understandable, then, that so many Central American artists gravitated to Clementina's gallery, which, perhaps to address the imbalance created by Inés Amor's specifically Mexican gallery, she chose to name Gallery of Central American Art. But Clementina had neither the social position, the connections, nor the money that were instrumental in Inés Amor's success. The Galería de Arte Centroamericano was not "professional"; it was, rather, a reflection of Clementina. As one observer described it to me, "it was an incredible environment, a vortex of writers and artists, the best and brightest intellectuals."

The way she blended the many roles she played has led to a wide variety of interpretations of Clementina's role in Central American culture and has contributed to the portrait of many faces that is the Clementina myth. She doesn't really care about art or know anything about it, they say; she only wants to make money from it. She doesn't really care about art; she's an egomaniac who only wants everyone to paint her portrait. She is a poor man's patron of the arts. She is a fairy godmother who helped many young artists get a start. She promotes Central American art: through her exhibits she helped establish its presence and consolidate its identity. She doesn't care about art; she just likes to have artists as lovers. She is a true egalitarian in her acceptance of young and old, revered artists and unknown talents. She only cares to associate with important people. And so on. And Clementina has contributed to the confusion by refusing to separate the strands of her life. Even today, her home is her gallery is her work is her income is where she has parties. She invites people in and kicks them out with equal ease. The artists she deals with are often also her friends and drinking companions, so when she charges a commission on a sale there is sometimes misunderstanding. But Clementina has placed the burden of comprehension and interpretation on the observer, because she long ago figured out that you can't please everyone, that whatever you do or say is bound to be misconstrued by someone, so you might as well do as you please and to hell with everyone else.

Francisco Amighetti is one of the many artists whose relationship with Clementina went beyond a superficial exchange of services. They first met in San José, Costa Rica, in the mid-1930s. He remembers that she didn't always have enough money to travel, but she would travel anyway, getting by as best she could. He considers her unique in that she was a woman who traveled alone. Being himself an inveterate traveler of limited resources, he was able to appreciate Clementina's wanderlust as well as marvel at her courage and independence. He traveled throughout Central and South America, often on foot, painting, drawing, engraving, and writing poems and travel memoirs.[7] In 1943 he received a scholarship to study art at the University of New Mexico. Realizing that the faculty did not have much to teach him, he traveled to Taos, where he met a number of the interesting individuals who formed part of the artistic community that centered around the home of Mabel Dodge Luhan. He then went to New York City and stayed in Harlem, drawn to yet depressed by the contrasts of wealth and poverty, violence and human solidarity. In 1947, when he went to Mexico to study mural painting, he showed Clementina the engravings and the journal-like prose text he produced in Harlem. He found himself in that typical impoverished predicament of many non-Mexican artists in Mexico. He had come to study, without a scholarship, so he got a job working with Nicaraguan poet and publisher Pablo Antonio Cuadra, who had started up a publishing house in Mexico. He received a salary only sporadically so was unable to pay the rent at his pensión. He had heard that Clementina had a boardinghouse of sorts, so he moved in, paying when he had the money, otherwise paying with artwork, primarily watercolors and portraits of Alba, Silvia, and Clementina. When Clementina saw the powerful woodcuts depicting scenes from Harlem—children playing in parks, prostitutes leaning out of windows, billiard parlors, dance halls, bars, glowing street lamps, violence, and alienation—she must have been reminded of her own lonely and difficult hiatus in New York.

Clementina was always full of cultural projects and good intentions, some of which she saw through to completion. Others were truncated because of the difficulties presented by lack of funds, public interest, or support or because some people interpret her efforts as attempts at self-aggrandizement. Other projects bloomed in the first flush of new enthusiasm, only to be abandoned when she was inspired by the need to move on. In the disorganized but creative atmosphere of her Mexican gallery-pensión, where it is rumored that Miguel Angel Asturias corrected drafts of *El Señor Presidente* at her kitchen table and Augusto Monterroso, Carlos Illescas, and Otto Raúl González discussed poetry and politics, Clementina dreamed of a cultural matriarchy with herself on the throne, encouraging Central American artists, promoting their work, publishing Central American poetry, sponsoring poetry readings and book-signing parties.

Her first such project was to found Ediciones Galería de Arte Centroamericano and publish Amighetti's Harlem memoirs in 1947 under the title *Francisco en Harlem* (Francisco in Harlem). The book is a sensitive, sometimes bemused, sometimes horrified vision of Harlem in words and pictures. The thirty-one woodcuts and the accompanying journal of the artist's solitude and penury were printed on rustic paper in an edition of one thousand copies. Clementina's introductory remarks succinctly describe the book as well as her grandiose plans for future publications.

> The Central American Art Gallery, in accordance with its program of artistic and cultural promotion, proposes to publish the works of new creative artists of the Isthmus, whose fresh interpretation of art breaks with the decayed and ivory-tower concepts of the past.
>
> At the same time we are working toward promoting Central American writing throughout the Continent, in an effort to make our literary movements known.
>
> We initiate our publications with *Francisco in Harlem,* the bitter tale of an artist who confronts the difficult conditions of the capitalist regime, where success is little more than a distant dream. The book is written in a plain style, sincere and suffused with a subtle irony. In addition, it contains 31 woodcuts by the author, which beautifully illustrate its contents.

Unfortunately for Central American art and literature, this initial effort had no successor during the life of the Galería. But Clementina did become more sophisticated at getting done the grass-roots work of cultural promotion, i.e. fund-raising, acquiring scholarships for young talent, gaining state and private support, and so her subsequent projects in El Salvador and Honduras were more numerous. Yet, given Clementina's talents and inclinations, her contributions to culture were often interpersonal: gatherings, encouragement, moral support, a place to sleep, locating buyers, organizing exhibits—which makes *Francisco in Harlem* a precious and palpable testimony to her unique brand of social commitment.

Gines Parra (French). Oil, not dated.

Above: Jorge González Camarena (Mexico). Oil, c. 1930.

Augusto Monterroso (Guatemala). Caricature, c. 1930.

Attributed to Diego Rivera (Mexico). Oil, c. 1930.

Francisco Amighetti (Costa Rica). Watercolor, 1947.

José Mejía Vides (El Salvador).
Charcoal drawing, 1948.

Below: Luis Angel Salinas
(El Salvador). Oil, c. 1957.

Francisco Zúñiga (Costa Rica). Oil, c. 1958.

Facing page: Miguel Angel Ruiz Matute (Honduras). Oil, c. 1960.

Aníbal Cruz (Honduras). Oil, c. 1970.

Facing page: Gelasio Giménez (Cuba). Oil (c. 1968).

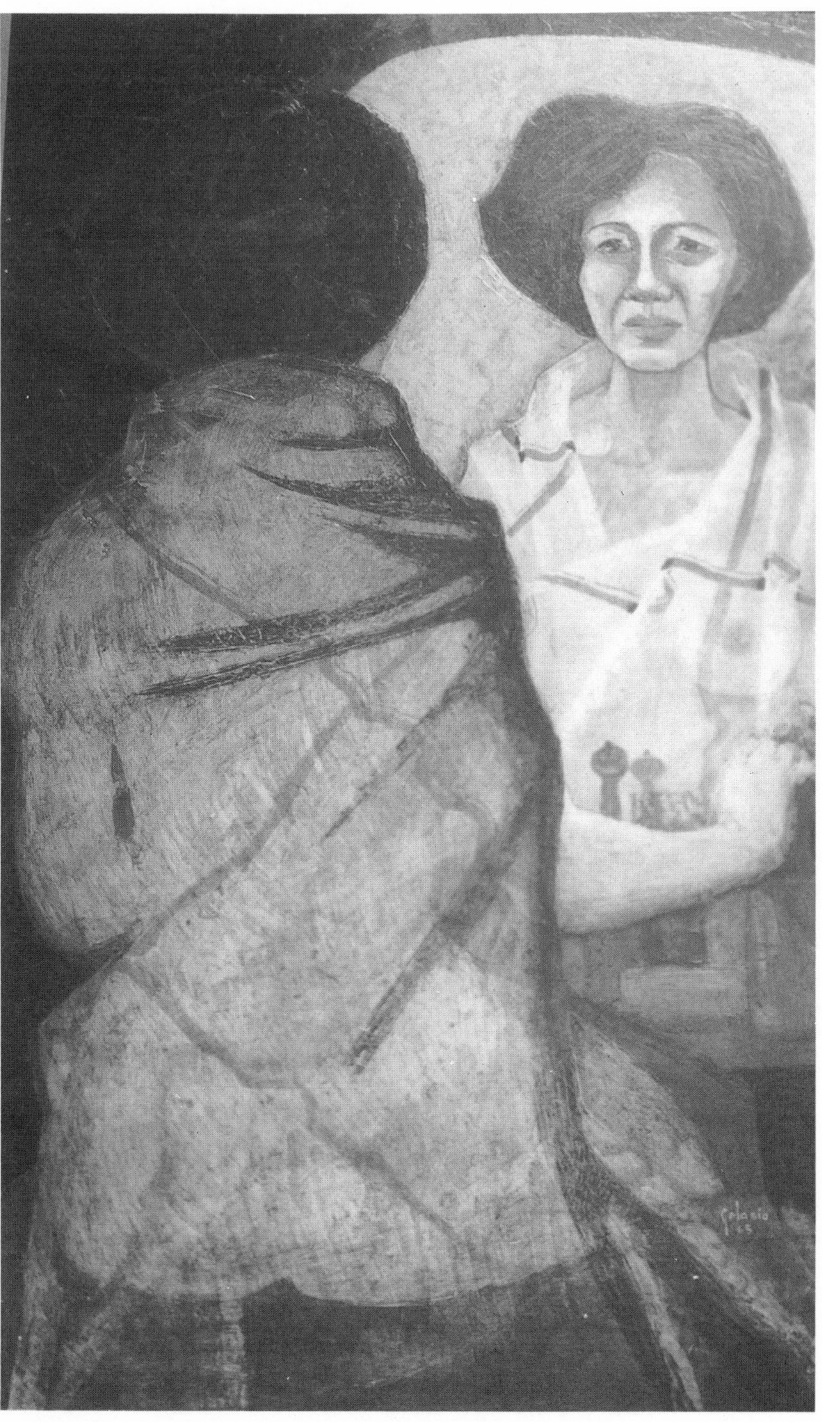

Luis Suárez (*seated*) flanked by his brothers Angel and Pío.

Amelia Zelaya de Suárez.

Victoria Bertrand,
a childhood friend of Clementina's
from Juticalpa, also a poet.

Clementina in Tegucigalpa, c. 1930. The poster on the wall is for a poetry recitation at the National Theatre, Tegucigalpa.

Clementina posing with her doll collection.

A seductive pose, c. 1930.

A publicity stunt to sell her magazine *Mujer,* c. 1935.

Cover illustration for *Mujer*.

Clementina with her daughters Alba and Silvia, c. 1933.

At an international peace conference, Mexico City.
Clementina (*center*) is the only woman present.

Clementina c. 1940.

José Mejía Vides, a Salvadoran painter and Clementina's second husband, c. 1950.

At Rancho del Artista with Costa Rican sculptor Francisco Zúñiga, c. 1955.

Clementina in El Salvador with Luis Angel Salinas (*left*) and Camilo Minero (*right*), c. 1957.

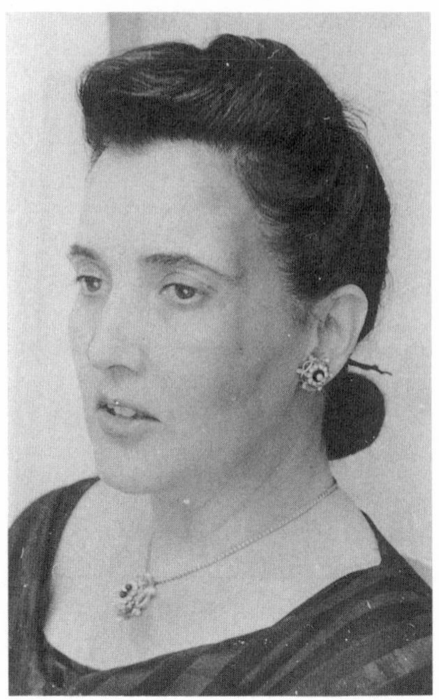

Claudia Lars, a Salvadoran poet and Clementina's friend.

Miguel Angel Asturias, Clementina's friend and fellow Central American writer.

Above: At a ceremony in her honor sponsored by the National Autonomous University of Honduras, Tegucigalpa, 1969. Medardo Mejía (*left*) and Cecilio Zelaya, rector of the university (*right*).

Reciting her poetry, Tegucigalpa, c. 1967.

Galería Clementina Suárez, Barrio La Hoya, Tegucigalpa, 1989.

Surrounded by her art collection, c. 1980.

In her gallery with Honduran artist Luis H. Padilla (*left*) and playwright Francisco Salvador (*right*), c. 1980.

With Nelly Sermeño, wife of Salvadoran ceramic artist Cesar Sermeño, Tegucigalpa, 1989.

At home, Tegucigalpa, 1989.

Growing with the Grass

After *From Disillusion to Hope* in 1944, Clementina published no more books of poetry until 1957, when *Growing with the Grass* was awarded a national poetry prize and subsequently published by the Ministry of Culture of El Salvador. However, there is evidence that at least some of the eight poems that form this book were written as early as 1945.[8] Because this work is central in her self-definition, and because it is strong and beautiful poetry, it is reproduced here in its entirety.

In the simple dedication, "Thus: / From comrade to comrade" (Así / De compañera a compañero), we encounter the essential ambiguity that marks the entire composition—the poet is in fact not her companion's comrade, perhaps not even his companion; rather, they are lovers. But she wants to transform a relationship based on sexual intensity into one that is both intimate as well as in touch with the world. She learned in the writing of *Sails* and *From Disillusion to Hope* that the individual self is nothing if it is not joined to the collective self. Her goal now is to convince her lover to embrace this new vision. We saw in *From Disillusion to Hope* that her efforts to achieve the longed-for multiple self had resulted in even greater solitude. She now focuses on the dyad as a possible conduit for the self to achieve fulfillment and transcendence.

The first poem prefigures the succeeding thematic structure: it juxtaposes possibility and failure, returning again and again to the sources of life and death, light and darkness. Metaphors that appear here are repeated later, their significance widening and becoming richer as they are used in ever expanding fields of reference. Rose, thorn, corola, blood, star, root, furrow, sprig, and ash are all objects of nature that suggest death or rebirth, transcendence or earthiness. They are called upon to construct an intimate story of a tender and once satisfying love that fails to grow in consciousness and comradeship. The spectre of destiny is ever present, implying that the poet has followed her star, has been faithful to her inner voice, implying further a superior vision that the lover either cannot or refuses to follow.

I.
It tried to be.
But there was the thorn,

the rose's eternal enemy.
And alone,
adrift,
the lost corola of my dream.

And it was.
In that sad fold
of my blood
where the smile paled,
turned to ice
on your vacant breast.

The rose, obeying its fate,
offered its flowery
candor.

Love will burn your bones.
Child of the air!
Dove of dawn!
Only in quickened blood
will the creative seed be safe.

Not for this will you
drop the star.
Human bonds hold no sway
over your visage, resurrected through the ages.

Graceful, body of angel,
a river runs its blood through your veins.
River that carries
the broken source of darkness.

Your fingers will never learn
to retain the lost gesture.
What seed has not found a furrow in your hand,
or an immaculate nest
in the hollow of your lap?

No road blocks the sky from itself.
All conspires to bring you to the level of your wound.

With myself. With you. Alone.
The blood is bound
to roots it does not comprehend.

Pudo ser.
Pero estaba la espina,
eterna enemiga de la rosa.
Y sola, sin orillas,
la perdida corola de mi sueño.

Y fue.
En aquel pliegue triste
de mi sangre
donde, pálida quedó la sonrisa
que se hizo hielo
sobre tu pecho ausente.

Obediente la rosa a su destino,
tuvo que ir mostrando
el candor de su rostro.

Te quemará el amor los huesos.
¡Niña del Aire!
¡Paloma del amanecer!
Ya que solo en la sangre despierta
estará el germen creador defendido.

No caerá por eso
la estrella de tu mano.
Ligaduras humanas no detienen
tu rostro, ya salvado en mil edades.

Esbelta, en tu talle de ángel,
un río es la sangre en tus venas.
Agua que trae y que lleva
la quebrada raíz de la sombra.

Tus dedos nunca sabrán
rescatar el ademán que va perdido.

¿Qué semilla no encontró surco en tu mano,
ni inmaculado nido
en el hueco de tu rodilla?

Ningún camino aparta al cielo de su cielo.
Todo te alza a la altura de tu llaga.
Conmigo. Contigo. Sola.
Atada va la sangre
a raíces que no entiende.

After establishing the truth of her vision, or her vision of the truth, the poet goes on to confess to her lover that she has realized that he is not the superior being she had hoped for. But because she loves him, she will continue her poem, hoping to make him see what she sees.

II.
So you see that
my breast illuminates
a magnificent truth.
The angels of my blood
are rebel angels.

And I am shamed by your soul bound
and your heart closed
by slavish laws.

When I first could hear they told me:
Little one: Don't turn your face from love.
For only thus will your flower have pollen
and float free,
showering multitudes,
your face growing with the grass.

Various are the ways of the flesh
and only the wind will save
your step, lost
in ashes . . .

Child of my love!
Only when the fire

carries you toward my cry,
will you recover intact
the wheat that ripens
inside your flesh.

I would have to die and not want you.
Beat my back
and bind my tongue
not to tell you
that the buds are weeping within you
the rivers are blocked,
because you deny the furrow
its due.

Ya ves cómo
mi pecho ilumina
una verdad tremenda.
Los ángeles que pasean por mi sangre
son ángeles rebeldes.

Y me humilla tu rostro atado
y tu corazón cerrado
por un mandato de siervos.

Cuando yo oí me dijeron:
Pequeña: No le niegues al amor tu cara.
Sólo así tu flor tendrá polen
y flotará libre,
goteando muchedumbres,
tu cara creciendo con la hierba.

Distintos son los rumbos de la carne
y sólo el viento salvará
a tu pie, que en la ceniza
quedó extraviado . . .

¡Criatura de mi amor!
Sólo cuando el fuego

te lleve hasta mi grito,
recuperarás intacta
la espiga que dentro
de tu piel madura.

Fuera necesario morirme y no quererte.
Golpearme la espalda
y atar mi lengua
para no decirte
que están en ti llorando los brotes
y detenidos los arroyos,
porque le niegas al surco
lo que es del surco.

But can he hear her? Is he even listening? She had been so happy with him, but now it is too late. Things changed, and their love was no longer a unifying embrace. She insists that poetry is her salvation—even though it is also what divides them.

III.
Do you hear me?
Are you listening to what I am telling you?
I who would hold back my song
and let death adorn
even my naked womb.

Before watching you from so far away,
from where
a planet breaks open
between my fingers.

I could say nothing more to you.
Every sign wounded me,
Without realizing it, I began to take my leave,
to loosen myself
from the bad habits of my feet,
your own words caused it.

Suddenly, something was different.
you were no longer you,
I was no longer myself.

Clay rose up
to unite and divide us
in concentric rings
of different ages.

I would have liked to bind myself to you
and ask you nothing.
Leave unwatered the vine
that grows in me.
But there was, between us,
an intractable sword
that would not allow it!

The word wandered free
in the air,
indestructible
within my cry.

I bruise so easily
that the sound of glass breaking
is painful.
It is enough that
your stony facade moves.
You don't see that I rise, tremble
with eyes closed.

I would exchange this blood
for one that could touch your roots,
strip you naked with my branch
of clean bones
of all that is not
an innocent cover
obedient to your pulse.

———

¡Me oyes!
¿Estás oyendo lo que te digo yo?
La que quisiera detener el canto
y dejar que la muerte decorara
hasta mi desnudo vientre.

Antes de mirarte de tan lejos,
desde donde
hay un planeta que se quiebra
entre mis dedos.

Y no pude decirte más.
Me dolían todas mis marcas.
Y sin saberlo, empecé a despedirme,
a despegarme
de los resabios de mis pies,
por tus mismas palabras.

De repente, algo fue distinto.
Ni tú te llamabas tú
ni yo me llamaba yo.

El barro crecido
nos unía y separaba
en mil anillos
de diferente edad.

Hubiera querido amarrarme a ti
y no preguntarte nada.
Dejar inconclusa
la vid que conmigo crece.
Pero habita, entre nosotros dos,
una espada arisca,
que no me lo permitió!

La palabra iba suelta
en el aire,
indestructible
dentro de mi llanto.

Es tan fácil herirme,
que un pequeño ruido
de cristal lo logra.
Basta que tu inmóvil
faz se mueva.
Y no me sientas subir, estremecerme
con los ojos cerrados.

Reemplazar quisiera esta sangre
por otra sangre que te tocara las raíces,
y te dejara desnudo mi ramo de huesos
limpios
de todo lo que no fuera
una inocente corteza
que acatara tu latido.

The life that the poet endeavors to articulate is a force, a conviction growing inside her. Melding with the romantic tradition of art perceived as a talisman against death, a creation that will live beyond the physical duration of its creator, the poet senses that love and communion with another human being will strangle her, cut off her voice. She gathers her strength to defy mortal love, choosing instead to be faithful to the call of poetic immortality. But, living out her destiny to long for human love although cognizant of its limitations, she tries to convince him to join her.

IV.
Go slowly,
for the child of air
kicking in my womb
grows.

Piece by piece
I cover
with rarefied air
that which will live
even after death.

The urgency of my step
is but a symbol

—nothing is mine—
an arrow bends me
inside your love.

Do you not sense petals
falling in my temples?
Do you not feel my hands
offering you the rose,
its touch and fragrance?

And that my dream
is an open artery
that burns the worm.
That you need a new name
to find
your childhood
smile.

That is what I had to tell you,
before your love
swallows my voice.

Tell you of this
double life
of night and insomnia
in the sobbing confusion.

Do not think I will come to you
barb in hand.
I had already abandoned
every thornbush
in order to find you.

Float in the radiance of my lightning!
Do not forget
that the fragile passing
of a miracle is fleet.

That the life I ask of you
is not yours

but full,
unquenchable,
immortal life.

Searching
I reach deep within you
to the tree that regales you
that embraces and holds you.
And perhaps even keeps you
from your best self.

———

Despacio,
que está madurándose
la criatura de espuma
que se queja en mi entraña.
Copo a copo,
voy cubriendo
de alta atmósfera
lo que vivirá,
aún detrás de la muerte.

La urgencia de mi paso
es un puro símbolo
—nada es mío—
una flecha me curva
dentro de tu amor.

¿No sientes deshojarse
pétalos dentro de mis sienes?
¿No sientes que mis manos
te adelantan la rosa,
el aroma y el tacto?

Y que mi sueño
es una arteria abierta
que calcina al gusano.
Y que precisas otro nombre
para encontrarte

con la sonrisa
de tu primer niñez.

Eso era lo que me faltaba decirte,
antes que tu amor
la boca me consuma.

Hablarte
de este doble vivir
en la noche y la trasnoche
de una sollozante bruma.

Nunca esperes que te traiga
una espina en la mano.
Para venir y para buscarte,
ya había dejado
todos los abrojos.

¡Flota en la luz de mi relámpago!
No olvides
que el paso frágil
de un milagro rápido huye.

Y que la vida que te pido,
no es tu vida,
sino que la copiosa,
inagotable.
La inmortal vida.

Buscando
voy dentro de tu fondo
al árbol que te viste
y te abraza y te estrecha.
Y tal vez hasta te separa
de tu mejor forma.

In the fifth section, the lyric voice calls out and in turn answers its own doubts. The dialectic that was established in the first poem and continues, still unresolved, in the fifth can be seen in various ways. It is the lyric voice engaged in bringing together the two major tones of its song; it is a soul in the throes of growth, determined to incorporate a new vision into itself; it is a woman calling on her mate to grow and change with her so they can continue to share their lives; it is a specific woman, Clementina Suárez, still in love with love, still looking for her Prince Charming to complete her life, still hard to please, except that her image of her ideal man has been modified. He is no longer only the virile and sensitive male who will bring her fully to life and be her inspiration; he is now a man who is strong enough to go beyond egotism, tradition, or self-centered knowledge to embrace a higher ideal. She never calls the ideal by name, but it is something new—an image of freedom, collectivity, and future. Her new image of the ideal man implies the primacy of relationship over the individual quest and suggests a relationship of equality and cross-fertilization. At this point in the poem, however, she is in control, hoping with her desire to fecundate man.

V.
How often
I have been
separate from you,
asleep
in love's water.
Intact behind you,
with you in absence.

And my voice,
that you never heard before,
spoke to you
of things between us
that my blinded eyes
never saw.

Since then
I knew
the day would come
when, looking in my eyes
you would find a flower gone mad.

Take it away from the mirror
you would say.
It changes your size,

chokes your face,
you are lost in its steady gaze.

In such uncontained gesture
will you find yourself
guarding waves in my forehead.

Leave your root behind!
Widen your world!
See the agony
and the affliction.

Perhaps
with kisses
we can conquer
our flowering verse-garden.

Burning words
awaken us.
We cannot remain alone,
arrive late, refuse to act
in this stubborn
half-light.

The dawn let loose
in the flesh
cries out to us,
that our marrow
carries a new brilliance
for the submissive shaft of wheat.

I know that the measure
I am giving you is not mine,
nor is the mourning,
nor the salt, nor the ash.

That there is a related tenderness
in my supple stem
that seeks its balance in you
to find herself.

Unbound,
in your endless blue
I attain a graceful
resurrection into life.

Perhaps
because I have come to see
that the sphenoid bone
is not the most important.
That there is scattered life
impaled on trenchant daggers
that we must release.

In this honorable vision,
hard-won and exemplary,
we are entwined,
no longer as if in a question,
or an adventure,
or in some elastic posture.

But as possessing unconditionally
a truth
that leapt from breast to sky
from sky to breast,
like an authentic world
free and without borders.

———

Cuántas veces
he estado
de ti separada,
dormida
en tu mejor agua.
Intacta detrás de ti,
contigo en la ausencia.

Y mi voz,
la que nunca antes oyera,
te hablaba

de cosas interpuestas
que mis quebrantados ojos
nunca vieron.

Y desde entonces
estuve segura
de que vendría un día
en que viéndome a los ojos
encontraras en mis pupilas
una flor enloquecida.

Quítala del espejo,
me dirías.
Transforma tu tamaño,
te ahoga el rostro
y te pierde en su vigilia.

En tal forma desmesurada,
te verás custodiando
olas en mi frente.

¡Echa tu raíz atrás!
¡Ensancha tu mundo!
Percibe la agonía
y la congoja.

Que acaso
con el beso y el beso,
lleguemos a conquistar
nuestro carmen florido.

Palabras encendidas
nos están despertando.
No podemos quedar solos,
tardar, estar inmóviles
dentro de esta
porfiada penumbra.

El alba que va suelta
dentro de la carne

nos está gritando,
que nuestra médula
arrastra un fulgor nuevo
para la espiga sometida.

Yo sé que no es mía
la pauta que te voy dando,
ni es mío el luto,
ni la sal ni la ceniza.

Que hay una conexa ternura
en mi dócil tallo,
que busca en ti su equilibrio
para encontrarse.

Sin contorno,
en tu inagotable azul,
alcanzo una resurrección
grácil para la vida.

Tal vez
porque he podido llegar a descifrar
que los esfenoides del cuerpo
no son lo más importante.
Que hay una esparcida vida
mordida por agudos puñales
que debemos librar.

Y con esta honrada visión
y esta ganada excelsitud,
quedamos enlazados,
ya no en una interrogación,
ni en una aventura,
ni en ninguna elástica posición.

Sino dueños absolutos
de una verdad
que saltaba del pecho al cielo
y del cielo al pecho,

como un auténtico mundo
libre y sin riberas.

The sixth poem is a tender love poem of beginnings and wonder. In the context of the larger poem in which it is embedded, it is more a vision of desire than a memory, although it has characteristics of both. The woman imagines that she has found her ideal lover, or that her current though imperfect mate has been transformed, and she describes the tenderness and joy she experiences with him. She touches his dewy eyelids, her soul leaps like a fish, they stand on the shores of the future, they are new in time—fresh, clean, childlike. The metaphors that integrate the previous poems and give them an earthy, primordial texture are absent here. We find instead an unfurrowed brow, a lifted face, a pure flower, eternal renewal, and joyful endurance.

VI.
From your warm bed
I rise up
singing.

With a radiant feeling
for the Universe
and for love.

Nothing hammers my brow
or my eyes!
I am sure of the size
of my dreams

and I flourish them gaily.

You have been a haven of tenderness!
In your arms I have seen
the ripening of all my fruit.

On this first of days
how lightly your lids
cover your eyes.

For my own
ingenuous joy
I told you again and again:

Close your eyes!
They look so
clean to me.

Drops of dew
cling to your lashes.
You are
new in time,
as in the first moment upon awakening.

For the first time you are balanced
by an unequivocal passion,
that does not rob the rose
of its harmony
or its memory.

I must have loved you
and heard you
in all your voices.

As if inside my body
you had left a child
who yet remained . . .

I was ready
to love you,
I could offer you
my lifted face
brimming with honey.

And what's more,
I knew
that dressed in white,
in blood or in sand,
the purity of my flower
is above reproach.

In you I can abide
with undiminished faith.
Leap like a fish
in wind or water.

Together now, clear,
not thinking that love
is a cross
to bear.

Being in your past,
remembering your presence,
yes, your impossible presence.

Walking your winters,
always beginning.
Insisting that time
reveal its secrets,
until it proffers us
an unweary sea.

Only thus,
on the shores of a life
that joyfully seeks
to endure,
will we begin to be happy, to want to be.

Taking on the task
knowing that only
through human love
can one be happy.

Without the sterility
of unequal,
solitary happiness.

De tu lecho tibio
me incorporo,
cantando.

Con un sentido radiante
del Universo
y del amor.

Nada golpea mi frente
¡ni mis ojos!
Estoy segura del tamaño
de mis sueños
y los agito con alegría.

¡Qué ternura la de tu regazo!
Madurar vi en ella
todos mis frutos.

Y en este primer día
qué livianos tus párpados
encima de los ojos.

Para mi propia
ingenua alegría.
Te decía y te volvía a decir:

¡Cierra los ojos!
qué limpios
los estoy mirando.

Cuelgan gotas de rocío
de tus pestañas.
Estás,
como en el primer despertar,
nuevo en el tiempo.

Estrenas el equilibrio
de un exacto ardor,
que no quita a la rosa
ni su armonía
ni su nostalgia.

Tendría que haberte amado
y escuchado
en todas tus voces.

Como si dentro del cuerpo
hubieras dejado un hijo
y estuviera todavía . . .

Que para quererte,
ya estaba despierta,
mi rostro levantado
podía ofrecerte
con sostenida miel.

Y además,
sabía
que vestida de azahar,
de sangre o de arena,
el pudor de mi trébol
no se discute.

Habitar puedo en ti
con inalterable fe.
En el viento o en el agua
saltar como pez.

Juntos ya, sin nieblas,
sin pensar que el amor
es una cruz
y lastima.

Estar en tu pasado,
recordar tu presencia
y hasta tu imposible presencia.

Andar tus inviernos,
empezando siempre.
Someter al tiempo
a que rompa sus cifras,
hasta que logre entregarnos
un mar sin fatiga.

Sólo así,
a orillas de la vida

que busca jubilosa
algo duradero.

Empezaremos.
A ser felices,
a quererlo ser.

Asumiendo el deber
de que sólo
por un camino humano
se puede ser feliz.

Sin lo estéril
de la desigual,
solitaria felicidad.

The weight of the material world has been momentarily lifted and the beauty of pure human communion envisioned in its place. But the respite is momentary, replaced in the following poem by doubt, disappointment, and pettiness. Meanwhile, the poet grows in self-assurance. She answers her lover's complaint that she is no longer the woman she once was by reminding him that he is still the man he always was, and that is not good enough. She returns to elemental metaphors, urging him to renew his commitment to life. In the final lines she is born, literally and figuratively. She rises from the ashes, she emerges from the womb, she creates herself in dialogue with him, not changing to be as he wants her to be, not waiting to be filled or inspired by him, but by breaking away.

VII.
My friend, you may say:
your heart, for you to love me,
is not where it should be.

It is too wide,
a harbor,
limitless dawn.

It is listening to
man's lament
and his urgent desire
to be free.

Today it knows that men,
if they work and suffer,
bled dry and agonizing,
do it to have life,
to love life.

All this I understand
with gentler care,
making my body smaller
in your memory.

But you have not been here yet
and the path of your star
is unsure.

For you to hear me,
I would have to wear
my bride's gown again.

I would have to light up
the corners
and find the dresses
where forgetfulness
molders.

Not even then. An ashen hoof
would crush my madness.
And we would never
reach the star.

You must waken.
Raise your bones
from their sleep.
Leave yourself naked,
voluntary,
changed.

You cannot wait
for the ants

to eat out
your eyes.

How can you sleep
in empty beds,
when there is a cry for help
and an open wound
that blood reclaims.

I am being born
before your eyes,
angels and seeds
cling to me.

———

Amigo, tal vez digas:
tu corazón, para quererme,
no está en su sitio.

Es más ancho,
más puerto,
más alba sin frontera.

Oyendo está la queja
de los hombres
y sus urgentes ansias
por ser libres.

Hoy sabe que los hombres,
si sufren y trabajan
estrujados y agónicos,
es por tener su vida
y por amarla.

Todo esto lo comprendo
con más suave cariño,
haciendo más pequeño
mi cuerpo en tu recuerdo.

Pero si no has podido llegar
y el paso de tu estrella
está indeciso.

Para que me oyeras,
tendría que vestirme
de novia nuevamente.

Tendría que iluminar
los rincones
y encontrar los vestidos
donde dejan su musgo
los olvidos.

Ni así. Pezuña de ceniza
apagaría mi frenesí.
Y nunca
llegaríamos al astro.

Tienes que despertar.
Levantar a tu esqueleto,
del sueño.

Dejarte desnudo,
voluntario,
distinto.

No puedes esperar
a que te coman
los ojos
las hormigas.

Cómo dormir
en los vacíos lechos,
cuando hay una queja
y un abierto costado
que reclama la sangre.

Naciendo estoy,
visiblemente,

y trepándome van criaturas
ángeles y semillas.

In the final arc of the dialectic, the poem's ambiguity reaches its resolution. The poet steps outside of the closed circle of the dyad and, in a twist of paradox, through her individuation becomes multiple.

VIII.
Before,
in our daytime,
I was only one.

Now,
in our night,
I multiply in my wounded
flesh
the voices of spent women,
of mothers
their furrows ripped
by daggers
and
of young girls with hands
full of thorns.

Before,
in our night,
my voice was a cry
and no more than a cry.

Today,
so close now to the dawn,
I carry rivers alive
with women who scream
as I do,
with worn air
for the liberated shore,
for the lily,
for barrenness and for love.

My pleas are both
life and joyful death.
You can dismiss my roses,
but not the burning corola
of my dream,
made greater with the need
of other dreams.

And you, tell me,
are you with me
in this circle of my blood,
or do you still search for me
in the tracks
of my sunken footsteps?

———

Antes,
en nuestro día
era yo sólo una.

Ahora,
en nuestra noche,
multiplico en mi carne
dolorida
voces de hembras deshechas,
de madres
con el surco
clavado de puñales
y
de niñas que tienen
las manos con espinas.

Antes,
en nuestra noche,
era un llanto mi voz
y sólo un llanto.

Hoy,
ya tan cerca del alba,

traigo despiertos ríos
de mujeres que gritan
como yo,
con el aire oxidado
por la salvada orilla,
para la azucena,
el yermo y el amor.

Mis ruegos se dividen
en vida o muerte jubilosa.
Tú puedes apartar mis rosas,
pero no la encendida
corola de mi sueño,
más grande con el ansia
de otros sueños.

¿Y tú, dime,
estás conmigo
en este círculo de mi sangre,
o me sigues buscando
por la huella
de mis pies hundidos?

Creciendo con la hierba, like an abstract dance, begins at the first moment in time, creating time and space with movement. There is no decoration in these poem dances; they exist on an elemental plane where powerful metaphors are placed in relation to nothing beyond themselves. Clementina's lyric voice has traveled to the source of her own inspiration to bring forth her own birth-resurrection. The space that the voice inhabits and creates is a place of male-female bonding as well as a woman space, where the individual female voice, while retaining its primordial identity, has achieved a new dimension, for the woman has seen and succeeded in identifying herself. She then calls on man to accompany her in this adventure of the soul, because surely it will be lonely on this new planet. She is the prophet calling man to see what she has seen, turning back to bring her companion with her; she is the seer who must return to tell her people so they too can see.

But what has she seen? Because some of her previous poetry is of a committed, combative nature, it is tempting to read this work as a poem of revolutionary consciousness-raising. Indeed, references such as "hombres / [que] sufren y trabajan" (men / who suffer and work) make that a legitimate interpretation. But it is also a poem about vision. It is about seeing life from the inside out, a joining of spirit and matter.

Clementina never lived this vision of male-female union in the world outside of poetry. When I asked her if she thought it was possible to achieve her ideal relationship, she said, "*Yes, but only if both people are truly revolutionaries.*" Unfortunately, she added, she has never known any couple who had attained this level of enlightenment. In her own case: "*the obstacle has been my poetry.*" The couples that stay together are never composed of two equally strong-willed or self-involved individuals. The kind of spiritual and physical communion that Clementina dreamed of she experienced only fleetingly, with different men for periods of time, but never on a sustained basis. Indeed, the men she actually married or lived with were men quite unlikely to be her soul mates. Getting married, as marriage is traditionally understood, implies settling down, something that Clementina was never able to do. The men she speaks of as being men with whom she felt she was able truly to communicate were all deeply centered in a belief or a life-style. She is evasive when asked if she might have liked to marry one of these exceptional men; perhaps she realized that part of the reason they were exceptional to her was precisely because her relation to them was not domestic.

One of these men was Medardo Mejía. Born in 1907 in a small town in Olancho not far from Juticalpa, he moved to Clementina's hometown as a young boy, and the two became close friends. He was from a poor family, but he managed to become a lawyer because of his intelligence and determination. A teacher, poet, and journalist, he was one of those dedicated revolutionaries who contributed to the fight for social change in Mexico, Guatemala, and El Salvador. He lived simply all his life but managed to travel to Europe and the Soviet Union, as well as throughout Central America. He founded *Ariel,* an important cultural and political journal of Honduras; he wrote numerous works of history, politics, and literature, including a comprehensive history of Honduras; and he received Honduras's Ramón Rosa National Literature Award in 1971. Yet for all his accomplishments, he remained unpretentious, even bohemian, in his habits.[9] He and Clementina loved and admired one another. Their paths crossed on occasion, there are rumors that they were lovers, but there was never any explicit commitment to complicate their friendship.

Francisco Amighetti was another soul brother to Clementina. They understood one another's restlessness, solitude, and love of travel. They are both great admirers of the opposite sex: Clementina loves men, and Francisco loves women, but their relationship remained platonic over the years, or so each insists. As Amighetti mused: "She was always telling me she loved me; she probably loved me the same way I loved her, but there was nothing amorous between us. Platonic. Platonic loves are the worst kind, in the sense of most intense. Platonic loves are never consummated, but they are very strong, they can produce poems. She used to dedicate poems to me. At parties when she recited she would say, 'This one is dedicated to Amighetti.' I think she improvised a lot."[10]

A third man with whom Clementina experienced a special communication, whom she once described as "*so esoteric, so removed from everyday concerns, so tremendously spiritual,*" was a unique figure in Central American letters, a man of multiple interests and talents, all of which took second place to an abiding devotion to spirituality. Salvador Salazar Arrué, who signed his name "Salarrué" to his stories, poems, novels, philosophical treatises, and paintings, was tall and charming, with fair skin, green eyes, and a look once described as that of one who "goes through life with his eyes open but dreaming."[11] A vegetarian and a theosophist, he projected an air of spontaneous and ingenuous simplicity. His writing was highly regarded not only in his native El Salvador, but throughout Central America.

Salarrué and Salvadoran poet Claudia Lars were great friends, and when Clementina moved to El Salvador in 1950 she renewed her friendship with both of them. She had known Claudia from the early 1930s in Costa Rica, and she had met Salarrué during previous visits to El Salvador. She felt that Claudia also understood her, because they shared a sense of the vital importance of poetry in their lives. "*Claudia and I would spend entire days talking! . . . Poetry was her life.*"

El Salvador

Clementina married José Mejía Vides after she had written *Growing with the Grass,* the poems that express so emphatically the desire for a mate whose love encompasses and transcends romantic love. One is tempted to think that she married him because she thought he was that man. When asked if she had achieved that relationship she was searching for with Chepe, as everyone called him, she answered, "*Once love is involved, it changes. One can love deeply, but there is always a part you hold back when you realize the other person's difference, when you realize there cannot be genuine communication with a being who is different.*"

José Mejía Vides had had a long and interesting career in art by the time he and Clementina married in 1949. In 1918, at the age of fifteen, he began his formal art studies at the Escuela Nacional de Artes Gráficas (National School for Graphic Arts) in San Salvador. This was the capital's first formal academy of art, barely five years old when José entered. In 1922 he was awarded a scholarship by the Mexican government to study art in Mexico City. He enrolled at the Escuela Nacional de Bellas Artes (National School for Fine Arts), where he took classes taught by the traditional method still prevalent at the time of copying paintings by the masters, but he was soon won over by the fresh, new approach to art practiced at the open-air schools. He became convinced that the practice of painting outdoors with live models was incomparably superior to the traditional academic method in use at the National School for Fine Arts. He was also impressed by the Mexican government's support of its artists through exhibits at the National University and through the purchase of their works. When he returned to El Salvador in 1927 he was full of enthusiasm and tried to convince the appropriate officials to support his efforts to found outdoor painting schools and to exhibit his work at the University, but El Salvador was not ready to adopt the radical experiments of the revolutionary Mexican government. There were no art galleries in El Salvador at the time, and no art museum, so José, undaunted, held his first exhibit in a basketball court in the National Gymnasium in 1929. One can begin to appreciate the dedication required to persist in an art career in El Salvador from the following anecdote. One day in 1934, José, in keeping with his practice of drawing and painting from life, went out to sketch a bridge in the neighborhood where he lived. He was arrested with the explanation that he was doing "something prohibited." He was handcuffed and taken to jail, where he stayed until a relative convinced the police chief to let him go. Upon being released he was warned: "The boss says you better not do it again."[12]

One of José's teachers at the open-air school in Mexico was Japanese artist Tamiji Kitagawa. Student and teacher became friends, and Kitagawa introduced José to the work of Van Gogh and Gauguin. José was particularly inspired by Gauguin's Tahitian journal *Noa Noa*. Gauguin had gone to Tahiti in search of its ancient mystery and indigenous traditions and beliefs. Depressed because he saw that in Papeete, the capital, these were things of the past, he resolved to withdraw even further from European influence. He felt that by living intimately with the natives in the wilderness he would gradually gain the confidence of the Maoris and come to know them. Inspired by a similar desire to retreat from the city and discover an earthier, simpler way of life, in 1940 José bought an old house in Panchimalco, a small village fifteen kilometers outside of San Salvador.

El Salvador is a predominantly mestizo country, but Panchimalco is one of a small number of Salvadoran towns in which the majority of the population is descended from the indigenous inhabitants of the country.[13] Consequently, the dress, customs, and physical features of the villagers were not those typical of the rest of the country. The women, in particular, because of their characteristic way of wearing their hair—piled atop the head with a woven scarf braided into it, or in long braids—and because of their colorful and graceful costume of long skirts worn with blouses decorated with lace and ribbons, were the inspiration for many local painters, especially those who favored regional portraits and landscapes. It was customary for the women not to cover their breasts, but the Catholic priests, scandalized by their nudity, preached against this fashion and punished those who continued the practice. Nevertheless, some women, particularly when they were washing their clothes along the banks of the river, still observed this custom into the twentieth century.[14] Although he has executed sculptures and murals in public places in San Salvador, Mejía Vides's best work was done in Panchimalco.

José returned to Mexico in 1948 to study the techniques of mural painting at the Instituto Politécnico Nacional (National Polytechnical Institute). He hadn't been there long when one day there was a knock on his apartment door. He opened the door and there "I find a lady dressed in black, wearing a red rose, come to give me a copy of the book by Amighetti she had just published. It was love. The courtship was brief. We were married the next year."[15] Clementina and Chepe first met in San Salvador in

1933, when Clementina gave a recital at the National Theatre. They did not see each other again until 1948 in Mexico, but they obviously lost no time getting reacquainted. Clementina recalls that Chepe shared an apartment with some other artists and was very involved in his art, but that he was sociable and would go to parties with her. He was part of a wide circle of acquaintances, a natural addition to her world, and she says she married him because she loved him. But though they may have been part of the same world in Mexico City, their personalities were very different. Chepe was friendly, but he was far from being a party-lover. As one old friend said: "Mejía Vides was a man who never drank. He was a saint, very abstemious, very respectful toward everyone, even Indians. I don't know why he married Clementina; maybe he really fell in love. He was a good person—it was lucky he didn't drink, because if they both did, they would have ended up killing each other."

Apparently their disagreements and personality clashes did not begin until they went to live in El Salvador, although even during the year they lived together in Mexico, Chepe remembers, "I had my doubts. I liked to work, and I would work from sunup til sunset. She didn't like that. If one wants to be faithful to painting, one shouldn't get married."

In 1949, Carlos Alberto Imery died, and José Mejía Vides was asked to return to San Salvador to take his place as director of the National School of Graphic Arts. He immediately left to assume his new position, while Clementina stayed behind to pack up her large and ever growing collection of books, art, clothes, and shoes, as she had this time stayed in one place long enough to collect a considerable number of possessions. She hoped to transplant her peculiar but flourishing cultural matriarchy to El Salvador. Besides her own energy and notoriety, she now also had the respectability of being married to the director of a prestigious art school. But her husband's projects were less ambitious, his personality more retiring, and his life-style more modest.

When Clementina arrived in San Salvador, Chepe had taken up residence in his house in Panchimalco, tenaciously clinging to his dream of living a simple life devoted to capturing on canvas the living images of this indigenous world. No longer in touch with the cosmopolitan circle of artists, writers, and assorted bohemians with whom he had associated in Mexico, Chepe fell under the influence of his very traditional and conservative family, who were not impressed by his choice of a wife. They found fault with Clementina's life-style, which she apparently modified very little from her premarriage days. For a time he and Clementina lived in the small, sparsely furnished house in this quiet town, and when he was not engaged in fulfilling his duties as teacher and administrator, he devoted every spare moment to his own art. So involved was he in his art that he seemed scarcely to notice or care about the amenities of life. He was happy with a simple cot for a bed and thought Clementina extravagant for buying linens and nice dishes, for wanting to go to the movies or eat in restaurants. But this spartan life-style is not reflected in his paintings and watercolors of the landscape and inhabitants of Panchimalco. They are warm and vibrant, suffused with a serene monumentalism and a contemplative tenderness that, while it may bear the imprint of his fascination with Gauguin, is also a unique blend of Central American colors and themes and the artist's own romantic vision. A number of his finest works are depictions of Indian women weaving, selling fruit, bathing, or washing clothes bare-breasted in the river.

He made several drawings and paintings of Clementina during their time together. In all of them her face and figure appear full, fleshy, and round. The features are recognizably hers, but they are executed with the same meditative softness that informs his paintings of Indian women. It was in the 1940s that Clementina took to wearing *huipiles* and embroidered blouses and dresses. Not exclusively, because she is also fashion-conscious, as a look through her photo albums attests, and she is as attracted to the currently popular shades of lipstick and eye shadow as she is to the traditional woven and embroidered indigenous clothing of Mexico and Central America. When Clementina modeled for her artist husband he saw something in her that was akin to the indigenous women of Panchimalco. Yet Chepe's portraits of Clementina are more convincing as studies for his Panchimalco paintings than versions of Clementina.

If their house in Panchimalco initially seemed romantic, Clementina soon felt trapped and isolated in the environment that produced such tranquillity and inspiration in Chepe. To go from being the center of a busy gallery-pensión in Mexico City to living in an Indian village fifteen kilometers outside of the significantly smaller city of San Salvador was frustrating at best. She also began to see that this man was more devoted to his art than he was to her. But wasn't this what she wanted, a companion whose vital concerns transcended the purely individual? It is interesting to compare the evaluation that each made of their relationship. He says, "She was too absorbing. I had to devote all my time to her, so I wasn't able to paint. She had a desire to live, to expand her horizons. I tried giving her her freedom, but she couldn't deal with that either." She, on the other hand, speaks with a certain remorse about not being able to continue living with him but sees it as having been inevitable largely for the same reasons that he offers. "*I've always regretted not having been able to spend my life with him, but he was a hindrance in my life, because his life is devoted exclusively to painting. So he absorbed me, and I was determined to make my own life, to shape my own life. But if I would have stayed with anyone, it would have been José Mejía Vides.*"[16]

Since Clementina was unhappy living in Panchimalco, they moved to what was a compromise between city and village, a house in Planes de Renderos, a neighborhood on the outskirts of San Salvador, on the road to Panchimalco. Their house was on a steep hill and had a sweeping view of the city and its surrounding hills.

Clementina has often remarked that her years in El Salvador were the happiest of her life. She had projects, she had lots of friends and good times, and she was a public figure. The space of El Salvador also suited her. It is the smallest of the Central American countries, as well as the most densely populated. In 1954 there were approximately 100 inhabitants per square kilometer. The capital had a population of 160,000.[17] In Tegucigalpa Clementina was stifled by provincialism. In New York she was overwhelmed by the size, the cold, the alienation, the language. In Cuba she was comfortable but too far from her daughters and hindered by the restrictions imposed on travel inherent in living on an island. In Mexico she established the contours of her dream. But in El Salvador Clementina blossomed. She was in a foreign country, but it was not so unfamiliar to her that she felt an outsider; she had found her queendom. Besides, she had begun to consider herself a citizen not of any particular country, but of no country, or of all countries. In a poem in *From Disillusion to Hope* she deals with the idea of being a foreigner:

Homeless

I come,
I go.
And then I think.

That it's all the same
here or there.
There is
no place
gained.

That here,
like there.
I am
what people call
a "stranger."

And like a stranger
I will come
and go.
Until here
like there.
Neither I
nor anyone
will be.

Sin residencia

Voy,
vengo.
Y luego pienso.

Que lo mismo
aquí que allá,
no hay
un lugar
conseguido.

Que aquí,
como allá.
Soy lo que
las gentes llaman
un "extranjero."

Y como un extranjero
iré
y vendré.
Hasta que aquí
como allá.
Ni yo
ni nadie
lo sea.

When Clementina arrived in El Salvador with her collection of books and art, the country was on the brink of a cultural and political renaissance, small-scale if compared to the earlier activity in Mexico, for example, but impressive when appreciated in its own context. The economy of El Salvador, as well as its long tradition of artists and intellectuals looking for support to the government or to wealthy or influential citizens, set the stage for a blossoming of activity during the presidency of Colonel Oscar Osorio. Since 1945, when the dictator Hernández Martínez stepped down and Osmín Aguirre Salinas, chief of police under Hernández, took his place in controlled elections, the military, working with landholding interests, has run El Salvador most of the time. This of course accords sweeping powers to the presidency, but there have been both liberal and conservative factions within the military, and Osorio leaned toward the Left. He allowed many of the intellectuals who had fled the country and were then in Guatemala working for Arévalo to return, and Miguel Angel Asturias, known for his leftist sympathies, was named ambassador from Guatemala in El Salvador. Osorio presided over the country's first social security legislation in 1949 and was influential in the enactment of a constitution in 1950 that provided public health programs and women's suffrage. He greatly expanded the government bureaucracy by creating the following institutions: Escuela Normal Superior (Teachers' College), Dirección General de Hospitales (Hospital Administration), Escuela Complementaria Rural

(Rural Schools), Aduana Aérea (Airport Customs), Certámen Nacional de Cultura (National Culture Awards), Junta Nacional de Turismo (National Tourism Council), Instituto de Colonización Rural (Rural Settlement Institute) and Instituto de Vivienda Urbana (Urban Housing Institute). In 1951 he created the Dirección General de Bellas Artes (Fine Arts Administration), which in turn opened schools of music, theatre, classical ballet, and painting. José Mejía Vides was appointed the first director of the new school of painting and served in this capacity until 1960.

One of the first things Clementina did upon arriving in El Salvador was to hold an exhibit of her art collection, which, besides portraits of herself by such well-known artists as Francisco Zúñiga, Fernando Leal, and Francisco Amighetti, included works by young artists such as Roberto de la Cueva and Ricardo Bárcenas, as well as drawings by José Clemente Orozco and Diego Rivera. She thus established her presence officially while at the same time taking full advantage of her position as wife of the director of the National School of Fine Arts and soon knew all the young artists in town. She became fast friends with Camilo Minero and Luis Angel Salinas, both of whom aligned themselves with the artists known as the "independientes." It was the beginning of a time of reaction and discontent, when Salvadoran artists separated into two fundamentally opposing groups: El Grupo de Pintores Independientes (Independent Painters Group), organized in 1947, mostly associated with the National School of Graphic Arts, and those who adhered to a more classical perspective and were associated with the Valero Lecho Academy. "As their respective names suggest, the academics adhered to the norms of painting of the Spanish academy, while the independents, sometimes called 'proletarian painters,' whose aesthetic followed the indigenous trend, used their art to question their cultural identity, their identity as mestizos. They characteristically took their work out into the streets. Their themes were the poor and the dispossessed, man and his landscapes, his activities and his infrequent joys. Their intention was to awaken man's social consciousness."[18]

Clementina favored the independents ideologically, and her life-style and cultural projects mirrored their tendency to take art into the streets. Her life-style definitely favored the street over the home. She never learned to drive and has never owned a car, so she would take the bus, or a cab if she had the money, from her hillside home in Planes de Rendero into the center of town. She would visit Camilo at the School of Fine Arts, in the studio where he painted theatre sets. Camilo was the prototypical starving artist, so poor that he slept on a straw mat in his studio. During breaks or at the end of the workday, groups of students from the art school congregated in the bars and cafés near the center. Their favorite hangouts were El Paraíso de Adán y Eva, La Praviana, El Principal, Gambrinus, and Lutecia. Clementina spent hours in these cafés, drinking and talking with Camilo and Luis Angel, as well as with many of the young writers of the group that came to be known as the Generación del '50 (the Generation of 1950), or, more descriptively, La Generación Comprometida (the Committed Generation). She didn't like staying home at night, either, and attended all the cultural events typical of a Central American capital: book presentations, gatherings in honor of a writer or artist visiting from another country, award ceremonies, lectures on cultural topics, concerts. These events usually included a reception in honor of the guest or speaker that often lasted late into the night. Many people involved in the cultural life of San Salvador in the 1950s have stories about Clementina being escorted home after these festivities. Camilo and Luis Angel often left her propped up against her door after ringing the bell, afraid to confront don Chepe, her husband and their teacher.

Besides attending all the local cultural events, Clementina created many of her own. Among her most popular and publicized were art exhibits in various public parks in San Salvador. The most significant of these exhibits was held in Parque Libertad, a centrally located park with a kiosk, brick walks, and tall trees. The park was used at all hours, but particularly in the evening and on Sundays, when the municipal band performed and groups of young men and women strolled the paths. The mayor, Dr. José Guillermo Trabanino, gave Clementina permission to set up her exhibit in the park; she in return promised him that Camilo and Luis Angel would each paint his portrait. The exhibit was a great success. "People who had never seen a painting in their lives could enjoy them in the park thanks to Clementina's dynamism. Newspapers praised the exposition because, besides being a novelty, it was a way of bringing the people and art together."[19]

The portraits were eventually painted. Luis Angel's contribution was somebody's portrait, although it bore scant resemblance to Dr. Trabanino.

One of the young artists who participated in this ongoing exhibit, which was held on Fridays, Saturdays, and Sundays, described the grass-roots nature of the project.

> People, particularly workers, enjoyed seeing the paintings on their way home from work. This had never been done before. The paintings were kept in the kiosk, where concerts were held in those days. Inside the kiosk, in a kind of basement where the caretaker kept his tools and brooms, that's where we kept the paintings and the easels. Sometimes we had to hang the paintings from trees because there weren't enough easels. But we enjoyed ourselves, because we were exhibiting our work, and there was no place else to exhibit it. Well, there was one other place, the main salon of the Ministry of Tourism, but it was the only one. It didn't last long because in the beginning we all pitched in enthusiastically, but then we got tired of always having to be there at certain times to hang the paintings, to take them down. We had to stay there and help her. And nothing ever sold. In those days it was very difficult to sell anything, in part because the bourgeoisie didn't know anything about art, in part because there wasn't the same national pride then that there is now. Every year, after the coffee harvest, they would leave the country and bring back European art, it didn't matter what, it was mostly for decoration.

Clementina also at this time organized more conventional shows, exhibited the works of Salvadoran artists in Honduras, and helped many artists sell their work. As one Salvadoran explained it, "Clementina believed that anyone who earned a good salary or who had money ought to buy paintings. Using that reasoning she sold many paintings by Salvadoran artists at a time when there were no art galleries in San Salvador and the only exhibition space was that room in the tourism building. Of course, Clementina would pay the artist the amount she thought he deserved—in other words, she charged for her services."

This practice of charging a commission for facilitating the sale of a painting, viewed not only as inevitable but as acceptable in today's art market, had not yet gained broad acceptance in El Salvador. Stories about Clementina's business practices portray her as both uninterested in profit and only interested in profit. The following two testimonies substantiate each opinion. A sculptor who knew Clementina well remarked that she had an unorthodox way of collecting art. "She was in the habit of acquiring paintings to exhibit them and never returning them. In fact, I once loaned her a bronze bust which she exhibited, and it took her years to return it to me. I had to go get it myself; I just took it—after all, it was mine. Everyone complained that she never returned their work to them. That's how she got her collection. She doesn't have a single receipt. Well, it is for a cause; she has used them to publicize our work, she has shown them around a lot."

Another artist, a young student of don Chepe's, remembers Clementina's generosity: "Clementina was a good person, she used to loan money to anyone who needed it, especially to artists." He also recalls that Clementina, to stimulate his youthful artistic ambitions, was the first person ever to pay him for a painting.

While there may be differences of opinion as to whether or not Clementina's art dealings were totally above reproach, there is no question that she did help many artists, financially as well as by encouraging them to do their best and providing them with an opportunity to exhibit their work. In Mexico she had been able to offer many young artists the hospitality of her pensión as well as the opportunity to display their work there. She realized that it would be impossible to recreate that open, intense, festive atmosphere in the home she shared with her quiet, serious painter husband, so she came up with an alternative space.

She called it El Rancho del Artista. It was a rustic adobe structure on the outskirts of the capital, on the road to Santa Tecla, on the property of Colonel Ascencio Menéndez, whose family had a country house nearby. Menéndez had a reputation for being a ladies' man and was referred to behind his back as "el cabrón loco" (the crazy old goat). Clementina was a favorite of his, so, capitalizing on his weakness for pretty women, she went to visit him one day with her friend, the Costa Rican poet Eunice Odio. Eunice was an excellent poet who a few years earlier had won the Central American poetry prize "15 de septiembre," for her work *Los elementos terrestres* (Terrestrial Elements). She lived a tempestuous life, moving from country to country, having numerous love affairs, and being intensely involved first in left-wing politics, only to make a radical conversion to conservatism later in life. She was a heavy drinker and had a reputation for being tempermental and fun loving. She was also very beautiful, with thick black hair and large green eyes. When she arrived in El Salvador on one of her travels, she stayed with Clementina and Chepe. This caused some unpleasantness between Clementina and her husband, because he was uncomfortable with the idea of his wife having a serious partier staying with her and accompanying her on her late-night revels. But she stayed there nevertheless. On the day of their visit to the colonel, Eunice got all dolled up, with long false eyelashes to complement her large green eyes. The colonel agreed to let Clementina use the house on his property for the Rancho, and President Osorio, allegedly another admirer of the female sex, helped her out financially. Thus began a period of five or six years when the writers and artists of El Salvador had a place to gather. To appreciate the character of this space, it is helpful to compare it with a similar space, the Galería Forma of Julia Díaz, Salvadoran painter, art collector, and energetic promotor of national art.

Julia Díaz studied first at the Valero Lecha Academy in San Salvador, then in Europe for five years. She returned to San Salvador in 1953, when El Rancho del Artista was in full swing, and installed her first studio in 1954, where she held bimonthly cultural activities such as poetry readings, lectures, and concerts. In 1958 she opened the Galería Forma, which served as her home as well as a place for cultural events. She refers to Galería Forma as "a center for culture and art," and "El Salvador's first art gallery."[20] Obviously she did not consider Clementina's Rancho to be a gallery, even though artists exhibited their work there. Julia Díaz has done more than anyone to professionalize Salvadoran art. The Museo Forma, El Salvador's only art museum, exists because of her efforts; in fact a number of the paintings in the museum are donations from her private collection.

Many people who remember the Rancho are quick to point out a fundamental difference between the space over which Julia Díaz presided and Clementina's. One artist described it: "Unquestionably Julita has had an art business. Clementina had a completely different place, an atmosphere with a bohemian flavor, where art was enjoyed all day long. One felt the artists' presence there. What was important was not the quality of your work or your age, but something else. You could show up at any hour of the day or night. Julia Díaz's place was another story altogether. There you had to wear a jacket and tie."

The Rancho was spacious enough so that visiting artists were able to stay there. When Francisco Zúñiga, for example, was commissioned by the Salvadoran government to execute the Monument to the Revolution, he and his workers stayed at the Rancho the entire time he worked on the sculpture. But not only well-known artists were invited. One young artist was only thirteen when Clementina recognized his talent and offered to help.

> She saw my first paintings and perhaps she thought, "That boy might become a good painter." She told me, "I'd like to help you in any way I can, I have the Rancho del Artista set up." So she invited me to her house and I was impressed to see a number of Salvadoran artists represented there: Ana Julia Alvarez, Camilo Minero, César Sermeño, Luis Angel Salinas, Alicia Osorio. There were very few artists at that time. You might say that most of the artists in the country showed their work there. She told me I could stay and live there. I told her I wouldn't be able to live there, but I would like to work there. So in return I swept out the ranch, helped with the housework. But it was very little that I did. She said, "I'm going to give you paper, watercolors." So I would go there to paint. I did some watercolors of her, some landscapes of the surrounding farmland. I used to go every day to paint. There were groves of trees outside; that's where I would work. She told me, "You're going to enjoy working here." She exhibited my work in the School of Graphic Arts. It was a great motivation for me to meet this person who made me feel this way, filling me with enthusiasm so I could continue to work and enjoy that artistic environment. I gave her a number of watercolors, which she exhibited throughout Central America.

In 1955 Clementina was appointed cultural affairs officer for the Honduran embassy in El Salvador. In this capacity she continued the work she had been doing right along, but now her projects acquired a certain aura of officialdom, even though nothing changed at the Rancho. It was during this time that the various facets of her life-style and her personality seemed most contradictory to the people who knew her. She would organize a reading by a visiting poet, for example, and she would preside at the event dressed conservatively and introduce the guest of honor with a serious and thoughtful speech. After the reading she would invite everyone to the Rancho for a reception. She would serve a few rounds of drinks and then pass around a basket so all present could contribute to the purchase of the next few bottles. As the evening wore on and she had consumed several drinks, her affectionate graciousness would disappear and in its place would surface an angry, contemptuous woman who, reacting to a real or imagined offense, would shout obscenities and summarily kick everyone out. An old friend described these episodes with a colorful flourish: "Clementina was a consummate partier. In those days she could have five drinks and still be more or less sober. But after the fourth or fifth drink she would start calling everyone imbecile, everyone, it didn't matter if she knew you or not, if you were her best friend or worst enemy. But she would say it so deliciously, not just imbecile, as anyone would say it, no, her delivery was grandiloquent: im-be-cile!"

It is one thing to act this way among friends who have come to know and accept one's peculiarities, but quite another to be unwilling to modify one's behavior in official situations or in the company of powerful or important people. But it was this characteristic unconcern for rank or authority that people loved and feared most in Clementina. As one acquaintance acutely observed: "Clementina is fantastic! Around here we used to say that if Clementina didn't exist we would have to invent her."

And she was in a way invented, or if not invented at least fictionalized, in a novel by Roque Dalton. Dalton was one of the Committed Generation that included Manlio Argueta, Roberto Armijo, Italo López Vallecillos, Tirso Canales, and others. From its beginnings as the Círculo Literario Universitario (University Literary Circle) this group has done much to reshape Salvadoran poetry and has contributed significantly to the ongoing and evolving debate that centers on the role of the writer in the class struggle and in revolutionary social change. Dalton is certainly the best known of this generation, in part because of the circumstances of his life and death. A son of the bourgeoisie who rejected his family's money and position, he was in his youth one of the primary voices of rebellious discontent with the hypocrisy of his class and the injustice of the political system. One critic has observed, "His tone, partly derived from Brecht and Nazim Hikmet, partly from the cynical 'anti-poems' of the Chilean Nicanor Parra, is both self-absorbed and self-mocking, secular, antiprophetic, aphoristic, didactic." He goes on to suggest that Dalton's persona is a combination of sentimentality and machismo.[21] But behind the writer's persona was an individual who chose to commit himself in deed as well as word to the cause of revolution in El Salvador. He became a member of the Communist Party, and his senseless death at the hands of his own comrades, the result of an internal dispute, immortalized him as a poet-martyr.

Roque Dalton frequented the Rancho and chose to include this space and its doyenne in his only novel, *Pobrecito poeta que era yo* (Poor, Unfortunate Poet That I Was). The title is from a poem by Salvadoran Pedro Geoffroy-Rivas that calls attention to the useless life the poet has lived, unconcerned with the human suffering around him, absorbed in his poetry for the sake of poetry. The narrator is a young intellectual whose time is spent criticizing the shallowness and hypocrisy of everyone in his society. No group is exempt, not even artists or intellectuals; there are only scattered individuals who merit his admiration. Clementina is one of them. She appears as the central figure in the chapter entitled "El Party." The narrator and a group of companions attend a gathering at the Rancho. The hostess is Cristina (Clementina). The narrator subjects Cristina to a series of witty criticisms, creating a caricature of her as indiscriminately inviting ignorant and pretentious conservatives to the same party as young, radical poets and artists. He jokes about her limited intellectualism: "my psychiatrist has limited my reading" (156). He paints her as promiscuous. He details her legendary three stages of drunkenness, which include "the alpha stage . . . of friendly affection . . . then . . . that of furious love . . . her least metaphysical stage . . . and the stage nominum vulgaris of collective hate and that's when she kicks everybody the hell out of her house without exception" (159). He then goes on to praise her gift for seemingly ingenuous though on-the-mark insults, referring to her language as "phrases worthy to be anthologized, precious jewels" (161). He especially delights in retelling an anecdote about how she told off the ambassador from Spain, to which the ambassador replied, " 'Madame, I am not used to being treated this way,' and she made me think of García Lorca's guardian angels, because she shot right back: 'Well, you'd better start getting used to it, you son of a bitch' " (160).

His conclusion is, " 'Right then and there I fell in love with Cristina, guys. I swear. Who wouldn't have? And I symbolically dedicated to her the statue of liberty, not the monstrous one in New York, but our own. . . . That statue doesn't belong to our pitiful fatherland, every day more enslaved. . . . It belongs to Cristina: the only relatively free person for a thousand kilometers around. . . . The day she leaves the country we're going to have to pray to God to send us at least a couple of earthquakes a week, to keep us from getting too bored" (161).

"If Clementina didn't exist, we would have to invent her."

CHAPTER FIVE

No Place to Call Home

Clementina Suárez Vive

As the play *Clementina Suárez Vive* (Clementina Suárez Lives) opens, Clementina is writing her memoirs. Pen in hand, she begins to tell her life to her interlocutor, Universal Love. Flashback. Clementina in Juticalpa in a forest, writing a poem in the shade of a tree. Enter physical love. They embrace. Love exits. Clementina on a street in a poor neighborhood, Clementina dressed in male attire, Clementina selling her magazine *Mujer* on a street corner, Clementina sitting in a café. Return to the present. Clementina continues her dialogue with Universal Love. Shift to Clementina walking by the sea. Universal Love bestows immortality upon her through her poetry. Enter Death, a Black Tree, and a Dancer in Red. Enter Agony. Grand finale: entire cast on stage, dancing. They invite the audience to participate. *Clementina Suárez Vive.*

This theatre piece, written and directed by Isidro España, was presented in Tegucigalpa in 1976, in Guatemala in 1988, and again in Tegucigalpa that same year. The text of the play is selections of Clementina's poetry. It was technically experimental, a lyrical interpretation of Clementina's life choreographed by César Guifarro with music arranged by Tito Estrada. The actors, dressed in black shirts and white pants, each represented a number of characters or emotions, their changes of identity indicated by the creative use of pieces of cloth of varying shapes, sizes, and colors. The actress who represented Clementina wore red.

Isidro wanted it to be a play that spoke to the youth of Honduras. The message he hoped to convey is that there can be life beyond death, and that it consists of the work one produces. He feels that Clementina will live in the memory of her country because of the example of her life's struggle and because of the poetry she leaves for future generations. He recognized the autobiographical nature of her work and used her poetry to dramatize her life.

Return to the Fatherland

Isidro was a young student in Tegucigalpa in the late 1950s when Clementina left El Salvador to return to Honduras. A creative young Honduran actor and playwright looking for a way to make a living with his talent, he dreamed of professionalizing the theatre in his country, just as artists, dancers, musicians, and writers dreamed of a government that supported their respective art forms. For the first time in many years there was even some hope that this dream would materialize. There was a sense of expectancy in the air, as well as an understandable tension caused by the political situation in the country.

The dictatorship of Carías had come to an end in 1948, although Carías wielded considerable power for a number of years afterward. He was followed by Manuel Gálvez, who served as president from 1948 to 1954. Gálvez was also of the National Party and the candidate chosen by Carías. Under Carías, talented individuals were sometimes aided in their creative endeavors with a scholarship or the publication of a book, mostly because of the intervention of his nephew, Marcos Carías Reyes, who served as his personal secretary. These official subsidies were sporadic and arbitrary, as would be the case when there are no predetermined criteria for selection of aid recipients, and this system of arbitrary support remained basically unchanged during Galvez's term.

In the election of 1954, no candidate received a majority of the votes cast. In the ensuing confusion, Gálvez left the country claiming ill health, and his vice-president, Lozano Díaz, took over. His presidency resembled a dictatorship more than a democratically elected government, but his power was tenuous and on 21 October 1956 the armed forces replaced him with a military junta, the first time in the history of Honduras that professional armed forces intervened in the political situation.

The military government called for elections in 1957, and Ramón Villeda Morales, the Liberal Party candidate, became the next president. The landowning oligarchy and foreign investors were nervous about what they saw as a Communist threat in the region after Arbenz's reforms in Guatemala, and they were particularly shaken by the well-organized and effective strikes in 1954 by agricultural workers on the North Coast of Honduras. But the conservative National Party had been in power since 1932, and many sectors of society were ready for a change. Some hoped the change would be radical, while some feared that same possibility.

The presidency of Villeda Morales was in many ways similar to the rule of Osorio in El Salvador. While Villeda Morales was not a radical reformer, he did initiate some social legislation, which has been interpreted as the reaction of a social-democratic government attempting to deflect the influence of communism in a country in great need of social reform. "During Villeda Morales's government there was some new legislation of a social nature, such as the Work Code, the Social Security Law, the Agrarian Reform Law and the Tenants' Rights Law, all of which were measures that, in an attempt to limit the influence of the Cuban Revolution, had been formulated and recommended by development theorists from the Alliance for Progress who postulated that development could be achieved through the capitalist free-market system within a protectionist framework but without altering the structure of domination and dependence that characterizes Central American society."[1]

Many factors contributed to a sense of growth and renewal during Villeda Morales's presidency: migration to the cities; the growth of an urban middle class; an expansion of government agencies and the consequent creation of jobs in the bureaucracy; economic diversification in the form of incipient industrialization; and the resultant shift in power away from the agriculture-export oligarchy that controlled the country under Carías and into the hands of those newly wealthy through banking and industry. In keeping with the belief that for Honduras to develop economically it must simultaneously develop on all fronts, including culturally and socially, the government of Villeda Morales did much to strengthen public education on all levels. When he took office in 1957, for example, there were, at the primary level, 2,417 public schools and 4,574 teachers in the country. By the end of his term in 1963 the number had increased to 3,697 schools and 8,771 teachers, and the number of students almost doubled.[2]

Clementina knew Villeda Morales, of course. He had visited El Salvador and they had talked about his dreams of progress and development for Honduras. He had urged her to return to her homeland, assuring her that there was money for cultural programs and that there would be a place for her in this growth if he were elected. So when he became president in December 1957, Clementina judged that the time was right for her to try to work in Honduras. Besides, the situation in El Salvador was no longer as exhilarating as when she first arrived with Chepe in 1950. President Osorio, who had helped support her cultural projects, had been replaced by Lieutenant Colonel José María Lemus, who was more conservative with government funds, and she found herself economically unable to keep the Rancho open in the spacious if rustic quarters she had enjoyed.

Her relationship with Chepe had deteriorated to the point where neither of them was committed to continuing to live together. Nor were they committed to a decisive and legal separation, because, for all their arguments, they were deeply attracted to one another, drawn to each other's difference. Through the blurring of time, both reconstruct their relationship and separation according to their own egos, each recalling that he or she was the one to leave the other behind. There was mutual affection, but they could not make their daily lives blend in any harmonious or satisfying arrangement. When the Rancho was open and active and Clementina enjoyed the almost daily companionship of her two young friends, Luis Angel and Camilo, she could ignore the obvious: that Chepe was not the ideal companion she longed for. While she was the cultural attaché to the Honduran embassy and had the financial support of the government for her projects, she found less time to berate Chepe for not wanting to accompany her to social and cultural events, which in turn allowed him to enjoy the solitude of his work and not be so bothered by his family's complaints about his libertine wife or by the constant activity at his home—the friends visiting Clementina, the laughing, the drinking, the boisterous talking.

So by 1957 Clementina was once again dissatisfied and in need of change. The quest for her destiny that had taken her to Mexico, New York, and Cuba had reached a dead end with her marriage to Chepe. She won the poetry prize sponsored by the Ministry of Culture for *Growing with the Grass,* which the ministry published in 1957 in a hardbound luxury edition with a cover design by Mejía Vides and drawings by Luis Angel, but she had written the poems years before. She says that she felt trapped in her marriage to Chepe. Even though she resisted conforming to anything that resembled a domestic life-style, she nonetheless felt stifled by the relationship. She felt that she wasn't attending to her own growth, she wasn't following the path of her poetry. In a word, she wasn't writing any poetry.

She was also aware that her sexuality was changing. Not that she experienced herself as a less sexual being, but she saw that a woman in her mid-fifties does not turn heads or attract lovers with the same regularity as a woman twenty or thirty years younger. It was around this time that she started shocking and entertaining friends and acquaintances by declaring, at a party, in a restaurant, in someone's living room, that her body had lost none of its grace and suppleness, demonstrating this by lifting her skirt or showing off a firm and indeed lovely bosom.

In her attraction to young artists that began in Mexico, there was—besides a genuine love of art and a selfless, even maternal, desire to nurture and promote—the pleasure of keeping company with young men full of energy and talent. She never lost that sensuality that flavors her friendships and informs her poetry.

Luis Angel and Camilo were both married during their close friendship with Clementina in El Salvador, but the three were inseparable. Clementina loved and needed their company, but she also was determined to help them with their careers, even if it meant being separated from them. She went out of her way to court Osorio's successor, President Lemus, even campaigned to help get him elected, finally persuading him to provide scholarships for Luis Angel and Camilo to study art in Mexico. In late 1956 the threesome dissolved when the two artists left for Mexico.

Another event occurred around this time to further complicate her emotional turmoil. Her mother's death in Juticalpa in 1955 estranged her from her already distant family. A disagreement over the division of property in Juticalpa and Jutiquile and the ensuing arguments in lawyers' offices and courts made her feel once more like the solitary, misunderstood black sheep of the family. A poem she wrote at this time recalls her dedication to *Bleeding Heart,* the words of a young woman grateful for her mother's unconditional love. The poem, "Ahora es que he crecido Madre" (Now That I Have Grown Up, Mother), was included in *The Poet and Her Signs,* an anthology of her poetry published in 1969.

You who knew nothing understood everything
silent and full you descended to me
spilling over my shores
your calm, serene worlds.
That's why I was able to leave you again and again, ascend,
be strong in life's battle
because I knew I could always
leave the clamor behind
and come home,
to the ageless root of your tenderness
where I was but a little girl
safe in your love.
Now I have grown up, Mother,
and despair licks at my heart,
the cold sweat of fear
paralyzes my eyes.
Dressed in mist, in blood, in night,
I spell your deepest name
naked and bright today in death.

———

Tú que nada sabías lo intuías todo
y callada y caudalosa descendías a mí,
y volcabas mi orilla
tus tranquilos y serenos mundos.
Por eso pude dejarte una y otra vez, ascender,
ser fuerte en la lucha, en la vida,
porque sabía que en cualquier minuto
podía apartarme del estrépito
y regresar,
a la milenaria raíz de tu ternura
donde nunca fui mas
que una niña sin crecer

arrullada por tu amor.
Ahora es que he crecido, Madre,
para que me lama el corazón la desesperación,
para que un helado sudor de espanto
paralice mis ojos en la sombra.
Y vestida de bruma, de sangre, de noche,
deletrée tu nombre profundísimo
hoy iluminado y desnudo en la muerte.

Her morale was so low that she began to lose her grip on herself. Always prone to flights of enthusiasm and bouts with despair, her depressions became more dangerous and suspiciously suicidal. She continued to drink heavily; she didn't eat properly or sleep regularly. In an article from 1957 that discusses *Growing with the Grass,* the author alludes to Clementina's reticence regarding her internal struggles. "Doubtless her pride and integrity as a woman prevent her from alluding to her psychological breakdowns, contrary to the norm in Hispanic American feminine poetry. One hears about, or rather one senses these turbulent and painful times, but one does not see the traces, is conscious only of a splendid serenity, of a dignified acceptance of a rather adverse destiny, of a dignified manner of dealing with failure and commanding respect." She goes on to mention an incident that Clementina no longer cares to remember. "One day this woman poet stood of her own volition before death's doors as a final protest against some deep disappointment. Saved in time by a group of friends and artists, her indomitable spirit survived the test and she appears not to remember this drama in her life."[3]

During the 1950s and 1960s foreign aid to Central America from the United States as well as from international aid organizations "focused on the need for Central American unity and engendered a spirit of cooperation. . . . The development of economic integration and its accompanying interstate organizations promoted cooperation and a sense of unity on the isthmus, as did the growth of interstate investments and the development of easier transportation and communication among the states."[4] In November 1957, in keeping with this spirit of Central American union, Clementina, under the auspices of the Salvadoran Ministry of Culture, brought an exhibit of Salvadoran art and literature to Honduras. Although cultural integration was never a major concern for the political proponents of this particular wave of pan-Americanism, the idea was appropriate for the time, and Clementina, for years a self-styled ambassador of cultural communication throughout the region, finally was able to convince government officials to fund a project that coincided perfectly with her restlessness, sociability, and love of travel. Her arrival created a stir in the Honduran capital. "Clementina's arrival has awakened the enthusiasm of the intellectual circles of the country. After ten years she has returned, this time bringing us, as Ambassador from El Salvador, the wonderful exhibit soon to open."[5]

She brought with her paintings by Salvadoran artists Mejía Vides, Salinas, Minero, Cáceres, and Salarrué. She brought books from El Salvador and copies of *Growing with the Grass.* She talked a lot about the open-air art exhibits that had been such a success in El Salvador and was careful to remind people that she was able to do this thanks to the "great effort of the Salvadoran government to support its national culture and the exchange of culture throughout Central America" (ibid.). She was politicking, hoping that the example of El Salvador would encourage Hondurans to do likewise.

Once back in Honduras, she says she wrote Chepe a letter telling him she would not be returning. He was relieved that this passionate complication was gone from his life, leaving him free to paint in peace. Neither ever remarried. Clementina says she once burned all her old love letters; the only ones she saved were those from Chepe.

For a while she was caught up in the excitement and optimism typically produced by those changes of government in Central America when the Left feels it is gaining an advantage. "*One never gives up the idea of returning to do something in her own country. I would say to myself: 'The truth is I am an outsider. Although I am loved and accepted in El Salvador, I am still a foreigner. I am going to take this movement to Honduras.' So I just decided to sell everything and go home. Villeda Morales had visited El Salvador a number of times and had invited me to return to Honduras. I thought that, once he was in charge of the government, that would be my opportunity to get involved. Medardo Mejía was staying at my house with his two children, and I told him my plan. 'Wonderful,' he said.*

'You know I've had the same idea, because one starts feeling like the lamplighter: always on the move. Let's pack up and go, because Villeda Morales will support our projects and we can do a lot of work.'"[6]

Her efforts did indeed constitute "a lot of work." All of the challenges she was facing—the deterioration of her marriage, her physical aging, her mother's death and her estrangement from her family, her long, dry period of writing little or no poetry—served to fuel her stubborn will to survive.

One of her first and most dramatic displays of solidarity with the hope and promise of the new Liberal Party government was the publication of *Canto a la encontrada Patria y su Héroe* (Song of the Found Fatherland and Its Hero) in 1958. Like *Growing with the Grass,* it is a single long poem. It consists of thirteen short compositions that range in length from six to fourteen lines. The individual poems, while typographically discrete, must be read as part of the larger poem to be fully appreciated. *Growing with the Grass* and *Song* are also visually similar: printed in large, bold typeface and bound in editions that measure twenty-nine and twenty-six centimeters, respectively, they give the impression of strength, simplicity, and clarity.

The discovery the poet shared in *Growing*—that she is her best self when "multiplicada"—is incorporated in *Song* in an ironic reversal. In *Song* she discloses that the multiplicity she had been striving for was in her all along. It was 1958, she was fifty-six years old, and her years of self-imposed exile were coming around to haunt her. She had been very critical of Honduras, the country that raised her but that rejected her desire to be free. Clementina's poetic quest, the search for herself through the other, began in earnest when her father died, and though it has often seemed that she was looking for her ideal male companion, she was also trying to bring her father back to life by finding him in a lover or a mentor. In *Song* the girl-woman reincarnates the father by becoming him and, in so doing, frees herself of the dichotomy of self and other, of belonging and being an outsider. *Song* is a hymn to the fatherland in which the poet claims the land and the father as her own. With this poem, Clementina empowers herself to be truly Honduran. She rejects any traditional or superficial understanding of homeland and insists that the nation is every individual as well as the collectivity, that the nation is earth and sea and sky, that it is eternal, immortal, and cannot be denied her, because she is in the father and the father is in her.

I cannot come home . . .
Because I have never left.
You are a country constructed
inside me.
You flow within me
like an open river.
You come from a distant past
rebellious and vegetal,
everything in you is new and old
a land for childhood
and to immortalize time.

———

No puedo llegar . . .
porque jamás me he ido.
Eres una patria construída
en lo interior.
Caminas dentro de mí
como un abierto río.
Vienes desde muy atrás
rebelde y vegetal,
todo en ti es nuevo y viejo
tierra para la infancia
y para inmortalizar el tiempo.

In the next five poems she constructs a profound identification with her country. In her individual birth her homeland is also born. The metaphorical blood of the land runs in her veins. She assumes for herself the power to bestow life, declaring that her return has brought new life to the land.

I have only to see you again
with my eyes of yesterday and forever
for you to be green once more.
Every blade of your grass
fills me with tenderness!
From there I watch you grow
with the tall, whispering pines.

From there I am born and populated
with your hot blood
that infuses hope.

———

Cómo te reverdeces
con sólo volver a verte
con los ojos de ayer y siempre.
Qué ternura me inunda
con cada hierbecilla tuya!
Desde ahí, te veo crecer
hasta el pino alto y rumoroso.
Desde ahí, nazco y me pueblo
con tu cálida sangre
que anima la esperanza.

She calls on childhood memories to bring forth images of newness and hope for the country where she grew up.

My country of dawn! Land of stone!
I don't even know how
to describe my love.
It is almost blind,
but its memory is intact.
It's like remembering your clay
or my new dress.
It's like playing in the sun
with the rays of your light.
Like being January in your veins
to learn to love you,
like being six years old
and learning to spell your name.

———

Patria de Aurora! Patria de Piedra!
No sé ni decirte la forma
en que te quiero.
Es casi un amor a ciegas,

pero con una memoria intacta.
Es como recordar tu barro
o mi vestido nuevo.
Es como jugar al sol
con las hebras de tu luz.
Cómo ser enero en tus venas
para aprender a quererte,
cómo tener seis años
para deletrear tu nombre.

She recalls her first kiss, and in her memory the place and the kiss merge. Her flesh is Honduran, and in her skin she becomes transparent, able to see and identify her immaterial self in the palpable reality of her country.

I love you as in the sand
I kissed my first love.
How full of the smell of earth
the mouth that kissed me!
It was you, my country
in your overflowing passion.
Your own fleshy cheek,
mystery of love intact;
I was she who walked in your skin!
Dressed in your flesh
I was perfectly transparent,
it was like seeing my soul's
reflection in your waters!

———

Te quiero como cuando en la arena
besaba el amor primero.
Qué olor a tierra tenía
la boca que me besaba!
Eras tú misma Patria
en su pasión desbordada.
Mejilla de carne tuya,
misterio del amor intacto;

la que en tu piel caminaba!
Vestida con carne tuya
qué transparencia tenía,
era como ver mi alma
en tus aguas reflejada!

In the fifth poem she introduces the possibility of going/growing beyond the homeland and the natural/national identity, concluding that this desire to expand her horizons is also her patrimony.

So one begins life
with a horizon in hand.
With an impetuous current
pulled by a jubilant sea.
Hunger for a grand destiny
moves forward bright and clear inside me!
A dream that never wanes,
a presence that stands firm,
a truth one has possessed,
suffering one has conquered,
This for me is my country!

———

Así se empieza la vida
con un horizonte en la mano.
Con una impetuosa corriente
que un mar jubiloso arrastra.
Avidez de un gran destino
que lúcido avanza por dentro!
Ilusión que jamás declina,
presencia que no se antepone,
verdad que se ha poseído,
dolor que se ha conquistado,
eso es para mí la Patria!

She courageously goes a step farther, to postulate that in fact she is the highest citizen who has internalized her nation and carried it beyond its borders and its own limitations.

If anyone carries you within her
it is she who walks in your blood,
who discerns your shadow,
leans over your abyss,
who made your image her own
and frees you when it seems impossible
from an impending servility.

Que si alguien te lleva por dentro
es quien camina en tu sangre
quien adivina tu sombra,
quien se asoma a tus abismos.
Quien ganada tiene su imágen
y te libera hasta lo imposible
de un posible vasallaje.

The next two poems, which introduce the hero who shares the book's title with *patria,* make us return to the previous verses to reread the subject as the poet herself and also as Honduras's national hero, Francisco Morazán (1792–1842), early champion of Central American union. She shares with Morazán an immortal vision; she has heard his message, and her own song echoes his call for union and pride. She relies on the authority of her own experience to validate her vision, reminding us that her own internal voice is sufficient.

There is a reason your hero
works faithfully
and is not forgotten.
His hand does not grow thin,
his life is not shortened.
His death has survived
because of his truth,
is reborn daily
in indestructible life.

Pushed into time
with my song that heralds the future,

Morazán wipes my forehead clean
and writes his message there.
My inner voice
assures me of this.
And if I am multipled
in his human presence,
Who could it be but you, my land,
in me, inexorably, overflowing?

———

Que por algo tienes tu héroe
trabajando sin olvido
y en todo aire exaltado.
Su mano no se adelgaza,
tampoco su existencia se acorta.
Que vivir pudo su muerte
por la verdad poseída,
y nace con ella a diario
con vida que no se destruye.

Así lanzada en el tiempo
con mi canción precursora,
Morazán desgarra mi frente
y su mensaje estampa en ella.
Me basta para saberlo
la voz que escucho por dentro.
Y si multiplicada voy toda
con su humanal presencia,
Acaso no eres tú, torrencial Patria
en mí, inexorablemente, desbordada?

In the following poem she fleshes out the hero, reversing the metaphorical process she employed in the first six poems. She dwells on the heart, the eye, the backbone, the head of the man, making them superhuman in their correspondence with nature and with the nation.

I am intrigued by your heart
made beautiful by history.
Such unexplored worlds

in your endless vision!
One must survive,
but in your backbone,
in your wonderful structure,
land and sea dweller.
People of tall pines
hold up your head.
Captain of ancient bravery
who knows not defeat!
The homeland is in your glory,
The homeland of your miracles.

Me intriga tu corazón
hermoseado en la historia.
Qué inexplorado mundo
en tu ilimitada pupila!
Hay que sobrevivirse
pero en la espina dorsal de tu cuerpo.
En tu fabulosa estructura,
habitante de mar y tierra.
Un pueblo de erguidos pinos
te sostiene la cabeza.
Capitán de antiguo coraje
que no sabes lo que es derrota!
En tu resplandor está la Patria,
La Patria de tus milagros.

Poems ten and eleven build to a crescendo, creating Morazán's heroic proportions by naming him and enumerating the objects and metaphors that define him. At the peak of the crescendo we return to the poet. She reinserts herself into the metaphorical construct, claiming that the homeland she has newly named, the country that acquires a clearer, broader identity through her poem, is the hero, the poet, and the dream.

You were like the earth
of indestructible vital impulse . . .
This is Morazán from the air,

from where I see him extended.
This is Morazán from his sword,
from his blood,
from his patient dream,
from his roads, his buildings.
This is Morazán from his birds,
this is Morazán from his homeland.

This is Morazán from the street,
from his hymns and his victory,
from his sky and from his roses.
This is my homeland,
this is my pure dream,
this is my song where words live,
this is my rock, my sun, my cry.

———

Eras como la tierra
con impulso vital indestructible . . .
Esto es Morazán desde el aire,
desde donde lo veo extendido.
Esto es Morazán desde su espada,
desde su sangre,
desde su sueño sin prisa,
desde sus caminos, sus edificios.
Esto es Morazán desde sus pájaros,
esto es Morazán desde su Patria.

Esto es Morazán desde la calle,
desde sus himnos y su victoria,
desde su cielo y desde sus rosas.
Esto es mi Patria,
esto es mi limpio sueño,
esto es mi canto donde viven las palabras,
esto es mi piedra, mi sol, mi llanto.

She completes the poem by completing her identification in time and space with her homeland and its best and bravest citizen.

I began here and here I return,
the homeland becomes all.
It is today, yesterday, tomorrow,
it is where the flesh is sustained,
where one finally dies.
It is the roundness of the earth,
it is the mother, the son,
it is tears, it is laughter,
it is the future that encompasses all.

It is the womb's promise,
it is hope ever present,
it is the name one never forgets,
it is poignant destiny,
it is the architecture of man,
it is the Homeland.

———

Desde aquí vine y hasta acá voy,
la Patria se apodera de todo.
Es hoy, es ayer, es el porvenir,
es donde se apoya el cuerpo,
donde se deja morir.
Es la redondez de la tierra,
es la madre, es el hijo,
es la lágrima, es la risa,
es el futuro que lo abarca todo.

Es el vientre promesa,
es la esperanza asomándose siempre,
es el nombre que no se olvida,
es el conmovido destino,
es la arquitectura del hombre,
es la Patria.

Song can be read as evidence of a narcissistic personality, the expression of a woman so involved in herself that everything she sees reflects that obsession. It is also a moment in her poetic time when she saw beyond herself, when she struggled to enlarge her vision and redefine her relationship with her past and her country in order not to lose it. Yet there is an inherent irony in a woman claiming identification with the patria, the fatherland. In Central America patria, a quintessentially male-defined and male-centered concept, resonates with the notions of struggle, battles, and heroism. Women have never been the creators or protectors of the fatherland, except for isolated cases that are the exception rather than the rule, but they are identified with it in other ways: they are the mothers of the nation's sons; they equate their fertility with that of the land; they nurture and educate its citizens; but they seldom claim identification with its heroes. Clementina's use of poetry to create a female identity for the patria is one of her most ingenious and radical poetic projects. But to meld her identity with a homeland she could not fully love or respect would not bring her peace, and her return home, as a citizen committed to participating in a cultural revival, was intense but brief. The fatherland's promise of plenitude continued to be illusory.

Cultural Worker

Around the time of the publication of *Song of the Found Fatherland and Its Hero,* Clementina was named cultural coordinator for the Ministry of Public Education in Honduras. One of her projects was the establishment of weekend libraries in the parks of Tegucigalpa, where she would set up tables and shelves and fill them with books, many from her own library, which she had been collecting over the years. Accumulating a respectable library is no mean task in Honduras, where price can be prohibitive, but even more problematic is access to books. But with her wide-ranging connections, Clementina was always receiving books from friends and acquaintances. If she knew friends were planning a trip to Nicaragua or Guatemala, she would ask them to bring back any new books that had been published there, or when writer friends published, they would present her with a copy of the book, as is customary even today among writers. Her library is now a treasure of most of the significant works of Central American literature of this century. It has been a constant struggle for her to maintain and increase her collection because she has moved so often and because the very scarcity of books makes them a temptation to visitors in her home.

Despite losses and damage, Clementina transported reading material to the parks of Tegucigalpa where residents could come to sit and enjoy a book on a Saturday or Sunday afternoon. As part of her job in the Ministry of Education she supervised the publication of easy-to-read and beautifully illustrated books on Honduras's national heroes, such as Francisco Morazán and José Cecilio del Valle, a contemporary of Morazán who fought to preserve Central American independence from Mexico. She also organized numerous art exhibits under the auspices of her government position.

One observer referred disparagingly to her job as "a position in the Ministry of Public Education befitting a country schoolmarm. An ant-size job for a woman of continental stature."[7] The reporter's intent in this article was not to belittle Clementina, but to criticize the government for not recognizing the merit of this Honduran poet who had achieved a measure of international fame—in short, for not coming up with the cash to fund her ambitious projects as the government had in El Salvador. In truth, no matter who is in power, there is never enough money to pay for cultural projects, scholarships, teachers' salaries, and the like. It is a longstanding complaint in Honduras that the party in power fills the jobs in the government bureaucracy with its supporters, and all available funds go to paying their salaries, leaving little or nothing to finance the programs that these individuals might wish to pursue. Things as simple but essential as light bulbs to illuminate an art exhibit or workers to hang the paintings can become insurmountable obstacles when there simply are no funds available. Clementina's salary was modest and her plans often frustrated by political and financial constraints, but she managed to participate in numerous projects, and her support and influence are remembered by many, particularly by individuals who in the late 1950s and early 1960s were the young art and theatre people.

The following description gives a sense of the energy that permeated the arts during this time. "During the optimistic days of the '60s a fleeting reform movement, subsequently frustrated, toward an ideological openness that was believed would strengthen cultural activities, began to transform the old-fashioned yet knowing facade of this old mining city. Symptoms of this transformation began to appear: new bookstores opened their doors, small, inexpensive restaurants for students and others of modest resources, new theatre groups, studios and art galleries became meeting places and a painting collective and a theatre group set up in the old 'La Merced' building. It seemed that finally a process was beginning which would put an end to the traditional Honduran uncommunicativeness, a logical consequence of centuries of repression and authoritarianism."[8]

Clementina participated in this revival in a variety of ways, besides the official role she assumed when she worked for the Ministry of Education. She contributed to newspapers and magazines, including *Correo Literario* (Literary Courier), a journal of arts and letters, and *El Día* (The Day), a daily paper for which she wrote the culture column. She organized art exhibits in Tegucigalpa, traveled with the exhibits to other cities within the country, and tried to convince officials to fund a Honduran exhibit that would visit other countries as well. She hoped to make a traveling exhibit one of her official responsibilities, but the Honduran government was not as generous as El Salvador's, and she had to look elsewhere for funds to carry through that idea. She associated with the young artists of Tegucigalpa much as she had with those of El Salvador and by her presence and encouragement stimulated a number of timid or perhaps insecure young talents to show their work and continue with their efforts. Francisco Salvador, now an accomplished actor, director, and playwright, recalls one of his first successes: "In 1963 I produced a play that was an important theatrical event here, a work by Sartre. It was an extraordinary success, thirty performances—this had never happened before in Honduras. And with a Honduran cast. That was when Lucy Ondina made her debut. After the opening performance we went to a restaurant in the center with the rector of the university. Clementina was with us, she was our muse, she had been at the opening, she was very encouraging to Lucy Ondina. I remember she told me that she had seen the play performed—I don't recall if in Mexico or in Cuba—but that she liked my production much better. I felt much more confident after that, because I had not yet studied directing, not until later when I went to Europe."[9]

In 1959 Clementina opened Honduras's first art gallery, Galería Morazánida, hoping perhaps to establish the Honduran version, on a smaller scale, of the Rancho del Artista. But she had no government support for this effort, and no sugar daddy to loan her a house, so she attempted to have a gallery that supported itself through the sale of art. Hondurans were not ready, however, to invest their money in local art. "*In those days paintings sold for thirty-five lempiras. . . . And that was when a gringo came along and bought one. . . . There were no painters here or people interested in buying anything. By the time I realized what the situation was, I was broke.*"[10]

Despite this bleak recollection, and certainly in part through her efforts, Hondurans were beginning to buy Honduran art. For the artists who dream of making a living from their art, it has been a slow process, often resulting in discouragement, poverty, or the decision to work outside of the country. One of the first and most tragic examples of Honduras's earlier disregard for its artists was Pablo Zelaya Sierra. Born in 1896 into a poor but artistic family (his father and aunt were both sculptors) in Ojojona, a small, picturesque town about thirty kilometers southeast of Tegucigalpa, Pablo went to the capital in 1911 and earned a scholarship to the Escuela Normal para Varones (Young Men's Teachers' School). After graduation he worked for a year teaching second grade before deciding to leave the country in search of further education and experience in art. He had already gone as far as his country could take him. "The Honduran environment has not been propitious for satisfying in any meaningful way the desire for knowledge of those young people who have not been content to graduate as teachers or accountants or to study for one of the professions. Honduran youth have not had access to postprimary education that would satisfy their needs in the arts or the various trades, nor have they had official support to get that education outside the country. Whenever a young person dares to solicit official support to leave the country to acquire advanced knowledge, an unequivocal no has been the answer, signaling the cruel end to any aspirations these youth might have had."[11]

In 1916 Pablo left Honduras, traveling on foot first to Nicaragua and then to Costa Rica, where, upon demonstrating his abilities in a national examination, he was chosen to teach painting and drawing at the Liceo de Costa Rica in San José. It became obvious that he was a talented artist who deserved to continue his development in a more stimulating cultural environment. In 1920 the Honduran government, at the request of some influential Costa Rican intellectuals, agreed to finance his studies in Spain. He studied at the traditional Academy of Fine Arts and in the museums of Madrid, turning later to the exciting new ideas of cubism. He stayed in Spain until 1932, painting, exhibiting his work in such prestigious cultural centers as the Ateneo de Madrid, and receiving the praise of critics. He was also struggling to make ends meet, as the promised scholarship from

Honduras failed to materialize after the first two months. He remained faithful to his dream of returning to Honduras to teach what he had learned in Europe. But nothing had changed, art and artists were still not a government priority, so, after exhibiting the work he had brought with him from Spain, he lived in abject poverty for five months until his death in March 1933.

Clementina, who was in Tegucigalpa during his brief return, described his hopeless situation. "*He would sit for hours in my living room; occasionally he would interrupt the silence to relate in a halting voice some episodes from his life, but then he would retreat inside himself again. . . . His happiness at being back in Honduras was brief, and then his Calvary began: you can just imagine what it was for a man like him to go knocking on doors, talking about his problem, about his immediate needs, his poverty, and to encounter deaf ears on all sides, nobody remembered the promises they had made to him.*"[12]

Clementina and Mercedes Agurcía, ever the nurturers of culture, were with him the night he died. His story, with all its painful details, has become a symbol in Honduras for truncated talent, a lesson in the foolishness of trying to be an artist in a society too preoccupied with political struggles to know how to appreciate artistic worth. His story has also become a symbol for those who insist that nothing has changed since his hapless return to Honduras in 1932. They use his example to berate the government for continuing to ignore the arts in the national budget. In a speech given at the Second Congress of Artists and Sculptors in Tegucigalpa in 1986, a professor from the National School of Fine Arts, reminding his audience of Zelaya Sierra's tragic experience as an artist in Honduras, declared: "The social, political and economic conditions at the time Pablo returned to the country are distorted officially. Nor will anyone talk about the circumstances of his death. To do so would be to demonstrate how little the government's attitude toward artists has changed in the last fifty-three years. Everyone knows that recently the Honduran (naturalized) painter Franz Bagus died and that the circumstances surrounding his death and burial were atrocious. It is extremely significant that just as was the case with Zelaya Sierra, there was no casket in which to bury him. But it is even more significant that the poet Clementina Suárez was the one who got the donation to buy one, just as she did when Zelaya Sierra died half a century ago."[13]

Nonetheless, the situation of artists has changed in Honduras, the result more of economic and social factors that have produced individuals with the financial means to purchase the work of Honduran artists for prices in keeping with the rest of Central America, than of changes in the government's attitude toward culture. During the 1980s a number of new galleries opened, and wealthy patrons compete to befriend the most talented or most commercially viable of the local artists. The Sandinista victory in Nicaragua in 1979 prompted many well-to-do and educated Nicaraguans to migrate to Honduras, some of whom have taken an active part in the art business, causing some local observers to wonder if this politically reactionary source of patronage will have an effect on the themes and techniques of Honduras's artists.

The story of contemporary art in Honduras began in 1940 with the opening of the National School of Fine Arts by decree of President Carías. One of Honduras's foremost art historians suggests that "one curious detail is that the school opened without a legal budget or formal documentation and to provide for its administative and teaching needs it relied on funds from the budget of the Ministry of Development and Public Works. This indicates that the school was part of what we might call a plan of authoritarian centralization and not an academic plan, which was in keeping with the administration of government under General Tiburcio Carías."[14] It has since come under the direction of the Ministry of Public Education and has evolved into an institution that has taken as its task the formation of art teachers destined for the public schools of the country. Many of Honduras's artists since 1940 have begun their art education at the National School of Fine Arts and then gone on to study in other countries, notably Italy, Mexico, and Spain. Some have received government scholarships, others have been aided by public service organizations such as the Lions and Rotary Clubs, and a few adventurous souls have tried to make it on their own. Of course there have always been families wealthy enough to send their children abroad to study, but privilege does not necessarily produce talent. In any case, all artists, upon returning to Honduras, have to confront the same realities.

Mario Castillo was one of the first generation of graduates of the National School of Fine Arts who attempted to professionalize their careers in a society taking its first tentative steps as consumers of art. He had returned to Tegucigalpa in 1957 after studying in Italy for six years, where he had become accustomed to exhibiting and selling his artwork. He met Clementina shortly after her return to Honduras. "I was very happy when Clementina approached me to get to know me better. She found out I was back and searched me out—we got along really well. She helped me exhibit my work and find buyers. She took me to the Central Bank, and she convinced them to buy my paintings. She had a way of practically compelling people to buy, she was everyone's friend, she knew everyone in the bank. . . . At that time in Tegucigalpa there were painters, but they didn't exhibit their work. They didn't earn a living with their painting. They taught at the School of Fine Arts and that was it, they didn't exhibit, never made paintings to be exhibited. It was hard, it still is, for a person who is dedicated to art. I took up art idealistically."[15]

Clementina astutely realized that, if one couldn't count on the government, one should try to educate the moneyed classes to support artists. Her method of cajoling, shaming, and pestering bankers and industrialists into purchasing art or donating money, goods, or services for exhibits was an important precedent, and the private sector's support, though not consistently generous, has been vital. "There is still no art museum on a national scale, nor is there a state-run gallery or collection of modern art. There are, however, excellent opportunities for the presentation of artistic works, thanks to the universities, both public and private, the National Library, and the cultural institutes from other countries, and especially due to the support from banks and private industries, such as the beer manufacturers."[16]

While this financial support can be a boon, it can also be dangerous. Difficult though it may be to maintain one's integrity in a world in which those who can afford art are not necessarily those who can appreciate an artist's need to experiment or to express social concerns in one's art, Clementina insists on the honesty of the artistic message in her critical appraisal. She has observed over the years that the growth of the market has led some artists to adapt their technique or message to the consumer. In her characteristic refusal to allow for human weakness, she has created some enemies with her unveiled remarks in this regard. Because of an opinion she expressed in an interview that was published in a local magazine, for example, painter Felipe Burchard was so angry that he went to her house, retrieved the portrait he had done of her, and refused to return it. They haven't spoken for years. The opinion in question was the following: "*Burchard draws and paints magnificently. But his problem is this: he has no ideology. The only thing that interests him is painting his canvasses and selling them. That's why he falls into decorative art, which no longer has any merit in other countries, because a work of art has to have unity, a message, something testimonial.*"[17]

In this same interview she spared no one in her evaluation of the depths to which the art scene in Honduras had descended. When asked what she thought of the School of Fine Arts, she answered, "*Awful. In the first place, the teachers don't even know what teaching painting means. Secondly, they have no idea what a school is. Consequently, that institution has never had what you could call a good period. López Rodezno exploited the school, when there were some magnificent artists there who ended up leaving because they couldn't work—obstacles were put in their way at every turn. Among Honduran painters the problem is that when there is no clear concept of how things are or what one is going to paint, then they fall into what Miguel Angel Ruiz did, which is to go after money and quick success. They don't have anything to paint. One day they paint this, tomorrow they paint that. They have no message, they have nothing to say*" (59).

But this opinion was recorded in 1981. In 1958 she was experiencing a period of energy and optimism, searching out the potential talents among Honduras's artists, befriending them, encouraging them, helping them exhibit and sell their work, and simultaneously building her own collection. The number of portraits of her continued to grow.

Mario Castillo has painted Clementina's portrait twice, solemn, simple portraits, reds and greens in blocks composing and surrounding her figure. He says he does not recall having any particular intention when he painted them, just that he tried to paint her as she was. In his understatement he has managed to capture an essential quality in her expression, a look that goes both inward and out. She seems to be projecting her thoughts while observing them before her, sphinxlike yet somehow communicative.

Another artist who became a close friend and painted several portraits of Clementina was Gelasio Giménez, known simply by his first name, which is also how he signs his work. One of Tegucigalpa's true eccentrics, Gelasio now seldom goes out. He stays in his apartment in Barrio La Hoya, just a few blocks from Galería Clementina Suárez, accompanied by his little dog Li-Po (who gnaws on carrots as if they were bones and eats cookies and potato chips offered by his master) and his cats, who now number nineteen. Gelasio spends his days visiting with friends who drop in to visit and painting series of canvasses on themes that obsess him until he exhausts the theme to move on to a new idea or technique. A series on pollution hangs in his sitting room—air pollution, noise pollution, moral pollution, and so on. He is currently fascinated with representations of the Madonna and Child. Born in Cuba, where he studied art in the 1940s, he left home on an adventure. His desire was to spend a year living in each of the Latin American countries in order to appreciate the differences in the culture of each country and to determine what if anything united them. He traveled to Ecuador, Mexico, Guatemala, and El Salvador. In El Salvador in 1958 the artists he met told him to be sure to meet Clementina when he got to Honduras. Shortly after they connected, he says: "She organized my first exhibit here. She helped me with the publicity, she introduced me to other painters. She has done a lot to encourage painters to exhibit their work, she's always organizing receptions and cocktail parties, she contacts the press, gets the posters. I think she had connections at the brewery, they used to donate beer for the parties. She used to get everything. I don't know why she was so interested in us, some people say it was because she wanted us to paint her portrait, or to give her paintings, but I don't think that was it, that she did it solely for personal gain. There should have been twenty people doing what she did, for whatever motive, that's what we need here, because painters here don't realize that you have to go to the papers, you have to work to make yourself known, to sell your work, but she understood this. She definitely helped us. She helped me with that first exhibit: she borrowed the easels from the School of Fine Arts, she got the exhibit space, she contacted the press, she did everything. She gave the orders. Yes, she has introduced many painters to the public."[18]

Gelasio never continued his adventure, never got any farther than Honduras, for something about the provincial atmosphere of Tegucigalpa proved conducive to his muse. Finding not much else to do, he disciplined himself to paint and sculpt. He was never formally connected with the School of Fine Arts, preferring to center his work and teaching in his own studio. Many artists from the 1960s, among them Alejo Lara, María Talavera, Aníbal, and César Rendón, owe much to his teaching and to the animated exchange of ideas that took place in his studio. He was considered a master, a teacher; he was a magnet, attracting the young art students, winning their affection when he overlooked their pranks and excessive drinking, although he has been known to kick them out of his house on occasions when they got too rowdy.

His friendship with Clementina developed into a love-hate relationship that, despite prolonged periods when they have not been on speaking terms, has endured. He has painted her portrait at least seven times, besides numerous spontaneous drawings sketched when she was in his studio visiting. It was a portrait that once caused them to be estranged for several years. In 1963 Gelasio and Clementina agreed that he would paint a portrait of her nude from the waist up, in honor of those lovely and by then legendary breasts. When he was finished, Clementina wanted to take it home. They got into a heated argument as to whether or not he was ready to allow her to take it. In the ensuing angry exchange, Gelasio grabbed a knife and slit the canvas in several places. He tells it this way: "'Now get out of my house,' I yelled, and I grabbed her and walked her to the door. She says I threw her down the stairs. It's not true. So, to make amends, I sent her a bouquet of flowers and three pounds of grapes. Francisco Salvador, a mutual friend, delivered them to her house. When she found out I was the one who sent them, she threw them out in the street. We didn't speak for two or three years. She didn't want to make up" (ibid.).

He eventually repainted the portrait, which she accepted when he presented it to her. It is one of the most interesting representations in her collection: a middle-aged woman with chiseled features sits with her back to the viewer, studying herself in her dressing table mirror, her hand extended to grasp one of the glass perfume bottles before her. Her expression is introspective, troubled, her upper body draped with a gauzy fabric, covering but not concealing her breasts.

One of the few artistic renderings of herself that Clementina does not have in her home is a bust that Gelasio was working on when they quarreled. Francisco Salvador was at Gelasio's studio when Gelasio attempted to dispose of it. Francisco salvaged it, and it sits atop a chessboard in the gracious old nineteenth-century living room of his family's hacienda in Jacaleapa, on the outskirts of Tegucigalpa. One of Clementina's projects, the one she would most like to see become a reality before she dies, is the construction of a national art museum, to which she intends to donate her collection of portraits. If it ever gets built, Francisco plans to see to it that the infamous bust sits among Clementina's other likenesses.

"My Exile Is Voluntary"

As election time approached in 1963, the army once again intervened in national politics, initiating with this coup a period of military rule that installed Colonel Osvaldo López Arellano as head of state. Under the guise of keeping Honduras safe from communism, now that Cuba had declared itself a Marxist state and the United States was supporting anticommunist governments in the region, López Arellano's government instituted a systematic program of repression against workers, farmers, intellectuals, and progressive university students, many of whom fled the country or were killed.[19]

Following the coup, and despite the danger, a group of students and other sympathizers staged a protest they called "No estamos conformes" (we will not comply), a jazz and poetry recital in which Clementina was invited to participate as guest of honor. She recited a new poem, "Combate" (Combat), which has become one of her most anthologized works. It is short and simple, powerful and direct, a statement that not only proclaimed the poet's allegiance to the popular struggle, but made the poem itself a weapon in the fight.[20]

> I am a poet,
> an army of poets.
> Today I want to write a poem,
> poems that cry out,
> poems that are weapons
> and hang them on doors,
> in prison cells,
> on school walls.
> Today I want to build and destroy,
> raise hope on the scaffolds.
> Awaken the child
> archangel of swords,
> be lightning, thunder,

of heroic stature
to raze, to ravage
the rotten roots of my people.

———

Yo soy un poeta,
un ejército de poetas.
Y hoy quiero escribir un poema,
un poema silbatos,
un poema fusiles
para pegarlos en las puertas,
en la celda de las prisiones,
en los muros de las escuelas.
Hoy quiero construir y destruir,
levantar en andamios la esperanza.
Despertar al niño
arcángel de las espadas,
ser relámpago, trueno,
con estatura de héroe
para talar, arrasar
las podridas raíces de mi pueblo.

Two years earlier, in March 1961, Clementina had been invited by the Instituto Cubano de Amistad con los Pueblos (Cuban Institute of Friendship with the People) to visit Cuba. She returned from her visit full of enthusiasm and praise for the Cuban people's revolution and did not hesitate to express her praise publicly. In the atmosphere of growing polarization and anticommunist fear, she was bold about which side she was on, but somehow the powerful arm of political repression never hurt her. While others have disappeared or been silenced in one way or another, she has continued to criticize the government with impunity, perhaps because she had so shrewdly cultivated friends on all levels of government and power, or perhaps because, with her notoriously sharp tongue, any attempt to silence her would probably have caused more embarrassment than anyone was willing to deal with.

With this new wave of repression came a renewed restlessness in Clementina. Honduras had proved to her that it was not the place where her vision of a community of creative artists with herself as matriarch would materialize. So once again she set her sights on El Salvador. She was nostalgic for what she had created but let slip away. If her memory of the Rancho was anything like this reminiscence of Salvadoran poet Roberto Armijo, written in exile in Paris, it is easy to understand why she would want to regain that time.

> I met Clementina in 1954, one Saturday when I went to visit the Rancho del Artista, a very pretty house that Clementina was renting from the owner General Ascensio Menéndez. On that first visit I was very impressed. I remember going up a steep paved driveway bordered by trees and gardens. At the end of the drive was a house with spacious rooms. I was wearing my student uniform from the National Institute. When I entered I found myself surrounded by paintings by Mexican and Salvadoran artists. . . . Clementina was at the far end of the room. She was a very beautiful woman, of slight build. She spoke very loudly, and when she had had a few drinks this characteristic was accentuated. Of course to me she was the legendary poet, the woman touched by the fire of strange things. From my provincial point of view she was something extraordinary. That was an unforgettable night for me, I remember especially the sense of mystery I intuited and the feeling of being in a different environment from anything I had known.[21]

She was also depressed by the political situation and the apparent lack of concern by the government for the welfare of its citizens, especially for the least fortunate. In a poem from this time, "En el café" (In the Café), she describes the hopeless poverty, both material and spiritual, that saddens her country.

> Every day I sit in the café
> as if I could push time ahead.
> Everything around us is misery and suffering
> even the way we speak.
>
> There are those
> who hope that someone
> will appear

to pay for their cup of coffee.
(My God, fifteen cents.)

Women worn out from life
with the true weariness of the flesh . . .

This immense solitude, this absence, when does it attack?
Where does the drama begin or end?
It would be enough just to close one's eyes
and enjoy seeing one's self
close, so close.

In fact who isn't happy that way
Like a peaceful sky
Still and deaf amid the blood's turbulence.
What a restful life. Will I ever know it?
No, it's not what I want,
I don't want to let go of my anguish.
I don't want a prison for my soul,
but prefer to swim in the shadows.

I tell myself:
I have to grow,
inevitably
children stand
before me

I am barefoot with them
looking for bread
in my small hands.

Todos los días me siento en el café
como para empujar la andadura del tiempo.
Todo, a nuestro alrededor es miseria, miseria
hasta en la forma de hablar.

Hay quien
espera que de pronto

aparezca quien le pague
una taza de café.
(Válgame Dios, de quince centavos.)

Mujeres gastadas de vivirse
con el verdadero cansancio del cuerpo . . .

Esta gran soledad, esta ausencia, cuándo ataca?
en dónde empieza o termina el drama?
bastará sólo con cerrar los ojos
y gozar de mirarse,
cerca, cerquísima.

De hecho así quién no es feliz
Igual que un sosegado cielo
Inmóvil y sordo a la turbulencia de la sangre.
Qué descansada vida. La gozaré?
No, no la quiero,
no quiero soltar mi angustia
No quiero cárcel para mi ser,
prefiero nadar entre tinieblas.

Me lo digo:
Yo tengo que crecer,
inevitablemente
criaturas interpuestas
me suceden

con ellas estoy descalza
y queriendo descubrir el pan
en mis manos pequeñas.

With her poetry she was preparing herself to leave again. The poverty and inertia were affecting her spirit. In "Navidad, 1966" (Christmas, 1966) she has lost completely the optimism of *Song of the Found Fatherland and Its Hero* and rejects her country's pettiness.

I cannot find a single person happy
with the joy of certain dialogue;

the word is impossible, lost:
the cry is withheld.

No one laughs in my country
How easy! Everything within reach, and no one risks
having, winning, what is his.
It is all so clear,
one only has to see the poor,
with their voice of warning.
They are the truth
in their collective body and name.

Merchants, in search of profit,
endlessly tally accounts . . .

Drown in this cup of wine! . . .

My country is made of stone. Sacrificial homeland!
heroes rest in your lap
but plural joy never comes,
years, centuries, time burying time
like the cross man bears. . . .

But this Christmas, 1966,
I see only hopeless horizons
for myself and my country:
Once again my body proclaims my desire;
I do not want an unworthy country
or small-hearted affections.

No encuentro a una sola persona feliz
con júbilo de diálogo cierto,
la palabra es imposible, perdida:
retiene el llanto.

En mi Patria nadie ríe
¡Qué fácil! Todo al alcance, y ninguno puede arriesgarse
a tener, a conquistar, lo que le pertenece.
Todo es bastante claro,

no hay más que mirar a los pobres,
con su altavoz de alarma.
Que ellos sí son la verdad
con su extendido cuerpo y su nombre.

Los mercaderes, que sólo buscan monedas,
cuentan cuentos sin parar . . .

¡Húndete en esta copa de vino! . . .

Mi tierra es de piedra ¡Patria inmolada!
en su regazo descansan héroes
pero el plural alegría nunca llega,
años, siglos, y el tiempo hundiendo al tiempo
como cruz en que pertenece el hombre. . . .

Pero en esta Navidad, 1966,
en que sin alternativa vigilo mi horizonte
y el de mi patria:
En forma corporal rubrico una vez más mi anhelo;
No quiero Patria mezquina
ni cariños con corazón de hormiga.

Unwilling to identify with a country she cannot respect, the poet is faced with the task of reconciling this pessimism with her earlier optimism. Her solution is to redefine *patria* and to reposition herself as a poet in relation to the new concept. Several of the poems from *The Poet and Her Signs* are experiments in a new way of looking at belonging. In "Con las espadas triunfales" (With Triumphant Swords) she announces, "My exile is voluntary." She explains that her absences from her country have been necessary for her to maintain her pride and determination. Every individual is a country, a microcosm of the patria.

Because one must know that the heart has its flags
and its great and small human epics,
where the voice emerges like the dawn
and we grow forever with a human root
with unshakeable faith in the people.

———

Porque hay que saber que el corazón tiene sus banderas
y sus grandes y pequeñas epopeyas populares,
donde emerge la voz como una aurora
y crecemos para siempre con una raíz humana
con fe inquebrantable al pueblo.

She rejects the romantic notion that the patria is a force or a presence that nurtures and protects its children. National myths are lies. The measure of the person is the measure of the nation.

It took me a long time to discover the meaning of *patria*
animosities opened and closed my eyes.
Slavery and freedom were the names
in which my unwritten heart fell.

Today I only know you live where I live
and nothing can dislodge you,
you are the wound where I suffer and delight
where I gather messages and tear pages from calendars
to affirm you exist and you should exist
as I want you to be,
among salt and honey, sweat and blood.

Until then, if there is a then,
I go forward, perhaps back
and again I pass by, Patria,
the waters of your bridge.

Tardé mucho en saber lo que era la Patria
los rencores abrían y cerraban mis ojos.
Esclavitud y libertad eran los nombres,
que en mi inédito pecho caía de bruces.

Hoy solamente sé que habitas donde yo habito
y que nada te desclava,
que eres la mordedura con que sufro y gozo
donde recojo mensajes y deshojo calendarios
para afirmar que existes y que debes existir

como yo quiero que existas,
entre sal y miel, sudor y sangre.

Ya para entonces, si es que hay entonces,
camino adelante tal vez regrese
y nuevamente atraviese, Patria
las aguas de tu puente.

She insists in "Con mis versos saludo a las generaciones futuras" (With My Poems I Hail the Generations to Come) that by choosing to be the measure of herself, she broke the chains of patria and now has friends and compatriots wherever she goes. Patria is now just one of many facets of a life devoted to poetry and justice. Transcendence is the key, to be beyond patria, above it, able to encompass it and more in her vision.

Alone,
for rejecting one road
and forging others,
with mounds of people I built my country.

Perhaps many tears have been shed in my past
but with them I fed hope.
Doors were tightly sealed from me
but my pain in its wisdom walked on
til it found the authentic path.

It is hard to see the truth
and the straight way of justice.

Now,
wherever I go
I will never be alone,
because I do not begin but rather end
in the blood of my offspring.

How distant is the solitude of my *Patria* and my blood!
today my small body pushes the stars
and with my poems I hail the generations to come.

———

Sola,
por dejar un camino
y amojonar otros caminos,
con terrones de pueblo construí mi país.

Detrás de mí quizá quedarán muchas lágrimas vertidas
pero con ellas fue que alimenté la esperanza.
Las puertas para mí estuvieron herméticamente cerradas
pero la sabiduría de mi dolor supo andar y andar
hasta encontrar el auténtico sendero.

Cuesta vislumbrar la verdad
y el camino recto de la justicia.

Ahora,
a cualquier lugar que llegue
ya nunca puedo estar sola,
porque no comienzo en la sangre de mis descendientes
sino que termino en ella.

Qué lejana la soledad de mi Patria y mi sangre!
hoy mi pequeñísimo cuerpo empuja las estrellas
y con mis versos saludo a las generaciones futuras.

But there is always the other side to this tough, self-made woman—the tender flesh that has borne children, the tired flesh that longs for comfort and protection. The tough side is usually uppermost, but sometimes in a poem the other need is exposed. In "Honduras, Alba, Silvia" she gathers up her children and her country in a maternal embrace. She calls them home, but her voice returns as an echo. Life goes on; they do not hear her.

The hills always before me, my country in between.
From everywhere I call you,
Again and again my cry resounds:

> Why do you not hear my voice?
> Patria, daughter.
> Honduras, Alba, Silvia.

On the shore, here before me,
Seeing that the river flows on.

Insane poetry of life,
My country, Alba, Silvia.
I call out to you:

> Can you hear me, can you hear my voice?
> Honduras, Alba, Silvia,

And the river flows on.

———

Los cerros siempre enfrente, mi patria en medio.
Desde cualquier parte te llamo,
Una y otra vez mi grito se repite:

> Por qué no escuchan mi voz?
> Patria, hija.
> Honduras, Alba, Silvia.

En la orilla, aquí enfrente,
Mirando que el río no se detiene.

Loca, loca poesía la vida,
Mi patria, Alba, Silvia.
Yo te llamo:

> Oyen, oyen mi voz?
> Honduras, Alba, Silvia,

Y el río no se detiene.

Having given up on Honduras as the site for the next Rancho, Clementina set to work to gather the necessary resources to rebuild in El Salvador. She knew that this time, besides contributions from wealthy patrons of the arts and from the government, she would have to come up with a plan to make the Rancho self-supporting. From 1963 until 1969 she traveled back and forth throughout Central America numerous times. In some ways her travels were not so different from those earlier vagabond days, except that now she was not so interested in staging poetry recitals, although she participated on occasion in collective readings or recited some of her poems at gatherings in her honor. She says that gradually she lost interest in reciting; instead, friends tell how she would often extemporize at parties, making up verses on the spot or reciting one of her poems with additional verses or repetitions. Her concern now was to seek support for her projects—the new Rancho, her traveling art exhibit. During these years she exhibited her own collection dozens of times and began collecting the work of young Central American poets with the intention of publishing an anthology. She found friendly support from President Schick of Nicaragua and once again at the Ministry of Culture in El Salvador. In a story on her that appeared in the magazine *Centro América Bohemia,* there is a photograph of her sitting at a table in a café with her Honduran friend Francisco Salvador, director of the University Theatre; Brazilian dance teacher and choreographer Rivo de Silva; Honduran actor Ricardo Licona; and Mario Vidal and René Figueroa, actor and director, respectively, from Guatemala. The interviewer asks her to describe her idea for a new Rancho in El Salvador. "*We now have more than 100 works—prints, paintings, sculpture—that will comprise the permanent exhibit. With this we will open up the market and be able to establish a presence in the Latin American consciousness. . . . We feel our project should have a spiritual base, so that the human element is understood and appreciated, this is the most important aspect.*"

Francisco Núñez Arrué, Salarrué's wealthy cousin, entrepreneur, patron of the arts, and longtime friend, admirer, and lover of Clementina, will be her primary source of funding. He had given her a piece of property on a hill overlooking San Salvador in the residential development that subsequently became the elite Colonia Escalón, where she planned to start construction. "*We have the land, as well as offers of construction materials and help with the expenses. There will be a lecture hall, a room for the permanent exhibit, and four guest rooms for visiting artists. We have a financial plan based on a framing shop and the sale of art supplies.*"[22]

While promoting her project she had also been working on other things. Two new books of hers were soon to be published by El Salvador's Ministry of Culture: *Salomar* (Sing Out), a book of poetry; and a departure for Clementina, *La Ronda* (Rounds), children's verses with illustrations by Mexican painter Ricardo Bárcenas, ex-director of the Academy of San Carlos and illustrator for Walt Disney Studios. In a letter from El Salvador to Francisco Salvador in August 1965, she sounds hopeful yet realistic. "*San Salvador is a big city now and life is hectic, even more so because I arrived full of projects that I am working on little by little. First: I have sent two manuscripts to the printer for publication. One is songs for children, illustrated, the other is poetry, unfortunately I had to select the poems the editor preferred. But it's better than nothing. It will be titled 'Salomar,' which means the singing out of travelers on the road, to feel less lonely more than to announce their arrival. Do you like it? My second project is that I am arranging to move here for good. Not because I don't love Honduras, but because I love it too much. But frankly, from a distance the situation looks bleak. It seems that one must jump through absurd hoops to accomplish even the most insignificant tasks. I hope you don't have to go through what I did, every day I feel more estranged from the petty details through which everything is manipulated at home. I have seen all my old friends here, everyone has been so loving! I am living in a house that belongs to don Francisco Núñez Arrué, it's charming: after that little room I was living in, this feels as big as the world . . . it's on Roosevelt Avenue. . . . But you know, Francisco, we can't just waste our time complaining, we have to move on with our projects, even if it's by the skin of our teeth.*"[23]

In the interview in *Centro América Bohemia* just mentioned, she said: "*I am leaving Honduras not because I don't love it, but because the best way to love it is by doing my work, and I am convinced that it is absolutely impossible for me to accomplish anything here. I don't want to become just one more of the many talented Hondurans who achieve nothing. I want to be active until the very last day of my life. I believe that politics, which is one hundred years behind the times in Honduras, is the reason we have not been able to establish a cultural movement here. Intellectuals are totally disregarded and never fight back. It's really a shame, because there is so much talent in Honduras.*"

War

How difficult, then, to have to return. Yet return she did, but not because she wanted to. In July 1969 Honduras and El Salvador entered a short but intense confrontation referred to in the foreign press as the "Soccer War." Although the period of actual fighting lasted scarcely a month, the reasons for the conflict reach back to the formation of the Central American Common Market in 1958 and even earlier, and hostilities between the two countries lasted for at least a decade after the battles. U.S. historians have a tendency to interpret the confrontation, which erupted during a soccer match, as the result of competition among workers from the two countries for scarce jobs.

Many Honduran observers attribute the conflict to more far-reaching causes. According to Quiñónez and Argueta, the causes included: the unequal development among the member nations of the Central American Common Market, Honduras being the least industrialized of the five; the attempt on the part of the Salvadoran oligarchy to expand its industrial and commercial base at the expense of the Honduran market; a growing Honduran middle class with aspirations to power; the demand by Honduran as well as Salvadoran peasants for land; and the unwillingness of the oligarchies of both countries to confront and attempt to solve their internal problems, this attitude leading to the acceptance of armed conflict as a political escape valve.[24]

Whatever the actual causes, the confrontation was angry and violent, and ordinary citizens found themselves caught in an atmosphere of passion and revenge. One woman recalls, "Many people, even politically enlightened people, went to war against those from the other country. I was in Honduras at the time; I had to leave, because I am Salvadoran. They were looking for Salvadorans to kill them. The same thing happened in El Salvador against Hondurans."

So Clementina, although there were times when she considered herself more Salvadoran than Honduran, had to return to Honduras until things cooled down. Assuming that her stay would be brief, and anxious to return to El Salvador as soon as possible, she stayed with relatives and friends in Tegucigalpa for periods of time, partly because she wasn't interested in setting up an apartment only to dismantle it, partly because she arrived with very little money. But the consequences of the conflict proved to be much more prolonged and devastating than anyone had anticipated. Honduras broke all economic ties with El Salvador, retired from the Central American Common Market, closed the Honduran portion of the Pan-American Highway to Salvadoran traffic, and closed the border between the two countries, making it impossible for Clementina to return. As one resident of Honduras recalls it, "Many Salvadorans had to leave the country, people who had practically grown up here—it was horrible. They closed the border for about ten years. Hondurans couldn't travel to El Salvador, there was no communication, one couldn't even send a letter. And if you did try to send a letter, you were under suspicion. It was somewhat of an artificial war; it wasn't a war that was the culmination of a process of which the people were conscious, no, but it brought out intense feelings."

A group of Honduran writers, caught up in the chauvinism of the moment, drafted an open letter condemning the Salvadoran people. Clementina refused to sign it. What a cruel twist of fate! Of course, even if she had somehow managed to return to El Salvador, there would have been little chance now of a Honduran getting any kind of government support there. So the weeks turned into months and then years, and Clementina remained in Honduras. Those books that the Salvadoran Ministry of Culture had agreed to publish never materialized. "*Lost,*" she says, shrugging her shoulders. And the Rancho? She still owns that piece of land in Colonia Escalón. But Francisco Núñez Arrué died, the construction materials disappeared, the promises of financial support were forgotten. A relative of Clementina's from the Salvadoran side of the family told of the tragic waste of culture and dreams that social unrest can cause. "Clementina had everything she needed to build the Ranch, she had the wood, everything. Núñez Arrué had a house where he let Clementina store the paintings in a back room. It was a kind of studio where she sometimes stayed, it was full of artwork. When she left she locked the room. When she returned much later she discovered that she had left the refrigerator connected and that water had drained out and damaged the paintings."

She lost another significant part of her collection as a result of the hostilities between the two countries. In May 1969 Clementina arrived in Tegucigalpa with more than one hundred paintings from her collection to stage an exhibit of Central American art. When the exhibit closed, she left the paintings for safekeeping in the Salvadoran embassy, as she was planning to return shortly to El Salvador with them. War broke out, diplomatic relations were severed between the two countries, and the Salvadoran ambassador, Colonel Horacio Melara Pinto, returned to El Salvador, locking the paintings in the embassy and leaving all official matters in the hands of the Mexican ambassador. But no one seemed to know or care who was in charge of what, and Clementina, despite repeated letters and visits to Mexican and Honduran officials, was denied access to her collection. At some point the Mexican ambassador tired of baby-sitting the Salvadoran embassy, and the building was left unguarded. Finally, in 1978, thanks to the Honduran ambassador in Mexico, Renato Irigoyen, Clementina was allowed to enter the embassy to recover her paintings. Upon examining the collection she discovered that forty-four of the most valuable paintings were missing. It was reported that "among the missing paintings were works by Miguel Angel Ruiz, Antonio Velásquez, Benigno Gómez, Pablo Zelaya Sierra and others, besides the legendary portraits of Clementina painted by Diego Rivera."[25]

CHAPTER SIX

Plenitude

Recognition at Home

While Clementina was angry, discouraged, and increasingly pessimistic about the possibility of returning to El Salvador, feeling trapped once again in what she experienced as the pettiness of Honduran society and its lack of cultural and revolutionary commitment, Honduras was busily recognizing the merits of its prodigal daughter. On 19 September 1969, a ceremony to honor her literary accomplishments was staged at the National University. Orchestrated by Leticia de Oyuela, director of University Extension, it was a gala affair. Speakers praised her, and Francisco Salvador prepared a lyrical biographical essay entitled "Clementina: Mujer, Maternidad, Revolución" (Clementina: Woman, Motherhood, Revolution), which he delivered dressed in a tuxedo, backed up by a chorus of young women who recited her poetry. Her lifelong friend Medardo Mejía bought her a gold lamé dress at an expensive boutique in town. She sat solemnly in the seat of honor, coifed in the high bouffant style popular then, wearing the thick-rimmed glasses that she preferred for public functions. There was music, theatre, art, poetry; the hall was decorated with trees and fountains. Clementina was pleased, but beyond surprise. Honduras had finally come around to applauding her talent. About time. To complete the homage to her, University Extension published two books, *The Poet and Her Signs* and *Clementina Suárez,* a compilation of semblanzas, critical essays on her poetry, anecdotes, interviews, and poems composed in her honor, interspersed with reproductions of the many portraits of her painted over the years. The essays tend to be admiring, some of them written in an awed tone, in wonder that such a dynamic and original woman could be from Honduras, notorious even in Central America for its provincialism. The book is a fascinating document in the cultural history of twentieth-century Central America, for the essays and portraits are from 1930 to 1969, and the authors and artists are names that students of Central American art and literature will recognize for their prominence and importance. A second edition of this book was published in 1982, updated to include the more recent portraits, interviews, and verbal sketches.

The selection and arrangement of the poems in *The Poet and Her Signs* was supervised by Leticia de Oyuela, known affectionately in Tegucigalpa as doña Lety. Doña Lety met Clementina in 1956 and was intrigued by this small, determined woman waiting to talk to the rector of the university and wearing a comfortable dress and flat-heeled, round-toed, little-girl shoes, who had been living in El Salvador and whose extended absences from Honduras had made her a mysterious figure and the subject of colorful gossip. Doña Lety is herself an important figure in Honduran culture; a woman of letters and a true intellectual, she is an authority on Honduran art and history. She is also a keen observer of human nature and derives great satisfaction from discovering and encouraging Honduran talent. She was responsible, for example, for encouraging Teresita Fortín to paint "Recuerdos" (Memories), a series of twenty paintings inspired by her dreams and memories, that doña Lety exhibited in her gallery Nuevo Continente in 1977. This exposure led to invitations to Fortín to exhibit her work in Rome and Washington, D.C., and to recognition of her work at home, where she was honored with the Pablo Zelaya Sierra National Art Award. Doña Lety was also one of the first to recognize the talent of primitive painter Roque Zelaya, who has since become Honduras's most respected painter in this field.

Clementina of course needed no introduction to Honduran society, but doña Lety was instrumental in reminding people that Clementina was one of theirs and that she deserved some public recognition. She and her family have maintained a close and supportive relationship with Clementina throughout the years. She knows Clementina as well as anyone, although as Clementina once said in a pensive moment, "*I know that Lety loves me very much, but how deep inside me does she see? There is always something lacking.*"

In *The Poet and Her Signs* Clementina continues her efforts to explain herself and to construct her identity. In "Mirando extasiada al cielo" (Looking Ecstatically at the Sky) she recognizes that one obstacle to fixing her identity in a readable or comprehensible form is that she changes over time.

Seated at the edge of life
I am three.
My dream, my poetry and I;
but what I say now
my blood erases in its rapid flow,
while the clock
—breakwater of days—
invents a new hour,
in time's gradual scale.
Before the pendulum's arc
and in the swallow's flight
is my moon, that laughs and cries
in an exact protectorate of words.
I don't know how to close my eyes,
regain afternoons,
memories,
landscapes,
in a single hidden source
that affirms definitively
the first-born moment;
at the level of the rose that does not wither
at the breast,
or of the cloud that would have stayed
at the window
looking ecstatically at the sky.

———

Sentada a la orilla de la vida
yo soy tres.

Mi sueño, mi poesía y yo;
pero lo que ahora digo
lo borra mi sangre con su veloz vertiente,
entretanto el reloj
—rompeolas de los días—
inventa una nueva hora,
en la escala gradual del tiempo.
Anterior al péndulo
y al vuelo de las golondrinas,
está mi luna que llora y ríe
en un exacto protectorado de palabras.
Yo no sé cómo cerrar los ojos,
reconquistar las tardes,
las memorias,
y los paisajes,
en una sola fuente recóndita
que afirme definitivamente
el soplo primigenio;
a nivel de la rosa que no se marchita
en el seno,
o de la nube que se hubiera quedado
prendida en la ventana
mirando extasiada al cielo.

She draws on memory to help her discern the pattern of her life. She begins "Poema al hombre y su esperanza" (Poem for Mankind and Its Hope) with an inward search that takes her back in time to her beginnings.

I look now within myself
and am so distant,
budding in hidden spaces
rootless, no tears, no crying out.
—Complete within myself—
in my own hands,
in the world of tenderness
created by my own flesh.

I have watched myself be born, grow, without a sound,
without branches of aching arms,
subtle, silent, with no words to wound,
nor womb overflowing with fishes.

Like a dream-rose my world was fashioned . . .

———

Ahora me miro por dentro
y estoy tan lejana,
brotándome en lo escondido
sin raíces, ni lágrimas, ni grito.
—Intacta en mi misma—
en las manos mías,
en el mundo de ternura
creado por mi forma.

Me he visto nacer, crecer, sin ruido,
sin ramas que duelan como brazos,
sutil, callada, sin palabras para herir,
ni vientre que rebace de peces.

Como rosa de sueño se fue formando mi mundo . . .

Her strongest and clearest self-construction is her declaration of autonomy and authenticity in "Rebeldía" (Rebellion). Her voice in this poem is emphatic; with it she dismisses those who in their small-mindedness and short-sightedness have obstructed her path.

. . . .

It doesn't matter that they try to deny
the light of my destiny,
that they unmercifully rend
the lace of my dream,
that they destroy the glass of my mirror,
that they submerge me in a night without goodbyes,
that they angrily deny me bread, salt and water.
Don't expect this to make me bow and scrape,

though flesh will always be flesh
my entrails are now like steel.

But those who attempt this
need not fear me
they ought to know
that I learned to sing with the right words.
That I have found the truth in the marrow of my bones
that's why I walk with my back to the dawn
as if she herself were born from my rib.

———

. . . .

No importa que pretendan negar
la luz de mi destino,
que rompan despiadadamente
el encaje del sueño,
que destruyan el azogue de mi espejo,
que me sumerjan en la noche sin adioses,
que con saña me nieguen el pan, la sal y el agua.
No esperen que por ello me doble dócilmente,
aunque la carne sea siempre la carne
mis entrañas ya casi son de acero.

Mas los que así pretendan
que por mí no teman
que haría falta para ello desconocer
que yo aprendí a cantar con las palabras justas.
Y que he encontrado la verdad en la médula de mis huesos
y que por eso marcho con espaldas de la aurora
como si ella misma naciera en mi costado

And she intends to continue her life's struggle, writing poems to stay alive.

To live is to keep on living,
searching minute by minute

to find the perfect word
that allows us to speak the message
of the truly eternal.

———

Que vivir es seguir viviendo,
buscarse minuto a minuto,
hasta encontrar la voz servidora
que nos permita dar el mensaje
de lo verdaderamente eterno.

In "Mi corazón en zozobra" (My Uneasy Heart) she asks, "Who marks the step? / Who determines the dream? / Who binds or loosens joy?" (¿Quién establece el paso / Quién norma el sueño / Quién ata o desata la alegría?) In answer, she sweeps back over her own life, retracing her steps—her changes and decisions—bringing herself back to the present. In poem after poem she draws the same conclusions as she tells the metaphorical tale of her life: that she has lived well because she has been free and she has loved; that life has been a struggle, but that she has learned to love the fight; that life is poetry, that poetry is hope and truth and humanity, that poetry is her life.

Solitude makes its inevitable appearance in these poems, but now it is her guide, woven into memory. It is a convergence of time and space that assists her in self-knowledge. She inhabits it; it is welcome. "Now I can hear my inner voice / and discover the small things that hurt me." (Ahora puedo escucharme por dentro / y descubrir las menudas cosas que me dañaron.)

Memory has also become a central force in her love poems. Love is now emotion recollected in tranquillity rather than the vivid passion that filtered through the pores of her language in her earlier work. In "Poema del amor, amor . . ." (Poems of Love, Love . . .) memory/absence has become as real as present/presence.

. . . .

I am remembering, no, loving,
coloring small things that I
put in order in my house,

in the sea-house I carry inside me
dressed in sand and shore and foam.

Remembering . . . rose by rose
asleep or awake,
with the humble opulence
of loving you, simply loving you,
blessed in my arms,
complete in your body,
parasol, sky, city of mine,
sweet land, warm paradise.

———

. . . .
Estoy recordando, no, amando,
coloreando minúsculas cosas
que voy ordenando en la casa,
en la marinera casa que llevo por dentro
vestida de playa, espuma y arena.

Recordando . . . rosa a rosa
despierta o dormida,
con la humilde opulencia
de quererte, simplemente quererte,
bendito entre mis brazos,
absoluto en tu cuerpo,
parasol, cielo, ciudad mía,
tierra dulce, paraíso tibio.

Memory, in fact, is sometimes more real than a palpable presence as she expresses in "Poema de su presencia."

If you were here
you would not be so close,
or so secure, or so transparent.
Or so preserved for perennial love
that fills body and soul
with pure happiness. . . .

There are no countries of yours
that memory does not visit,
I trace them step by step,
walk in and out of them . . .

———

Si estuvieras aquí
no estarías tan cerca,
ni tan seguro, ni tan transparente.
Ni tan guardado para el perenne amor
que de dicha cristalina
el alma y el cuerpo llena. . . .

Ya no hay país tuyo
que la memoria no recuerde,
paso a paso iluminada los recorro,
salgo y entro en ellos . . .

Two of the new poems in *The Poet and Her Signs* are a return to the voluptuousness of her early work. "Mágicamente iluminada como en un paraíso" (Magically Illuminated as in a Paradise) is a celebration of physical femininity. It is a tropical poem, full of sunlight, warm air, and sensuality. She takes off her dress, kicks off her shoes.

I have absorbed, breathed, shouted,
live, live, live,
as if I were waking up again and again
a bee busily
sipping its heavenly honey. . . .

I throw open
the doors of my house
and scatter the bedclothes.
I look in the mirror, a dwelling
that cannot contain me. . . .

———

He absorbido, he olfateado, he gritado,
vivir, vivir, vivir,

como si despertara una y otra vez
y fuera abeja laboriosa
que libara su miel astral. . . .

Abro precipitadamente
las puertas de mi aposento
y tiro lejos la sábana.
Me asomo al espejo como a una morada
que no habrá de retenerme. . . .

"El regalo" (The Gift) echoes the central gesture of *Temples of Fire:* the poet is a cornucopia of treasures, all of them gifts for her lover. She offers "a piece of my skirt" (un pedazo de mi falda); "my feet intoxicated with fruit" (la ebriedad de mis pies frutales); "the shadow of my errant body" (la sombra de mi errante cuerpo); "the mouth that bites you" (la boca que te muerde); "the skin that clothes me" (la piel que me viste). But most of these new poems point to a shift in the locus of her poetic center from her sensual self to a wiser, more contemplative space. Around this time she decided to stop lying about her age. Articles about her usually claim 1903 or 1906 as the year of her birth. She once said that she had added and subtracted years so often that she was no longer sure exactly how old she was. A search for records in the town hall in Juticalpa produced her birth certificate, fixing her arrival on 12 May 1902. Sometime in her sixties she knew she was an older woman, not yet old, but no longer young. In her eighties she told her sister that perhaps she should look ahead and begin to plan for her old age.

With its tribute at the University and two books published, 1969 was a big year for Clementina, but it was just the beginning of a series of honors, awards, and invitations, in Honduras and elsewhere, recognizing her efforts in the domain of culture and rewarding her for all those years of not giving up. One of the most significant of the many awards was the Ramón Rosa National Literature Award, which she received in 1970. This distinction, created in 1949 by President Gálvez, was awarded for the first time in 1951 to Luis Andrés Zúñiga and in subsequent years to Clementina's first husband Guillermo Bustillo Reina, to Claudio Barrera, Jacobo Cárcamo, and Daniel Laínez. No writers were honored from 1957 to 1967, but, through the instigation of congressional representative Manuel Luna

Mejía, it was reactivated in 1968 and presented to novelist Argentina Díaz Lozano. In 1970, by popular demand, Clementina was chosen to receive this honor.[1]

Clementina's acceptance speech was short and to the point and expressed her refusal to speak the official language of insincerity. "*I'm not going to say that I don't deserve this distinction, because that would be false modesty; yes, I deserve it, because I have been faithful to my vocation and have maintained it with the highest dignity. . . . I have never enjoyed official favor or the privileges of other writers, but have made it on my own with hardship and unpleasantness. I have lived modestly and have not compromised the dimensions of my humanity . . . I am grateful for this honor and must say that I have earned it thanks to the affectionate stubbornness of my friends who year after year have worked for my candidacy.*"[2]

The awards continued to pile up, and with them came invitations to speak at all kinds of events and gatherings. Some of the more prestigious plaques and medals have found a space on the walls of her bedroom and kitchen, and more than once she has attempted, with partial success, to gather together all the newspaper and magazine articles, the catalogues from all the art exhibits she has organized, the documents and paraphernalia and photographs that form a paper trail of one woman's struggle to be a poet and a worker in the fields of culture.

The awards and invitations that Clementina has most appreciated were the ones that included a trip, for she has never lost her wanderlust. She continued to carry canvasses around, organizing exhibits in the United States, the Dominican Republic, and throughout Central America and Panama. But now she insisted on traveling with a modicum of comfort—no more knapsack, although she still stayed with friends, settling in and making herself at home. In 1970 she traveled to Europe as the guest of Miguel Angel Asturias, who was living with his wife in Paris. She visited Russia and China thanks to invitations she received at the prompting of her friends Asturias and Pablo Neruda. She went to Spain as a guest of the Association of Latin American Writers in 1971 and to Argentina in 1985 to receive an honorary degree from the University of Argentina. She attended numerous literary congresses and peace conferences, always shocking and delighting the younger generations of writers and revolutionaries with her outspokenness, her stamina, and her willingness to criticize repressive governments and denounce U.S. intervention in Central America. She became a living emblem to them of an earlier generation that, through the lens of time and nostalgia, seemed brave and wise to the young people battling imperialism, death squads, and the militarization of their countries.

In 1979, to celebrate the twentieth anniversary of the revolution, the Cuban government organized the Festival Mundial de la Juventud (World Youth Festival). The group of students from the University of Honduras who were in charge of selecting the young people who would represent Honduras at the event decided to invite Clementina to accompany them. Although the focus of the celebration was youth, the committee agreed that she should go as an honorary guest because of her youthful enthusiasm and because she had contributed to revolutionary culture by being a role model to younger generations. One of the young poets in the group recalled that because of travel restrictions to Cuba, they had to go via Panama. Clementina had been asked to bring a selection of the work of young Honduran artists. On the return trip, some of the paintings were lost in Panama. He remembers Clementina's presence in Cuba: "There were people from all over the world. It was impressive seeing Clementina there, surrounded by young people and their activities, and she participated in everything. We had to walk a lot. At the end we had to walk about ten blocks to get to the Plaza of the Revolution, where Fidel was going to give the closing speech. Clementina marched along with the rest of us, she did everything we did. There were very few old people. The idea was that there be representation from the various Latin American revolutionary movements; each country sent an exemplary individual. She was known as a revolutionary poet."

A House of One's Own

In 1975 Clementina bought a house in Barrio La Hoya, one of Tegucigalpa's oldest neighborhoods, the first house she ever owned. In the years since she left Chepe she had had some hard times: lots of different apartments, sometimes only a single room; staying with friends or family here and there; moving her books and art collection around; losing things, leaving things behind, having things stolen. She drank a lot; whenever there was a party or any excuse to drink with friends she took advantage of the opportunity to get drunk, sometimes such that she would have to be carried home. For a time she rented a single large room in La Leona, a steep, winding hill near the center of town that in places one must climb steps to ascend. Arriving tipsy one night, she fell on the stairs and broke her arm. For a while she seemed to lose interest in taking care of herself. She didn't eat regularly and became decalcified and had to wear a leg brace and use a wheelchair.

But the pendulum always swings back for Clementina. Despite her bouts with despair she maintained a strong and visible presence in Tegucigalpa. There was Clementina visiting a government office, trying to get someone to come up with some money so some young artist could exhibit his work; Clementina standing on a street corner holding onto someone's hand and talking animatedly; Clementina on the phone trying to get the Nicaraguan ambassador to write her a letter so she could buy Nicaraguan primitive art and take it out of the country. There was Clementina's picture in the paper again, her small hands, as always, folded across her lap. There was Clementina talking at a high school graduation about the importance of social commitment in poetry. Wasn't it just like Clementina—yelling to the driver to stop the car so she could get out and pee, or celebrating her eightieth birthday by closing off the street, bringing in the band from the nearby penitentiary, and inviting her friends to dance and drink and eat all night.

Once she bought her house, life became easier. Now she could unpack her books for good and put them on shelves. She could unpack her paintings and hang them anywhere she wanted—in the kitchen, the bedroom, the hallway. She set up large glass cases to display her sculptures; she hung her collection of folk-art crucifixes among her paintings; she put plants in the windows. She once again created her space in her image and likeness, but this time it was all hers, paid for with money from the sale of land from her inheritance from her mother. She became more protective of her space. She had lost many valuable works of art over the years through theft and damage, and she was taking no chances of losing more.

But this did not mean that her house was off-limits. She continued to associate with artists, and one young painter in particular became her favorite. Luis H. Padilla, today considered one of Honduras's finest artists, spent a number of years painting at her home. She trusted him and let him live there when she was away traveling. She would sometimes prepare him a meal, but mostly she let him do as he pleased. He would lay out his materials and paint for hours, immersed in his work. They loved talking to each other about art, politics, ideas. He listened to her stories about her adventurous life and respected her opinions on art. He says he was like a son to her, but also something more. Sometimes he thought she was jealous when he spent time away from her. She says she loves him because she respects his work and his dedication, because he is intelligent and a good artist. People would jokingly refer to Padilla as "el protegido de Clementina" (Clementina's protectee). She enjoys remembering this gender reversal, although he did not find it flattering.

Numerous are the artists who have loved or hated Clementina, or who are indebted to her generosity. Most of them have also been estranged from her at some time, but those who know and understand her take this for granted. As she once explained, when asked why she was sometimes so aggressive, "*I am totally aggressive, not just once in a while. I have had to fight tooth and nail to defend myself and now that I don't need to any more, it's become a habit. But deep down my friends know that this is just an attitude that I have adopted in life.*"[3]

Of Time and Old Age

The portraits from this period reflect not only the physical reality of a middle-aged woman getting plump and wearing loose-fitting, comfortable clothes, hanging around the house barefoot, but also the ever-present force of the legend. Miguel Angel Ruiz and Alvaro Canales painted her in housedresses with everyday hairdos. For Rendón she is a bronze-skinned Indian woman, for Miglorissi a psychedelic matriarch. Ezequiel Padilla captured her granite will, Aníbal her revolutionary spirit, and Vizquerra her iconoclasm. There are portraits from Italy, Argentina, Paraguay, Nicaragua, and Mexico documenting her still frequent travels.

Her friends began to fear for her safety. Would she be able to handle the crowds in the airports, the responsibilities of overseeing the transport of canvasses through customs, the long hours of sitting in conferences listening to speeches, the parties and the drinking? In November 1987 the Honduran American Cultural Association of New York invited her to New York to accept an award for her contributions to Honduran culture. On the plane she began to feel ill. It was a bitterly cold November for New York, and Clementina's tropical constitution succumbed to the herpes virus that attacked her nervous system. She cut her visit short and flew back to Tegucigalpa, terrified of being incapacitated in that northern metropolis that she remembered only too well. She took to her bed for months, life edging away from her. Something in her had finally aged, some fiber at her core was giving up, was looking death in the eye and thinking, well, maybe I should just let myself go.

That was how I found Clementina in January 1988, a tiny old woman with rose petal–soft skin and large opaque eyes, suspicious, tired, silent. "If only you'd come just six months earlier, you would have met the real Clementina," I was told again and again. "She is a shadow of her former self." Everyone thought she was going to die.

If Clementina had died in January 1988 I would have had a different story to tell. I could have gathered her from among the back issues of the *Revista Tegucigalpa,* her long dress gracefully falling over her chair, her feet in fashionable high-heeled shoes. It is her birthday, 12 May 1933, our poetess, Clementina Suárez. I could have imagined her as always thirty years old, hanging out at Mamá Yaca's estanco with the bohemian poets of Tegucigalpa, decorating her apartment with colorful scarves and lengths of bright material, straw baskets, and dozens of dolls. I could imagine her coming home well after midnight, draping herself languidly on her divan to compose melancholy sonnets or exalted poems of passion. Sometimes a fellow poet, or more likely a distinguished patron of the arts, anxious to protect her from vituperous tongues and material want, would accompany her home. They would have another drink. She would feel beautiful. She would feel like a poet, a woman full of power and mystery, Scheherazade of a thousand verses, a thousand possible caresses. Would this man be the key that unlocks her poetry?

But Clementina recovered from her battle with death and is living out her eighty-eighth year in Barrio La Hoya. I sit beside her and see loose folds of skin hanging from her arms. Those shapely ankles are swollen; it is painful for her to walk. She pats Moon Drops moisturizing lotion onto her silky soft and wrinkled skin. She dusts her face with a powder puff and smoothes rouge on her cheeks. "*I have to use makeup,*" she says, "*because my skin is yellow from being sick for so long*." She paints her eyelids a silvery blue and draws high arches for eyebrows. She applies Charles of the Ritz lipstick to her famous mouth and inspects herself in the mirror. She puts on an undershirt because brassieres have become uncomfortable and struggles into a shift dress of colorful Guatemalan fabric. I help her straighten the fabric over her hips. We rummage in her drawers, looking over the dozens of sashes to choose the right one for the dress. She wraps a red one around her waist but later removes it because she's more comfortable without a belt. From among the boxes piled in her bedroom labeled brown sandals, medium heel; red pumps, high heel; and so on, she extracts a pair of sensible black flats. This is tiring. She leans back on her pillows and pulls her legs up onto the bed. Clementina's legs. How many times has she lifted her skirt, crossed her legs enticingly? Her left leg has been swollen and painful. The doctor gave her some medicine to reduce water retention. At eight o'clock we take a cab to the cocktail party. Some old friends from El Salvador will be there—César Sermeño, a successful ceramicist who was one of the young men that hung around the Rancho, and his gentle wife, Nelly. They reminisce about the good times with Luis Angel and Camilo, about the time they brought her home after a party and stood outside the door singing in the middle of the night. Chepe peered over the balcony to see what was going on and pushed over a heavy ceramic pot that crashed behind them, a warning that it was late and time to leave. Surrounded by friends, drinking whiskey and sodas, Clementina was back in El Salvador, queen of culture, courted and happy.

Clementina recovered. In August 1988 she went to Juticalpa to receive the keys to the city and to reign for three days as her hometown honored her with songs, dances, poems, and speeches. The elders rummaged in trunks looking for handwritten copies of that poem about a virgin's dream that they had furtively handed around in their school days, convinced it had been written by Clementina. The youngsters sang and danced and had a party, wondering who this old woman was. Clementina was radiant. She promised the town that they would inherit her library if they constructed a building to house it. The Rotary Club pledged to do so.

In October, from her bedroom, she pushed and prodded, phoned and sent messengers, to organize an exhibit of Central American primitive art at the Honduran American Cultural Institute. She was born to a mother whose guiding principle in life was "demand and you shall receive," and she absorbed that principle at an early age. From her bed she reigns in the space she has created for herself. Bring me that; I need this; do that. She knows every painting she owns, she places each ceramic or sculpture in the spot she chooses for it. She is frail now and needs a housekeeper, someone to cook for her, go to the store, wash her clothes in the stone sink. But she loses her patience with them, and they all leave sooner or later.

In November Ediciones Paradiso published *Con mis versos saludo a las generaciones futuras* (With My Poems I Hail the Generations to Come), an anthology of her work that included only two new poems, both of them meditations on time and old age. She seldom goes out now. She sits at home contemplating the slippers by her bedside. She eats very little—fruit, milk, a piece of cheese. She loves company but tires soon after her visitors arrive. Sometimes I catch glimpses of what must have been the other Clementina.

I visit her every day. She tells me stories about Antonio Rosa, León Felipe, Chepe, Camilo, Claudia, Eunice. She tells me to straighten a picture on the wall, to bring her glasses, to answer the phone. Drop by drop, inch by inch, she lets me into her space. She lets me look through her photo album, borrow pictures to reproduce. She lets me study her scrapbooks as she sits across from me at the kitchen table. She wants to know what I've done, whom I've met. When I return from my visit to El Salvador I tell her I met Chepe, that he is lonely in his blindness, unable to paint, which is the only thing he ever really wanted to do. She can't sleep for thinking about how difficult it must be for him, all he ever cared about was his art, and now he can only imagine the colors of his palette. She lets me climb up the shaky metal staircase to her second-floor library and storeroom. I come down with books to borrow. She hesitates. I assure her I will be careful. She allows me to take the books home to read.

A college freshman knocks on her door. "May I speak to the poet?" She asks the typical first-year questions: "Which are your best poems? What is the message of your poetry? What are the stages of your development?" Clementina looks at her as if she were speaking a foreign language. She looks at me, waiting for me to answer for her. After all, I am her biographer. I go into the kitchen and make coffee on the three-burner Tropigas stove, letting the boiling water drip through the muslin strainer. I notice that Gelasio's portrait is crooked. I stand on a chair and straighten it. The phone rings. It is ninety-two-year-old Fernando Pineda Ugarte, calling to tell Clementina that a beautiful rose had opened that morning in his garden. He is going to send it to her in a cab.

At home in Camden, Maine, I read one of Clementina's poems from *The Poet and Her Signs* and think about how she sometimes said or wrote one thing and did another. "El poema" (The Poem) expresses what she thought her *ars poetica* should be.

> If you start to write a poem
> think first of who will read it.
> Because a rhyme is only a rhyme
> when someone understands it and it lives on
> over and above all,
> having escaped the mediocrity
> that flippancy or wordiness exalts.
>
> ———
>
> Si comienzas a escribir un poema
> piensa de antemano en quién lo leerá.
> Pues una rima es solamente una rima
> cuando alguien la comprende y sobrevive
> ante todo y sobre todos,
> escapando de las mediocridades
> que exaltan la petulancia y la palabrería.

When I started writing this biography I thought I should decide beforehand for whom I was writing. Would this portrait be for Clementina, for Hondurans, for North Americans? But I realized that I had to write it for myself, that I was speaking to myself, forming sentences and paragraphs that would illuminate Clementina to me, just as I think that Clementina was always writing for herself, to explain herself to herself. But, as she so wisely realized in the second stanza of this poem:

> The poem is not necessarily as it is
> but as it should be in its spirit of justice.
> A word is sufficient to love hope

and to speak of this is more important
than the most beautiful but ordinary poem.

———

El poema no es necesariamente tal como es
sino como debe ser en su aliento de justicia.
Una palabra es suficiente para amar la esperanza
y hablar de ella tiene más importancia
que el más bello pero intrascendente poema.

During the writing of this biography I often dreamed about Clementina and Honduras, and nighttime images would fuse with more conscious speculations. In one dream Clementina was moving out of her house in Barrio La Hoya. Everyone was helping her pack. Her paintings were being wrapped and stored, her ceramics put in boxes. She was radiant, dressed up and made up, climbing the gleaming white stairs to her new bedroom. Young women helped carry her things to their appropriate storage places. "I am so happy," she said. I kissed her and said, "When can we talk?" One of the women approached and asked me if I would like to make an appointment to come back and see Clementina. I thought of her old house, filled to the brim with signs and symbols of herself, full of shadows and plants and dust, paintings hanging from the ceiling, her bed, her shrine to herself, its alcove of portraits. Her kitchen with its tiny stove, its miniature refrigerator, watched over by dozens of Clementinas of various ages, charcoal and pencil sketches, oils, watercolors. How could I visit her now, how could I talk to her about herself in this sterile environment? How would she know who she is without her stuff? I left, walking home on ridges overlooking Camden, thinking what a long walk it is now that she/I/we have moved. I realized how I cherish her space, with her in it, and how completely she has made it her own. I realized how much I will miss her, but I take comfort in remembering that the legend will live even when the woman is gone. The legend and the woman had become one for me, and I understood that they are inseparable.

Epilogue

Tegucigalpa is only a four-hour trip from New Orleans, but I return to Clementina's city feeling as if I am entering another dimension. When I ride from the airport into the old center of the city I am reminded of proportions, relativity, hierarchies of values. I remember how narrow the cobblestoned streets are, how pungent and fetid and warm and sweet are the smells in the alleys. I wonder if I've even come close to getting any of this right in my writing.

More than anything I want to go to Clementina's house in Barrio La Hoya. She left no will, so her daughters inherited everything. Three residents of Juticalpa are upstairs cataloguing the library. Clementina's publicly stated wish to donate her books to her hometown is being honored, and Juticalpa now has a Casa de la Cultura in the center of town in which to house them. The portraits of Clementina have been given to the Rotary Club because that long dreamed of art museum in Tegucigalpa is becoming a physical reality. The invaluable art collection, representative of a century of regional artistic expression, has been divided in two. One half has been sold already. The other half, Alba's, is still in Clementina's house, packed up and covered over while the painters apply clean white paint to the walls. Alba plans to put everything back together just as it was when her mother was alive and turn the house into a living museum. I keep remembering my dream, the white walls of Clementina's house, what will become of her if she doesn't have her stuff?

I wish this story could have ended differently. But—on Saturday, 7 December 1991, in the early afternoon, in broad daylight, someone gained entry to Clementina's house. She was found a few hours later, brutally beaten, unconscious. She was taken to the hospital, where she died in the early morning of Monday, 9 December, without having regained consciousness.

Who? The murderer (murderers?) has not been found. All of us who knew her are talking and talking about her death, taking the pieces of evidence and reconstructing her story for her. The local papers couldn't get enough of the gruesome tale. They carried descriptions of her ravaged home, photographs of an old woman beaten beyond recognition, speculations as to possible motives. Shock and pain flooded the artistic community. This heinous crime was so unexpected that people have had to stretch their imaginations to come up with possible explanations. Lacking any conclusive evidence, speculation has run wild in Tegucigalpa.

Some observers insisted that she had lots of money stashed away and that it was surely a thief. Hadn't the police found the contents of her drawers strewn around her bedroom? But of course whatever she had was in the bank, she was too smart to leave money around the house. She was always so *lista,* so street-smart; Tegucigalpa was her home, and she knew it only too well. Others shake their heads sadly and say, no, it's a symptom of the times. Too much poverty, too much misery. It had to be some poor beggar desperate for money to feed himself and his family. Or more likely a drug addict, there are so many drugs in Tegucigalpa these days, yes, it was a drug addict, they'll do anything to get a fix, even beat up an old woman. Then again, maybe it was politically motivated, although it doesn't seem likely. Yes, Clementina was outspoken in her criticism of politicians, but she was an old lady, no real threat to anyone. Maybe it was one of the local artists or writers, you know how one or another of them was always fighting with her because of some criticism or indiscretion. But so angry as to beat her, leave her dying? They found her on the kitchen floor, bones broken in her face.

And how did they get in, with the bars on the windows, the bolted doors? Did she open the door? Did she know them? They ransacked her house but took none of the art. Perhaps they broke in, or perhaps they just made it look like a break-in. Perhaps it was a family member with some old grudge. Curiosity, envy, admiration, affection, and misunderstanding continue to forge the Clementina legend, but she is no longer around to defend herself. Tegucigalpa now has no choice but to gaze into her murder as if in a mirror and see itself.

I try to make sense of this act of violence. Clementina survived suicide attempts, unwed motherhood, being broke, traveling alone. She was strong. But who is stronger than senseless aggression? She was unique, yet in the end she was treated no differently than other victims of anonymous violence. Death is the great leveler (the moral of the story is not hard to find), yet I resist having to accept so ignominious an end for her.

She should have died at a party—her own birthday party, perhaps—drinking her seventh whiskey and soda and flirting with some young painter. Or even in her bed, Queen Clementina journeying to her colorful queendom in the sky from her throne of blue satin pillows. She waged a lifelong battle against mediocrity. Surely her last act, her last gesture, was to go out fighting.

Notes

Introduction

1. Juan Ramón Agüero exemplifies this exalted prose in *Reflexiones y semblanzas hondureñas.* He begins his semblanza of Clementina Suárez: "This resplendent Honduran woman was born to take on the forms of a melodious song and to unfold into the world of dreams like a message of love, vibrant and eternal" (Nació esta fulgurante hondureña, para tomar las formas de un canto sonoro y expandirse por el mundo del ensueño como un mensaje de amor, de vibración y de eternidad).

2. The following titles demonstrate this tendency: Luisa Zanelli López, *Mujeres chilenas de letras* (Chilean Women of Letters) (Santiago: Imprenta Universitaria, 1917); Sidonia Carmen Rosenbaum, *Modern Women Writers of Spanish America* (New York: Hispanic Institute, 1945); Yvette E. Miller and Charles M. Tatum, eds., *Latin American Women Writers: Yesterday and Today* (Pittsburgh: Latin American Literary Review, 1975); Celia de Zapata, "100 Years of Women Writers in Latin America," *Latin American Literary Review* 3,6 (1975): 7–16; Lucía Fox-Lockert, *Women Novelists in Spain and Spanish America* (Metuchen, N.J.: Scarecrow, 1979). It can be noted from the dates of publication that this inclination has continued well into the second half of the twentieth century.

3. Julieta Carrera, *La mujer en América escribe,* 268–74.

4. The first two quotations are from Juan Ramón Agüero, *Reflexiónes y semblanzas hondureñas,* 79, while the last is from Fausto Lara, *Aspectos culturales de Honduras,* 444.

5. Victoria Glendinning, "Lies and Silences," in *The Troubled Face of Biography,* ed. Homberger and Chomley, 49.

6. This dictum has been challenged or ignored recently by a number of scholars. A notable example in the field of anthropology is Ruth Bejar, *Translated Woman: Crossing the Border with Esperanza's Story* (Boston: Beacon, 1992).

7. For a discussion of the ethical problems faced by Anglo-American feminists researching Third World women, see María Lugones and Elizabeth Spelman, "Have We Got a Theory for You!" and Daphne Patai, "Ethical Problems of Personal Narratives."

8. Rose, *Writing of Women,* 77.

9. Letitia de Oyuela, "Presencia humana de Clementina Suárez," 6.

10. Autobiography criticism has eloquently discussed the notions of the essential and contingent self. See, for example, James Olney, ed., *Autobiography;* Paul Jay, *Being in the Text;* and Paul Eakin, *Fictions in Autobiography.*

11. For discussions of women's creative expression as autobiography, see Bella Brodzki and Celeste Schenck, *Life/Lines.*

12. See for example Sara Alpern et al., *The Challenge of Feminist Biography.*

Chapter One: A Childhood of Privilege

1. Clementina's own words are indicated in the text by italics. They are from numerous taped and untaped interviews with the author from 20–31 January 1988 and from 28 September 1988 to 10 April 1989, in Tegucigalpa, unless otherwise indicated by a note. All translations are the author's.

2. Medardo Mejía, "Clementina Suárez," *Clementina Suárez,* 9.

3. William Wells, *Explorations and Adventures in Honduras,* 420.

4. Leticia de Oyuela, "Las haciendas de Tegucigalpa," 63–64. Much of the information included here on the Zelaya family up to the mid-nineteenth century is from Oyuela's manuscript.

5. Medardo Mejía, "Doña Apolinaria," *Comizahual,* 337–40.

6. Francisco Morazán (1792–1842), who fought for Honduran independence and Central American union, and José Trinidad Reyes (1797–1855), founder of the Honduran National University, are two of the figures universally loved and respected in Honduras.

7. Medardo Mejía, "Felipe Bustillo repitió la palabra de Cambronne," *Comizahual,* 333.

8. Wells, *Explorations and Adventures in Honduras,* xiii.

9. This genealogical information was obtained from the family tree in the possession of Alba Rosa Suárez, Clementina's oldest daughter, who resides in Tegucigalpa.

10. Wells, *Explorations and Adventures in Honduras,* 272.

11. Elvia Alvarado, *Don't Be Afraid, Gringo,* 82. Another account of the massacre can be found in George Black, "The Unquiet Death of Father Guadalupe Carney," in *Honduras,* ed. Nancy Peckenham and Annie Street, 186–91.

12. See Daniel Faber, *Environment under Fire,* for a description of the ecological destruction of Honduras. Also informative is Faye Henderson, *Honduras.*

13. Froylán Turcios, *Memorias,* 81. Subsequent quotations from Turcios in the text are from these memoirs, unless otherwise noted.

14. The highway connecting Juticalpa with Tegucigalpa was paved during the administration of Policarpo Paz García, 1978–82.

15. Victor Rubí Zapata, *Mi Juticalpa y yo,* 10.

16. I thank Juan Darío Euceda of Juticalpa for allowing me to read his unpublished manuscript of a historical novel set in Juticalpa at the end of the nineteenth century, from which I derived some of the information on the local wares available on market days. Further details are from interviews with Juticalpa residents.

17. Clementina Suárez, "Memorias."

18. René Pauck, *Clementina Suárez.*

19. Medardo Mejía, "Ramón Lobo Herrera," 6–7.

20. Information about the school is from Olimpia Varela y Varela, "La mujer hondureña en la obra cultural y social de su patria," 10.

21. One of the poems from her first book, *Corazón sangrante,* is entitled "Mi luminosa soledad" (My Luminous Solitude).

22. Pedro Salustio Hernández, "La carreta chillona."

23. In an interview in April 1978 ("Entrevista con Clementina Suárez," *Presencia Universitaria* 5, 41 [1978]: 8–9), Clementina is characteristically inaccurate in her chronology, for she states that she was ten years old at the time of the epidemic, although she would have been sixteen.

Chapter Two: Forging a Poetic Identity

1. Suárez interview, *Presencia Universitaria.*

2. José Muñoz Cota, "A través de mi cámara en el cumpleaños de Clementina," in *Clementina Suárez,* ed. UNAH (1982), 69.

3. Clementina Suárez, Interview by Manuel Salinas, 1972.

4. Pauck, *Clementina Suárez.*

5. Martín Paz, "Clementina Suárez o la perennidad en la poesía," in *Clementina Suárez,* ed. UNAH (1982), 55.

6. Jorge Fidel Durón, "Cosas de tiempos pasados," in *Elogio de Tegucigalpa,* ed. Acosta, 277–78.

7. María Guadalupe Carías, "¿A dónde fue la Tegucigalpa de mis amores?" in *Elogio de Tegucigalpa,* ed. Acosta, 307–8.

8. Argentina Díaz Lozano, *Peregrinaje,* 169–71.

9. Marco Antonio Rosa, *Tegucigalpa, ciudad de remembranzas,* 136–50.

10. Alejandro Castro Díaz, *Cartas al Terruño,* 75. This is a collection of these fictional letters, with a prologue by Jorge Fidel Durón.

11. Patricia Meyer Spacks, *Gossip,* 11.

12. See Ramón Oquelí's prologue to *Boletín de la defensa nacional,* ed. Turcios, for a concise description and analysis of this important event in Honduran history.

13. See Turcios, *Memorias,* 304–20, for a colorful description of these dramatic months in Tegucigalpa.

14. Visitación Padilla, "La mujer en el altar de la patria," in *Boletín de la defensa nacional,* ed. Turcios, 60. The Choluteca River runs between Comayagüela and Tegucigalpa. Some think of them as sister cities; others consider them a single urban area. The population figure of 30,000 cited previously includes both areas.

15. Clementina Suárez, interview, Zöe Anglesey, 15 September 1985. The term *feminist* has had a long and troubled history in women's movements in Latin America. Many Latin American women choose not to use the term to describe themselves because they believe it represents a typically North American perspective and does not correspond to their priorities.

16. José Francisco Martínez, *Literatura hondureña y su proceso generacional,* 231.

17. Guadalupe Gallardo, "A Danlí," in *Indice general de poesía hondureña,* ed. Manuel Luna Mejía, 428. Shortly before my book went to press, a Honduran writer alerted me to the possibility that Guadalupe Gallardo may have been a man. Because of the gender ambiguity inherent in Spanish syntax, it is not possible to determine the poet's sex from the description of his/her life in Luna Mejía's work, but because Guadalupe can be a man's name or woman's name, further research is necessary before we can make a determination.

18. While some literary scholars claim that *Angelina* by Carlos F. Gutiérrez, published in 1898, is the first Honduran novel, Julio Escoto claims in "*Angelina* y *Blanca Olmedo:* Las dos caras de la moneda," *Aportes* 1 (1974), that there are records of Gamero de Medina's novels *Amalia Montiel* and *Adriana y Margarita,* both published in 1893, although there are no extant copies of either work.

19. For a brief biographical sketch and an appreciation of her work, see Betty LaDuke, "Painter of Memories," *Compañeras,* 53–56, as well as Leticia de Oyuela's remarks in the catalogue of Fortín's exhibit at the National Library in Tegucigalpa, 8–26 November 1980.

20. Emma Moya Posas died in 1991.

21. Suárez, interview, Anglesey.

22. A few other women, such as Angela Ochoa Velásquez and Paca Navas, seem to have taken their poetry seriously, but their inability to promote or project themselves has resulted in their being marginalized or ignored by literary historians. In addition, none of these women attempted to break into the male literary circles, thereby establishing no presence for Clementina to observe or emulate.

23. Some critics have also referred to this group as La Generación de la Dictadura, because of their coetaneity with the dictatorship of Tiburcio Carías Andino (1932–48). For a thoughtful analysis of the nature and importance of this group, see Roberto Sosa, "La Generación de la Dictadura," *Prosa armada,* 91–107.

24. Castro Diaz, *Cartas al terruño,* 244.

25. In *Frida,* Hayden Herrera's biography of Frida Kahlo, one of Rivera's wives, Herrera points out that Frida, as well as Frida's sister Cristina, Tina Modotti, Lupe Marín (another of his wives), and others appear in his murals.

26. Guillermo Bustillo Reina published two books of poetry: *Romances de la tierruca* and *Opalos de Erandique.* In 1925 he coedited with Arturo Martínez Galindo the magazine *Continente* in New Orleans. He also wrote two handbooks on Honduras: *Honduras* and *El libro de Honduras.* He received the Ramón Rosa National Award for Literature in 1953.

27. Claudio Barrera, prologue to *Antología de poetas jóvenes de Honduras desde 1935.*

28. In an interview she is quoted as saying, "La llamé *Mujer* porque era yo quien la hacía" (I called it *Woman* because I was the one doing it) (*Alcaraván* 9 [1981]: 22).

29. Two other books by Clementina Suárez, probably commemorating recitals, are listed in Miguel Angel García, *Bibliografía hondureña, 1620–1930,* vol. 1; they are *Recital en el Teatro Nacional* (Tegucigalpa: Tipografía Nacional, 1931) and *Recital para Marco A. Ponce* (Tegucigalpa: Teatro Nacional, 1932), but I have been unable to locate either of them.

Chapter Three: "Ever Widening Horizons"

The chapter title is drawn from Alfonso Cravioto's prologue to Suárez's *Veleros,* which refers to Clementina's "horizontes cada vez más amplios."

1. There has been much debate regarding the terms used to refer to persons of Spanish or Latin American origin in the United States. Whenever possible I have used the country of origin as the descriptor. When referring to a number of individuals from various Spanish-speaking countries, I have used *Hispanic.*

2. Angel del Río, introduction to Federico García Lorca, *Poet in New York,* xiv; see Sally Ortiz Aponte, "Federico de Onís, Paladín de la cultura hispánica," and Oyuela, "Presencia humana de Clementina Suárez," 7.

3. Besides the articles by Alejandro Castro in the *Revista Tegucigalpa,* her working-class exploits were recorded by José Rodríguez Cerna in his memoirs, *Itinerario.*

4. Judd Ahlander, "Mexico's Muralists and the New York School," 20. Antonieta Rivas Mercado gives an insightful and opinionated account of the Mexicans and the Americans in New York in the early 1930s in her letters to the Mexican

painter Manuel Rodríguez Lozano. She disparagingly refers to the two groups, whose relationship was a kind of cultural and economic symbiosis, as "la mexicanada" and "Mexican folkways" (*Cartas a Manuel Rodríguez Lozano [1927–1930]*). See Helen Delpar, *The Enormous Vogue of Things Mexican,* for an idea of the scope and character of this international cultural exchange.

5. Louis Pérez, *Cuba,* 237.

6. Robert Manteiga, "Politics and Poetics," 7. See Mary Low and Juan Breá, *Red Spanish Notebook,* for a firsthand account of the rapturous idealism that the Spanish Revolution inspired in so many non-Spaniards. For a balanced account of the political movements in Cuba in the 1920s and 1930s, see Pérez, *Cuba.* A more biased (anti-Communist) but also more detailed account can be found in Carlos Márquez Sterling, *Historia de Cuba desde Cristóbal Colón a Fidel Castro.*

7. See Jean Franco, *The Modern Culture of Latin America,* for a good general discussion of the evolution of the artist's social consciousness in Latin America, and her "Vallejo and the Crisis of the Thirties" for a discussion of some of the strategies that evolved among revolutionary poets of the 1930s.

8. Luis Alemán (Claudio Barrera, pseud.), "Entrevista a Nicolás Guillén," *La pajarita de papel* 5–6 (1949–50): 80–81.

9. *Poesía negra en Honduras,* selection and prologue by Claudio Barrera, which anthologizes the poesía negra of fifteen Honduran poets, illustrates the popularity of this style.

10. Franco, "Vallejo," 43.

11. Clementina Suárez, interview by Roberto Sosa, "Entrevista con Clementina Suárez," *Tiempo,* 24 June 1976.

Chapter Four: Bohemian Revolutionary

1. *Nuevo Diario,* 5 January 1939; *El Pueblo,* 18 January 1939; *La Epoca,* 9 February 1939.

2. The final three quotes are from the Suárez interview by Salinas.

3. Ibid.

4. Graciela García, *Páginas de lucha,* 28–29.

5. Besides numerous volumes of poetry, short stories, biography, and history, Rafael Heliodoro Valle has produced some works of fundamental bibliographical importance, such as *Bibliografía del periodismo en Honduras* and *Diccionario biográfico de Honduras.* For a complete list of his work, see Oscar Acosta, *Rafael Heliodoro Valle, Vida y obra.*

6. Inés Amor, *Memorias,* 168–69. These recollections of the Mexican art scene from 1935 to 1975 are a vivid and thoughtful testimony of this time.

7. Francisco Amighetti's autobiographical travelogues include *Francisco y los caminos* and *Francisco en Costa Rica.*

8. In a semblanza of Clementina that appeared in the journal *Pan-América* 3,33 (1947): 20, the author mentions that a fragment of *Creciendo con la hierba* was published in Guatemala in 1947 and that Clementina had recited the poem at the National University of Guatemala on 25 July 1945.

9. For insights into Medardo Mejía's life and character, see his autobiographical essay, "Refiere, Anisias, el paso de aquel milpero."

10. Francisco Amighetti, interview by author.

11. Nelson DeVega, "Mito y realidad en la obra de Salarrué," 11.

12. This story is retold in an article by Eugenio Martínez Orantes based on an interview with the painter that appeared in the Saturday cultural supplement of *Diario Latino,* 24 May 1986.

13. Nahuizalco, Izalco, and Juayúa also retain vestiges of their indigenous past.

14. See Alejandro Dagoberto Marroquín, *Panchimalco,* for a study of the land and people of Panchimalco.

15. José Mejía Vides, interview by author.

16. Pauck, *Clementina Suárez.*

17. Emmanuel Robles, "Imágenes de El Salvador," 13.

18. Carlos Cañas, prologue to *Pintura salvadoreña del presente siglo* by Julia Diaz, 14–15.

19. Eugenio Martínez Orantes, "Clementina Suárez en El Salvador," 7.

20. Díaz, *Pintura salvadoreña del presente siglo,* 27.

21. John Beverley, "Poetry and Revolution in Central America," 169–70.

Chapter Five: No Place to Call Home

1. Edgardo Quiñónez and Mario Argueta, *Historia de Honduras,* 129.

2. Stefania Natalina de Castro et al., *Significado histórico del gobierno del Dr. Ramón Villeda Morales,* 85.

3. Juanita Soriano, "Una poetisa hondureña: Clementina Suárez," in *Clementina Suárez,* ed. UNAH (1969).

4. Ralph Woodward, *Central America,* 271.

5. "Clementina en Honduras en misión cultural," *Gráfico* 3,33.

6. Súarez interview, *Alcaraván* 9 (1981): 23.

7. Filadelfo Suazo, "Se va definitivamente de Honduras Clementina Suárez," in *Clementina Suárez,* ed. UNAH, 117.

8. Oyuela, "Luis Hernán Padilla," 15.

9. Francisco Salvador, interview by author, Tegucigalpa, 25 October 1988.

10. Suárez interview, *Alcaraván,* 23. The lempira was worth $0.50 U.S. at this time.

11. José Vásquez, *Pablo Zelaya Sierra,* 11–12.

12. Clementina Suárez, "Ausencia y presencia de Pablo Zelaya Sierra," 7.

13. Juan Domingo Torres, "Las artes plásticas en Honduras," 27.

14. Oyuela, "Las orígenes de la Escuela de Bellas Artes y Arturo López Rodezno," chap. 14 of "Honduras y el trabajo artistico," unpublished ms. on the history of art in Honduras.

15. Mario Castillo, interview by author, Tegucigalpa, 22 December 1988.

16. "Pintura actual de Honduras," *Arte* 9 (1988): 59.

17. Suárez interview, *Alcaraván,* 24.

18. Gelasio Giménez, interview by author, Tegucigalpa, 21 December 1988.

19. Mario Posas, "Notas sobre política y sociedad en la Honduras de post-guerra," 4.

20. "Combate" has appeared in various newspapers and magazines. It was anthologized for the first time in 1969 in Clementina Suárez, *El poeta y sus señales,* and subsequently in *Volcán,* ed. Alejandro Murguía and Barbara Paschke, and in Clementina Suárez, *Con mis versos saludo a las generaciones futuras.*

21. Letter from Roberto Armijo to the author, January 1989.

22. I found this interview in Clementina's scrapbook but have been unable to verify the date of publication. The content, however, locates it around 1967 or 1968.

23. *Clementina Suárez,* ed. UNAH (1969).

24. Quiñonez and Argueta, *Historia de Honduras,* 135–39.

25. Victor Meza, "Los cuadros de Clementina Suárez o la historia de una valiosa pérdida," 9.

Chapter Six: Plenitude

1. Oscar Acosta, ed., *Los premios nacionales de literatura Ramón Rosa,* 20.

2. Clementina Súarez, acceptance speech, ibid. 21–22.

3. Clementina Súarez, interview by Ramón Oquelí, in *Clementina Súarez,* ed. UNAH, (1969).

Bibliography

Works by Clementina Suárez

Corazón sangrante. Tegucigalpa: Tipografía Nacional, 1930.
Iniciales. Mexico: Libros mexicanos, 1931.
De mis sábados el último. Mexico: Libros mexicanos, 1931.
Los templos de fuego. Mexico: Libros mexicanos, 1931.
Recital en el Teatro Nacional. Tegucigalpa: Tipografía Nacional, 1931.
Recital para Marco A. Ponce. Tegucigalpa: Teatro Nacional, 1932.
Engranajes. San José, Costa Rica: Borrasé, 1935.
Veleros. Havana: Editorial Hermes, 1937.
De la desilusión a la esperanza. Tegucigalpa: Tipografía Nacional, 1944.
Creciendo con la hierba. San Salvador: Ministerio de Cultura, 1957.
Canto a la encontrada Patria y su Héroe. Tegucigalpa: n.p., 1958.
El poeta y sus señales. Tegucigalpa: Universidad Nacional Autónoma de Honduras, 1969.
Antología poética. Tegucigalpa: Secretaría de Cultura y Turismo, 1984.
Con mis versos saludo a las generaciones futuras. Tegucigalpa: Ediciones Paradiso, 1988
"Memorias." Manuscript.

Anthologies that contain Clementina Suárez's poetry

Anglesey, Zoë, ed. *Ixok Amar Go.* Penobscot, Maine: Granite, 1987.
Escoto, Julio, ed. *Antología de poesía amorosa de Honduras.* Tegucigalpa: n.p., 1975.
Lagos, Ramiro, ed. *Mujeres poetas de Hispanoamérica.* Bogotá: Ediciones Tercer Mundo, 1986.
Luna Mejía, Manuel, ed. *Indice general de poesía hondureña.* Mexico: Editora Latinoamericana, 1961.
Meyer, Doris, and Marguerite Fernández Olmos, eds. *Contemporary Women Authors of Latin America.* Brooklyn, NY: Brooklyn College, 1983.
Murguía, Alejandro, and Barbara Paschke, eds. *Volcán.* San Francisco: City Lights, 1983.

Critical appraisals of Clementina Suárez's work

"Entrevista con Clementina Suárez." *El Heraldo.* 10 Aug. 1988.

Gold, Janet N. "Clementina Suárez: Comunicación con una poeta." *SobreVuelo* 1, 4 (1988): 13–16.

———. *Clementina Suárez: Su lugar en la galería de mujeres extraordinarias.* Tegucigalpa: Guaymuras, 1990.

González y Contreras, G. "Veleros de la poesía." *Repertorio Americano* 34 (1937): 184.

Gutiérrez Pacheco, Azucena. "La mujer hondureña y sus limitantes en el campo de la creación poética." *Tragaluz* 1, 6 (1985): 18–19.

Martínez Orantes, Eugenio. "Clementina Suárez en El Salvador." 1989. Typescript in possession of author.

Mejía, Medardo. "Entrevista con Manuel José Arce." *Gráfico,* 23 July 1972.

———. "Presentación de Clementina Suárez." *Ariel* 11, 214 (1969): 26–28.

Naranjo, Carmen. "Una mujer muchas veces pintada." *Imaginaria* 1, 1 (1986): 12.

Oquelí, Ramón. "Clementina." In *Gente y situaciones,* by Ramón Oquelí, 153–54. Tegucigalpa: UNAH, 1969.

Oyuela, Leticia de. "Presencia humana de Clementina Suárez." *Tragaluz* 1, 5 (1985): 6–8.

Pauck, René, dir. *Clementina Suárez.* 1982. Video.

Polasky, Sulema. "La visión erótica de Clementina Suárez." *Presente* 78 (1973): 3–5.

Price, Julia. "Faces of Rebellion: Critical Commentary and Translation of the Poetry of Julia de Burgos, Rosario Castellanos, and Clementina Suárez." Master's thesis, University of Cincinnati, 1981.

Rodríguez Barahona, Heriberto. *Clementina Suárez.* N.p., n.d.

Salinas, Manuel. "El mundo poético de Clementina Suárez." In *Cultura hondureña contemporánea.* Tegucigalpa: Editorial Universitaria, 1991.

Soriano, Juanita. "Una poetisa hondureña: Clementina Suárez." *Armas y letras* 2, 2 (1959): 49–58.

Umaña, Helen. "Una teoría del amor en la poesía de Clementina Suárez." In *Literatura hondureña contemporanea,* by Helen Umaña, 217–27. Tegucigalpa: Guaymuras, 1986.

———. "Voces femeninas en la poesía hondureña." *Tragaluz* 1, 11 (1986): 6–8.

Universidad Nacional Autónoma de Honduras (UNAH). *Clementina Suárez.* Tegucigalpa, 1969. 2d ed., 1982.

Wyld Ospina, Carlos. "Apunte acerca de una poetisa y un poema." *Revista de la Biblioteca Nacional* (1948): 73–75.

Works consulted on Central America, Mexico, and Cuba

Acevedo, Ramón Luis. "Apuntes sobre Roque Dalton y la violencia en la literatura salvadoreña." *Renacimiento* 1, 2 (1981): 31–39.

———. *La novela centroamericana.* Río Piedras, P.R.: Editorial Universitaria, 1982.

Acosta, Oscar. *Rafael Heliodoro Valle: Vida y obra.* Rome: Instituto Italo-Latino Americano, 1981.

———, ed. *Elogio de Tegucigalpa.* Tegucigalpa: Consejo Metropolitano del D.C., 1978.

———. *Los premios nacionales de literatura Ramón Rosa (1951–1972).* Tegucigalpa: Ministerio de Educación Pública, 1973.

———. *Poesía hondureña de hoy.* Tegucigalpa: Nuevo Continente, 1971.

Acosta, Oscar, and Pompeyo del Valle, eds. *Exaltación de Honduras.* Tegucigalpa: Nuevo Continente, 1971.

Agüero, Juan Ramón. *Reflexiones y semblanzas hondureñas.* Trujillo, Honduras: n.p., 1952.

Ahlander, Leslie Judd. "Mexico's Muralists and the New York School." *Américas* 30, 3 (1978): 19–25.

Albizúrez Palma, Francisco, and Catalina Barrios y Barrios. *Historia de la literatura guatemalteca.* Guatemala City: Editorial Universitaria, 1982.

Alcaraván. Tegucigalpa. 1980–82.

Alvarado, Elvia. *Don't Be Afraid, Gringo.* Translated and edited by Medea Benjamin. San Francisco: Institute for Food and Development Policy, 1987.

Amighetti, Francisco. *Francisco en Costa Rica.* San José, Costa Rica: Editorial Costa Rica, 1980.

———. *Francisco en Harlem.* Mexico City: Ediciones Galería de Arte Centroamericano, 1947.

———. *Francisco y los caminos.* San José, Costa Rica: Editorial Costa Rica, 1963.

Amor, Inés. *Una mujer en el arte mexicano.* Mexico City: UNAM, 1987.

Arellano, Jorge Eduardo, ed. *Antología general de la poesía nicaragüense.* Managua: Ediciones Distribuidora Cultural, 1984.

Argueta, Manlio. *Caperucita en la zona roja.* Havana: Casa de las Américas, 1977.

———, ed. *Poesía de El Salvador.* San José, Costa Rica: EDUCA, 1983.

Argueta, Mario. *Diccionario de escritores hondureños.* Tegucigalpa: n.p., 1986.

Ariel. Tegucigalpa and San José, Costa Rica. 1930–70.

Armijo, Roberto, and Rigoberto Paredes, eds. *Poesía contemporanea de Centro América.* Barcelona: Los libros de la frontera, 1983.

Arte. Tegucigalpa. 1982–88.

Ayes Rojas, Edgardo. *Estampas de Olancho.* Tegucigalpa: n.p., 1986.

Baciu, Stefan. *Centroamericanos.* San José, Costa Rica: Libro Libre, 1985.

———. *Francisco Amighetti.* Heredia, Costa Rica: Universidad Nacional, 1984.

Barrera, Claudio, ed. *Antología de poetas jóvenes de Honduras desde 1935.* Tegucigalpa: n.p., 1950.

———. *Poesía negra en Honduras.* Tegucigalpa: n.p., n.d.

Bayardo Brito, Javier. *Conspiración contra el olvido.* Tegucigalpa: Ediciones Breve Repertorio, 1978.

Bayón, Damián, ed. *América Latina en sus artes.* Mexico City: Siglo XXI, 1974.

Becco, Horacio J., and Osvaldo Sranasani, eds. *Poetas libres de la España peregrina en América.* Buenos Aires: Ollantay, 1947.

Benedetti, Mario. "Situación del intelectual en América Latina." In *La identidad cultural de Hispanoamérica,* edited by Jaime Giordano and Daniel Torres, 13–18. Santiago de Chile: Instituto Profesional del Pacífico, 1986.

Bermúdez, Antonio. *Ester, la cortesana.* Tegucigalpa: n.p., 1939.

Beverley, John. "Poetry and Revolution in Central America." In *The Year Left: An American Socialist Yearbook,* edited by Mike Davis, et al., 155–79. London: Verso, 1985.

Beverley, John, and Marc Zimmerman. *Literature and Culture in the Central American Revolutions.* Austin: University of Texas Press, 1990.

Brenner, Anita. *Idols behind Altars.* New York: Payson and Clarke, 1929.

Burchard, Felipe. Interview. *Tragaluz* 1, 10 (1986): 4–5.

Bustillo Reina, Guillermo. *El libro de Honduras.* Tegucigalpa: n.p. [1958?].

———. *Honduras.* Havana: n.p., 1930.

———. *Opalos de Erandique.* Tegucigalpa: n.p., n.d.

———. *Romances de la tierruca.* Tegucigalpa: Calderón, 1950.

Callan, Richard. *Miguel Angel Asturias.* Boston: Twayne, 1970.

Cárcomo, Jacobo. *Antología.* Tegucigalpa: Editorial Universitaria, 1982.

Cárdenas Amador, Galel, ed. *Primer simposio de la literatura hondureña.* Tegucigalpa: Editorial Universitario, 1991.

Carías Reyes, Marcos. "Bohemio." *Revista Tegucigalpa,* 13 June 1928.

Carrera, Julieta. *La mujer en América escribe.* Havana: Ediciones Alonso, 1956.

Carteles. Havana, 1934–39.

Castillo, Mario, ed. *El arte contemporaneo en Honduras.* Tegucigalpa: USIS, 1968.

Castro, Stefania Natalina de, et al. *Significado histórico del gobierno del Dr. Ramón Villeda Morales.* Tegucigalpa: Editorial Universitaria, 1985.

Castro Díaz, Alejandro. *Cartas al terruño.* Tegucigalpa: Aristón, 1976.

Cerámica: César V. Sermeño. Compiled by Eugenio Martínez Orantes. San Salvador: Editorial Abril Uno, 1988.

Chase, Alfonso, ed. *Las armas de la luz: Antología de la poesía contemporanea de la América Central.* San José, Costa Rica: Departamento Ecuménico de Investigaciones, 1985.

Constantine, Mildred. *Tina Modotti: A Fragile Life.* New York: Rizzoli, 1983.

Correo Literario de Honduras. Tegucigalpa. 1958–59.

Cueva, Agustín, ed. *Centro América: Una historia sin retoque.* Mexico: UNAM, 1987.

Cultura. San Salvador. 1956–58.

Dalton, Roque. *Pobrecito poeta que era yo.* San José, Costa Rica: EDUCA, 1982.

———. *Poesía escogida.* San José, Costa Rica: EDUCA, 1983.

Danby, Colin, and Richard Swedberg. *Honduras: Bibliography and Research Guide.* Cambridge, Mass.: Camino, 1984.

Darío Euceda, Jorge. Novel in progress.

Delpar, Helen. *The Enormous Vogue of Things Mexican: Cultural Relations between the United States and Mexico, 1910–1945.* Tuscaloosa: University of Alabama Press, 1993.

Depestre Catony, Leonardo. *Cuba en citas, 1899–1952.* Havana: Editorial Gente Nueva, 1987.

DeVega, Nelson R. "Mito y realidad en la obra de Salarrué." *Presente* 133–38 (1988): 11–14.

Diario Latino Cultural. San Salvador. 1987–88.

Díaz, Julia. *Pintura salvadoreña del presente siglo.* San Salvador: Museo Forma, 1985.

Díaz Chávez, Filander. *Carías: El último caudillo frutero.* Tegucigalpa: Guaymuras, 1982.

Díaz Lozano, Argentina. *Peregrinaje.* Santiago de Chile: Zig-Zag, 1944.

Echeverría, Carlos Francisco. *Historia crítica del arte costarricense.* San José, Costa Rica: Editorial Universitaria Estatal a Distancia, 1986.

Esfinge. Tegucigalpa. 1916.

España, Isidro. *Clementina Suárez vive.* Typescript.

Exposición colectiva y homenaje. Tegucigalpa: Instituto Hondureño de Cultura Interamericana, 1985. Exhibition catalogue.

"Extensión Universitaria." *Presente* 5, 48–49 (1968): 14–16.

Faber, Daniel. *Environment under Fire: Imperialism and the Ecological Crisis in Central America.* New York: Monthly Review Press, 1993.

Ferrero, Luis. *Zúñiga.* San José, Costa Rica: Editorial Costa Rica, 1985.

Festival de arte de nuestros vecinos de Centro América y Panamá. San José, Costa Rica, 1984. Exhibition catalogue.

Fishman, Lois R. "Bittersweet Memories." *Américas* 36 (1984): 30–35.

Franco, Jean. *The Modern Culture of Latin America: Society and the Artist.* New York: Praeger, 1967.

———. "Vallejo and the Crisis of the Thirties." *Hispania* 72, 1 (1989): 42–48.

Galería de Arte "Banco Central de Honduras." Tegucigalpa, 1978. Exhibition catalogue.

Gallegos Valdés, Luis. *Panorama de la literatura salvadoreña del período precolombino a 1980.* San Salvador: UCA, 1981.

Gallegos Valdés, Luis, and David Escobar Galindo, eds. *Poesía femenina de El Salvador.* San Salvador: Ministerio de Educación, 1976.

García, Graciela. *Páginas de lucha.* Tegucigalpa: Guaymuras, 1981.

García, Miguel Angel. *Bibliografía hondureña, 1620–1930.* Tegucigalpa: Banco Central de Honduras, 1971.

García Lorca, Federico. *Poet in New York.* Translated by Ben Belitt. New York: Grove, 1955.

Gauguin, Paul. *Noa Noa.* 1919. New York: Dover, 1985.

Gonzaga, Quino. *Semblanzas.* Tegucigalpa: n.p., n.d.

González, José. *Diccionario de autores hondureños.* Tegucigalpa: Editores Unidos, 1987.

González-Camino, Fernando. *Alta es la noche, Centro América ayer, hoy y mañana.* Madrid: Instituto de Cooperación Interamericana, 1990.

Guifarro Mercadel, Salatiel [Virgilio Cardona]. *Tierra del oro y del talento cuna.* Tegucigalpa: n.p., 1979.

Guillen, Nicolás. Interview by Luis Alemán. *La pajarita de papel* 5–6 (1949–50): 78–82.

Henderson, Faye. *Honduras: A Country Profile.* Washington, D.C.: Office of U.S. Foreign Disaster Assistance, 1981.

Henríquez Ureña, Pedro. *Historia de la cultura en América Hispánica.* Mexico City: Fondo de Cultura Económica, 1947.

Hernández, Pedro Salustio. "Datos proporcionados por una de las últimas sobrevivientes del siglo pasado en esta ciudad de Juticalpa, Doña Concepción Urbina V. de Hernández." Typescript.

———. "La carreta chillona." Typescript.

———. "Serapio Romero, El Cinchonero." Typescript.

Herra, Rafael Angel. *El desorden del espíritu: Conversaciones con Amighetti.* San José, Costa Rica: Universidad de Costa Rica, 1987.

Herrera, Hayden. *Frida: A Biography of Frida Kahlo.* New York: Harper and Row, 1983.

Howard-Reguindin, Pamela F. *Honduras.* Oxford: Clio, 1992.

Ideas, Revista Femenina de Letras. Tegucigalpa. 1988–89.

LaDuke, Betty. *Compañeras: Women, Art and Social Change in Latin America.* San Francisco: City Lights, 1985.

Laínez, Daniel. *Antología poética.* Tegucigalpa: Aristón, 1950.

———. *Manicomio.* Tegucigalpa: Editorial Universitaria, 1980.

Langdon-Davies, John. *Behind the Spanish Barricades.* New York: McBride, 1936.

Lara, Fausto. *Aspectos culturales de Honduras.* Tegucigalpa: Imprenta Ariel, 1951.

Lars, Claudia. "Entrevista con Mercedes Durand." *Presente* 4, 38–39 (1967): 13–14.

León Felipe. "Poesía integral." *Repertorio Americano* 15 (1935): 106–9.

Lindo, Hugo. *Recuento: Anotaciones literarias e históricas de Centro América.* San Salvador: Ministerio de Educación, 1969.

López, Matilde Elena. "¿Crisis en la poesía salvadoreña o la poesía salvadoreña en la crisis actual?" *Presencia* 1, 3 (1988): 128–51.

———. "Entrevista con André Cruchaga." *Diario Latino Cultural,* 16 January 1988.

———. "Sobre la poesía social en El Salvador." *Presente* 94 (1984): 15–23.

Low, Mary, and Juan Breá. *Red Spanish Notebook.* 1937. Reprint, San Francisco: City Lights, 1979.

Luna Mejía, Manuel. *Indice general de poesía hondureña.* Mexico City: Editora Latinoamericana, 1961.

Manteiga, Robert C. "Politics and Poetics: England's Thirties Poets and the Spanish Civil War." *Modern Language Studies* 19, 3 (1989): 3–13.

Márquez Sterling, Carlos. *Historia de Cuba desde Cristóbal Colón a Fidel Castro.* New York: Las Américas, 1969.

Marroquín, Alejandro Dagoberto. *Panchimalco.* San Salvador: Ministerio de Educación, 1959.

Martínez, José Francisco. *Literatura hondureña y su proceso generacional.* Tegucigalpa: Editorial Universitaria, 1987.

Martínez, Roger. "La presencia de la mujer en la literatura hondureña." Typescript.

Martínez Orantes, Eugenio. "Claudia Lars la Divina." *Diario Latino Cultural,* 25 July 1987.

———. "Clementina Suárez en El Salvador." Typescript.

———. "José Mejía Vides." *Diario Latino Cultural,* 24 May 1986.

———. "La generación del '50 y Mercedes Durand." *Diario Latino Cultural,* 14 November 1987.

———. "La magia cautivadora de Salarrué." *Diario Latino Cultural,* 26 July 1986.

Martínez S., Luz Ivette. *Carmen Naranjo y la narrativa femenina en Costa Rica.* San José, Costa Rica: EDUCA, 1987.

Mejía, Martha Luz. "35 años de 'Grupo Ideas.'" *El Heraldo,* 30 May 1989.

Mejía, Medardo. *Comizahual: Leyendas, tradiciones y relatos de Honduras.* Tegucigalpa: Editorial Universitaria, 1981.

———. "Ramón Lobo Herrera: Hasta el monismo alemán de Heackel." *Ariel* 1965, 6–11.

———. "Refiere, Anisias, el paso de aquel milpero." *Ariel,* May 1975, 13–28.

Méndez Dávila, Lionel. *Art in Latin America Today: Guatemala.* Washington, D.C.: Organization of American States, 1966.

Meneses, Carlos. *Miguel Angel Asturias.* Madrid: Ediciones Jucar, 1975.

Meyer, Harvey K. *Historical Dictionary of Honduras.* Metuchen, N.J.: Scarecrow, 1976.

Meza, Víctor. "Los cuadros de Clementina Suárez o la historia de una valiosa pérdida." *Presencia universitaria* (78): 99.

Miller, Beth, and Alfonso González. *26 Autoras del México actual.* Mexico City: B. Costa-Amic, 1978.

Molina Chocano, Guillermo. *Estado liberal y desarrollo capitalista en Honduras.* Tegucigalpa: Banco Central de Honduras, 1976.

Montero, Carlos Guillermo. *Amighetti: 60 años de labor artística.* San José, Costa Rica: Museo de Arte Costarricense, 1987.

Moraña, Mabel. *Literatura y cultura nacional en Hispanoamérica.* Minneapolis: Institute for the Study of Ideologies and Literatures, 1984.

Morris, James A. *Honduras: Caudillo Politics and Military Rulers.* Boulder, Colo.: Westview, 1984.

Oquelí, Ramón. *Los hondureños y las ideas.* Tegucigalpa: Editorial Universitaria, 1985.

Orantes, Alfonso. "¿Crisis o advenimiento de una nueva literatura?" *Cultura* 14 (1958): 213–16.

Orozco, José Clemente. *Autobiografía.* 1945. Reprint, Mexico City: ERA, 1970.

Ortega Díaz, Adolfo. "Salarrué." *Repertorio Americano* 15, 686 (1934): 337–39.

Ortiz Aponte, Sally. "Federico de Onís, Paladín de la cultura hispánica." *Américas* 30, 2 (1978): 41–45.

Osses, Ester María, ed. *Para el combate y la esperanza: Poesía política en El Salvador.* Santo Domingo: Editora Taller, 1982.

———. *La novela del imperialismo en Centroamerica.* Maracaibo: Universidad del Zulia, 1986.

Oviedo, Jorge Luis. *Antología del cuento hondureño.* Tegucigalpa: Editores Unidos, 1988.

Oyuela, Leticia de. *Evolución histórica de la mujer en Honduras.* Tegucigalpa: Fundación de Asociaciones Femeninas de Honduras, 1989.

———. "Hacienda y estancia ganadera en la alcaldía mayor de Tegucigalpa." Typescript.

———. *Historia mínima de Tegucigalpa.* Tegucigalpa: Guaymuras, 1989.

———. "Honduras y el trabajo artístico (Apuntes para una historia del arte)." Typescript.

———. "Las haciendas de Tegucigalpa." Typescript.

———. "Luis Hernán Padilla, una vocación comprobada." *Arte* 4 (1987): 15–18.

Padilla, Luis H. Interview. *Alcaraván* 19 (1983): 33–34.

Padilla H., A. León. *El machismo en Honduras.* Tegucigalpa: Editorial Universitaria, 1983.

Pagoaga, Raúl Arturo. *Itinerario histórico de la poesía hondureña.* Tegucigalpa: López y Cía., 1973.

———. *La mujer hondureña bajo el cielo del arte, la ciencia y su influencia social.* Tegucigalpa: Imprenta Calderón, 1985.

Pan-América. Tegucigalpa. 1945–60.

Paredes, Rigoberto. "Aníbal, Sabillón y Vizquerra: 3 pintores hondureños en España." *Alcaraván* 4 (1980): 19–21.

Paredes, Rigoberto, and Manuel Salinas Paguada. *Literatura hondureña.* Tegucigalpa: Editores Unidos, 1987.

Peckenham, Nancy, and Annie Street, eds. *Honduras: Portrait of a Captive Nation.* New York: Praeger, 1985.

Pérez, Louis A. *Cuba: Between Reform and Revolution.* New York: Oxford University Press, 1988.

Pineda, Adaluz, ed. *Poesía: Antología femenina.* Typescript.

Posas, Mario. "Notas sobre política y sociedad en la Honduras de postguerra." *Alcaraván* 2 (1980): 2–5.

Presencia. San Salvador. 1988–89.

Presente. Tegucigalpa. 1969–90.

Quiñónez, Edgardo, and Mario Argueta. *Historia de Honduras.* 4th ed. Tegucigalpa: Escuela Superior del Profesorado "Francisco Morazán," 1986.

Ramírez, Sergio, ed. *Antología del cuento centroamericano.* San José, Costa Rica: EDUCA, 1984.

Reber, Vera Blinn. "Art as a Source for the Study of Central America, 1945–1975: An Exploratory Essay." *Latin American Research Review* 13, 1 (1978): 39–64.

Repertorio Americano. San José, Costa Rica. 1919–59.

Revista Tegucigalpa. Tegucigalpa. 1917–36.

Rivas Mercado, Antonieta. *Cartas a Manuel Rodríguez Lozano (1927–1930).* Mexico City: Secretaría de Educación Pública, 1975.

Robles, Emmanuel. "Imágenes de El Salvador." *Síntesis* 1, 10 (1955): 11–22.

Rodríguez Cerna, José. *Itinerario.* N.p., n.d.

Rosa, Marco Antonio. *Tegucigalpa, ciudad de remembranzas.* Tegucigalpa: Imprenta Calderón, 1972.

Rubí Zapata, Víctor. *Mi Juticalpa y yo.* Juticalpa, Honduras: n.p., 1986.

Salinas Paguada, Manuel. *Cultura hondureña contemporánea.* Tegucigalpa: Editorial Universitaria, 1991.

Sarmiento, Sergio. "Starting Over." *Américas* 36 (1984): 36–42.

Schlesinger, Stephen, and Stephen Kinzer. *Bitter Fruit: The Untold Story of the American Coup in Guatemala.* New York: Doubleday, 1982.

Síntesis. San Salvador. 1956–59.

Smerdon Altolaguirre, Margarita, ed. *Manuel Altolaguirre: Las islas invitadas.* Madrid: Castalia, 1972.

SobreVuelo. Tegucigalpa. 1987–89.

Sosa, Roberto. *The Difficult Days.* Translated by Jim Lindsay. Princeton, N.J.: Princeton University Press, 1983.

———. *Prosa armada.* Tegucigalpa: Guaymuras, 1981.

Suárez, Clementina. "Ausencia y presencia de Pablo Zelaya Sierra." *Arte* 1 (1982): 7–8.

Teja Zavre, Alfonso. "Marcos Carías Reyes, hombre de arte." *La pajarita de papel* 5–6 (1949–50): 95–97.

Thais, Eva. "Personalidades: Valores femeninos hondureños." Typescript.

Tiempo, César. "El mecenazgo oficial en El Salvador." *Presente* 4, 46 (1968): 17.

Torres, Juan Domingo. "Las artes plásticas en Honduras." *Tragaluz* 2, 14 (1986): 27.

Traba, Marta. *Crítica de arte en Latino América.* Bogotá: Museo de Arte de Bogotá, 1984.

Tragaluz. Tegucigalpa. 1985–90.

Turcios, Froylán, *Memorias.* Tegucigalpa: Editorial Universitaria, 1986.

———, ed. *Boletín de la defensa nacional.* 1924. Reprint, Tegucigalpa: Guaymuras, 1980.

Umaña, Helen. *Literatura hondureña contemporanea.* Tegucigalpa: Guaymuras, 1986.

———. *Narradoras hondureñas.* Tegucigalpa: Guaymuras, 1992.

Valle, Rafael Heliodoro. *Historia de la cultura hondureña.* Tegucigalpa: Editorial Universitaria, 1981.

———. "Peripecias de la cultura en Centro América." *Cultura* 8 (1956): 55–64.

Varela y Varela, Olimpia. "El feminismo." *Pan-América* 2, 29 (1946): 6–11.

———. "La mujer hondureña en la obra cultural y social de su patria." *Pan-América* 15, 182 (1959): 9–11.

Vásquez, José V. *Pablo Zelaya Sierra.* Tegucigalpa: Ministerio de Educación Pública, 1976.

Verani, Hugo. *Las vanguardias literarias en Hispanoamérica.* Rome: Bulzoni, 1986.

Villars, Rina. *Quiero vivir mi vida: Testimonio de Graciela García.* Tegucigalpa: Guaymuras, 1991.

Vizquerra, Julio. Interview. *Arte* 5, 9 (1988): 51–53.

Wells, William V. *Explorations and Adventures in Honduras.* New York: Harper and Row, 1857.

Woodward, Ralph Lee, Jr. *Central America: A Nation Divided.* 2d ed. New York: Oxford University Press, 1985.

Ycaza, Alberto. "Arte naif contemporaneo de Centro América." *Arte* 5, 10 (1988): 47–49.

Zelaya Sierra, Pablo. "Hojas escritas con lápiz." *Arte* (Tegucigalpa, Escuela Nacional de Bellas Artes) 1 (1958): 5–12.

Zepeda, Mariana. *Galería de Arte de IHCI: Su primera década, 1961–71.* Tegucigalpa, Calderón, 1971.

Zimmerman, Marc. "Salvadoran Literature: Lyric, Collage and Testimony in the Making of a National Narrative." Paper presented at the annual meeting of the Latin American Studies Association, 1986.

Works consulted on life writing

Aaron, Daniel. *Studies in Biography.* Cambridge: Harvard University Press, 1978.

Alpern, Sara, Joyce Antler, Elizabeth Israels Perry, and Ingrid Winther Scobie, eds. *The Challenge of Feminist Biography.* Urbana: University of Illinois Press, 1992.

Auerbach, Nina, ed. *Tulsa Studies in Women's Literature* (special issue: "Woman and Nation"), Fall 1987.

Belenky, Mary Field, Blythe McVicker Clinchy, Nancy Rule Goldberger, and Jill Mattuck Tarule. *Women's Ways of Knowing.* New York: Basic Books, 1986.

Benstock, Shari, ed. *The Private Self: Theory and Practice of Women's Autobiographical Writings.* Chapel Hill: University of North Carolina Press, 1988.

Berry, Thomas Elliott. *The Biographer's Craft.* New York: Odyssey, 1967.

Brodzki, Bella, and Celeste Schenck, eds. *Life/Lines: Theorizing Women's Autobiography.* Ithaca, N.Y.: Cornell University Press, 1988.

Clifford, James L. *From Puzzles to Portraits: The Problems of a Literary Biographer.* Chapel Hill: University of North Carolina Press, 1970.

Culley, Margo, ed. *A Day at a Time.* New York: Feminist Press, 1985.

Diamond, Stanley. "The Beautiful and the Ugly Are One Thing, the Sublime Another: A Reflection on Culture." *Cultural Anthropology* 2, 2 (1987): 268–71.

Eakin, Paul John. *Fictions in Autobiography.* Princeton, N.J.: Princeton University Press, 1985.

———. *Touching the World: Reference in Autobiography.* Princeton, N.J.: Princeton University Press, 1992.

Ellmann, Richard. *Golden Codgers: Biographical Speculations.* New York: Oxford University Press, 1973.

Freedman, Diane P., Olivia Frey, and Frances Murphy Zauhar, eds. *The Intimate Critique: Autobiographical Literary Criticism.* Durham, N.C.: Duke University Press, 1993.

Gilbert, Sandra. "Life Studies, or, Speech after Long Silence." *College English* 40, 8 (1979): 849–63.

Gittings, Robert. *The Nature of Biography.* Seattle: University of Washington Press, 1978.

Groag Bell, Susan, and Marilyn Yalom, eds. *Revealing Lives: Autobiography, Biography, and Gender.* Albany: State University of New York Press, 1990.

Heilbrun, Carolyn G. *Writing a Woman's Life.* New York: Norton, 1988.

Homberger, Eric, and John Charmley, eds. *The Troubled Face of Biography.* New York: St. Martin's, 1988.

Jay, Paul. *Being in the Text.* Ithaca, N.Y.: Cornell University Press, 1984.

Jelinek, Estelle C. *The Tradition of Women's Autobiography: From Antiquity to the Present.* Boston: Twayne, 1986.

Juhasz, Suzanne. "The Critic as Feminist: Reflections on Women's Poetry, Feminism, and the Art of Criticism." *Women's Studies* 5 (1977): 113–27.

Kendall, Paul Murray. *The Art of Biography.* New York: Norton, 1985.

Kennard, Jean E. "Personally Speaking: Feminist Critics and the Community of Readers." *College English* 43, 2 (1981): 140–45.

Kirschner, Suzanne R. "'Then What Have I to Do with Thee?': On Identity, Fieldwork, and Ethnographic Knowledge." *Cultural Anthropology* 2, 2 (1987): 211–34.

Lejeune, Philippe. *On Autobiography.* Translated by Katherine Leary. Minneapolis: University of Minnesota Press, 1989.

Lippard, Lucy R. *From the Center: Feminist Essays on Women's Art.* New York: E.P. Dutton, 1976.

Lugones, María C., and Elizabeth V. Spelman. "Have We Got a Theory for You! Feminist Theory, Cultural Imperialism, and the Demand for 'The Woman's Voice.'" *Women's Studies International Forum* 6, 6 (1983): 573–81.

Lutz, Catherine. "Emotion, Thought, and Estrangement: Emotion as a Cultural Category." *Cultural Anthropology* 1, 3 (1986): 287–309.

McConnell-Ginet, Sally, Ruth Borker, and Nelly Furman, eds. *Women and Language in Literature and Society.* New York: Praeger, 1980.

Meyer Spacks, Patricia. *Gossip.* Chicago: University of Chicago Press, 1985.

Myers, Jeffrey. *The Spirit of Biography.* Ann Arbor, Mich.: UMI Research Press, 1989.

Oates, Stephen B. *Biography as High Adventure.* Amherst: University of Massachusetts Press, 1986.

Olney, James, ed. *Autobiography: Essays Theoretical and Critical.* Princeton, N.J.: Princeton University Press, 1980.

Ostriker, Alicia. *Writing like a Woman.* Ann Arbor: University of Michigan Press, 1983.

Pachter, Marc, ed. *Telling Lives: The Biographer's Art.* Washington, D.C.: New Republic Books, 1979.

Patai, Daphne. "Ethical Problems of Personal Narratives, or, Who Should Eat the Last Piece of Cake?" *International Journal of Oral History* 8, 1 (1987): 5–27.

Raymond, Janice G. *A Passion for Friends* Boston: Beacon, 1986.

Rosaldo, Renato. "Ideology, Place, and People without Culture." *Cultural Anthropology* 3, 1 (1988): 77–87.

Rose, Phyllis. *Writing of Women.* Middletown, Conn.: Wesleyan University Press, 1985.

Smith, Sidonie. *A Poetics of Women's Autobiography.* Bloomington: Indiana University Press, 1987.

Spiro, Melford E. "Cultural Relativism and the Future of Anthropology." *Cultural Anthropology* 1, 3 (1986): 259–85.

Walter, James. *Reading Life Histories.* Nathan, Queensland: Griffith University, 1981.

Index